Dad - Merry Xmas
- Jim, Donna

Crossing Home Ground

Opposite: *Junction Sheep Range Provincial Park*

Crossing Home Ground

A GRASSLAND ODYSSEY
THROUGH SOUTHERN INTERIOR BRITISH COLUMBIA

David Pitt-Brooke

HARBOUR
PUBLISHING

Harbour Publishing Co. Ltd.
P.O. Box 219, Madeira Park, BC, V0N 2H0
www.harbourpublishing.com

Edited by Cheryl Cohen
Indexed by Sarah Corsie
Dust jacket design by Anna Comfort O'Keeffe
Text design by Mary White
Map by Roger Handling
Photographs by David Pitt-Brooke
Printed and bound in Canada

Harbour Publishing acknowledges the support of the Canada Council for the Arts, which last year invested $153 million to bring the arts to Canadians throughout the country. We also gratefully acknowledge financial support from the Government of Canada through the Canada Book Fund and from the Province of British Columbia through the BC Arts Council and the Book Publishing Tax Credit.

Library and Archives Canada Cataloguing in Publication

Pitt-Brooke, David, author
    Crossing home ground : a grassland odyssey through southern interior British Columbia / David Pitt-Brooke.

Includes bibliographical references and index.
Issued in print and electronic formats.
ISBN 978-1-55017-774-9 (hardback).--ISBN 978-1-55017-775-6 (html)

    1. Pitt-Brooke, David--Travel--British Columbia. 2. Naturalists--Travel--British Columbia. 3. Hiking--British Columbia. 4. Natural history--British Columbia. 5. Human ecology--British Columbia. 6. Grasslands--British Columbia. 7. British Columbia--Description and travel. I. Title.

FC3817.5.P58 2016   917.11'5045   C2016-904712-1
                                                      C2016-904713-X

*To all who have stood in defence
of wild country, beauty and grace,
the beloved home places.*

*Also to Scott Steedman and Michelle Benjamin,
who got me started.*

We shall not cease from exploration
And the end of all our exploring
Will be to arrive where we started
And know the place for the first time.
Through the unknown, unremembered gate
When the last of earth left to discover
Is that which was the beginning;
At the source of the longest river
The voice of the hidden waterfall
And the children in the apple-tree

—T.S. Eliot, "Little Gidding"

I only went out for a walk and finally concluded to stay
out till sundown, for going out, I found, was really going
in.

—John Muir,
John of the Mountains: The Unpublished Journals
of John Muir, ed. L.M. Wolfe

Contents

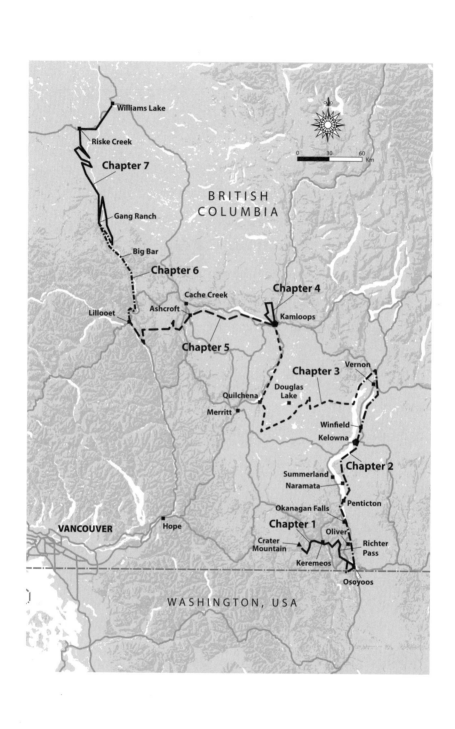

Preface

*Something there had been, something delicate, wild
and far away. But it was shut out behind the doors of
yesterday, lost beyond the hills.*
                    —Robin Hyde (Iris Guiver Wilkinson),
                                    The Godwits Fly

In autumn 2004, my editor at the time, Scott Steedman, treated me to a celebratory lunch, long promised. That spring Raincoast Books had published my first book, a collection of observations and reflections on a series of seasonal experiences in the wild and beautiful country along the west coast of Vancouver Island. *Chasing Clayoquot: A Wilderness Almanac*, as the book was titled, had done well. It had collected some nice reviews and readers seemed to enjoy it.

When we'd finished our meal, Scott paused, looked me in the eye and asked the inevitable question: "What now?"

I was still living in Tofino, still enjoying life on the west coast, but starting to feel the need of a change, fresh horizons, new adventures (plus a chance to dry out, perhaps, and maybe catch a little more sunshine than one might reasonably hope for on the wet coast).

Also, much as I loved Vancouver Island it wasn't home ground. I'd grown up in the valleys of British Columbia's southern interior and that warm, dry, open country—big lakes and rivers, ponderosa pine and bunchgrass meadows—was still, for me, the "home of the heart," my place in the world, and I still felt the attraction.

Even before Scott asked his question, I'd begun to wonder if I might approach and appreciate that home ground in much the same way as I'd approached my adopted home on the west coast of the island, with an intense, consciously planned, systematic campaign of exploration,

1

venturing out, month by month, to witness the particular events and attractions of each season. I would think and I would read and then I would write about what I'd seen, partly to bear witness to the beauty and grace of the countryside and partly to share my experiences, especially with readers who might not in their lives have the opportunity to see things as I'd seen them.

Ironically, I'd never taken time to pay that kind of close attention to the countryside I grew up in. Now, it seemed, I might have a chance to make up the deficit. The result would be a companion to *Chasing Clayoquot*, a testament to beloved home places and a homecoming as well.

It was going to be a challenge. I knew that from the first. The valleys of southern interior British Columbia are a very different sort of environment, more populated, not as wild and tumultuous as the coast, not as magnificent, not nearly as renowned. It's a place of more modest beauty, though certainly with its own quiet charm: open, sunny, welcoming.

And very much in need of a little loving attention and testimony, as it turned out.

When I was a child, the Okanagan was still blessed with one of the world's truly beautiful landscapes: leafy little towns, hardly more than villages, clustered along the shores of Okanagan Lake. And beyond the little towns, a countryside of fields and orchards. And beyond the fields, swelling hillsides of bunchgrass, groves of trembling aspen, open parklands of ponderosa pine and Douglas-fir climbing to forested uplands of spruce and fir. From that height, turning around, one could look down across the great bowl of the valley, the hills and the orchards, the fields and the little towns, to the glittering waters of the lake beyond. Space and light everywhere. It was something else.

That countryside had yet to feel anything like the full weight of humanity. I could bicycle in a morning to places where groves of ancient Douglas-firs still stood, huge and windswept. I could walk pristine meadows of native bunchgrass. I remember meadowlarks singing in the spring and killdeers calling around little ponds in the heat of summer. The scent of wild roses in June and the pungent fragrance of big sage on warm September days. Snowy winters, the hillsides gleaming white at noon, blushing gold at sunset, fading to indigo after dusk. The cold wind hissing through bare stalks of bunchgrass. Beauty and grace in all seasons.

But time has not been kind.

It's an oft-repeated story nowadays. Rapid population growth. An explosion of urban and industrial development. The disappearance of beautiful places, one after another, to be replaced by a rising tide of ugliness, ruin and clutter. The old Douglas-firs are long gone to fatten somebody's bank account. The bunchgrass has turned to hobby farms and subdivisions and highways. A time traveller, extracted from the towns of sixty or seventy or eighty years ago, would hardly recognize those places as they are today and would not, I think, find the new any sort of improvement on the old.

Even more grievous, perhaps, those developments have engendered a creeping alienation or estrangement from the natural world, a fracturing of the sustaining bond between the human beings who live here and the landscapes they inhabit, so that the once-beloved places have dwindled to mere scenery, real estate, a supply of resources, an afternoon's adventure playground, a remote backdrop to the more immediate events of everyday life. The countryside has ceased to be a home for the heart and has become mere commodity.

All rather depressing.

But what to do? How to keep from sinking into despondency? And how to compass such an enormous area, such a variety of country, such ecological and biological diversity? I soon realized the month-by-month approach that had served so well in *Chasing Clayoquot* wasn't going to work here. Much of what is interesting and vivid (at least biologically) in this warm, dry environment is crammed into the three or four months of spring and early summer when moisture is adequate for plant growth. For the rest of the year, the living world is mostly marking time, waiting for spring to roll around again.

For a time I was stumped.

Then I had an inspired thought.

I've always loved the idea of the young John Muir (who would, of course, become America's pre-eminent wilderness advocate of the nineteenth and early twentieth centuries) stepping out of some doorway in Jeffersonville, Indiana, in September 1867 and walking all the way to the Gulf of Mexico, a thousand miles away, seeking out, as he later wrote, "the wildest, leafiest, and least trodden way I could find."

So there you had it. I would take myself out for a walk. A long walk. After all, that was part of the essence of this countryside, the characteristic openness that positively invites you to step out, makes you feel you could walk practically anywhere, follow any course you chose, very different from the salal thickets and dense forests of Vancouver Island.

The route I plotted would carry me a thousand kilometres or more through the network of deep valleys (Okanagan, Nicola, Thompson and Fraser) that furrow the highlands of southern interior British Columbia from the forty-ninth parallel of latitude at the Canada–US border to the fifty-second parallel at Williams Lake on the edge of the Cariboo and Chilcotin plateaus.

I covered that whole distance on foot (believe me, you never really know a country until you've measured it out, pace by pace), seventy-five days of walking, divided into two- to fourteen-day stretches, depending, carrying all the necessities on my back, across great mountain ranges and wild rivers, blown by all the winds that pass and wet with all the showers. It took me over a year, from summer to summer and into the next fall, to finish the project.

It was my very own quest, a secular pilgrimage. I progressed, as pilgrims do, from one piece of sanctified ground—the little green patches on the map—to the next, testifying along the way to what had been lost, certainly, the harm that had been done, but also celebrating whatever bits of grace and beauty still remained.

I went in search of special places and special moments, surviving fragments of indigenous ecosystems, little opportunities for reflection, enduring sparks of loveliness that had managed to survive, amazingly enough, despite all. And not just loveliness, but wildness too. That secret life that endures outside human regulation or control.

And then I came home to write.

This book, *Crossing Home Ground: A Grassland Odyssey through Southern Interior British Columbia*, is the result.

It's been a long haul, much more time and effort than I could have imagined when I started out, back in the autumn of 2004. The world has changed. Raincoast Books has ceased publishing; Scott Steedman is doing other things. Happily, Howard White at Harbour Publishing has stepped up to see the book through into print.

A pilgrimage should be shared. I wish we could have done this journey together.

But at least, through these pages, you can get a taste of the thing.

Drop what you're doing, lace up your walking shoes and we'll step out to see what can be seen.

We'll be taking our chances, of course, luck of the journey. I make no promises. Indeed, I'm pretty sure, especially at the beginning of our walk, through the more populated southern sections of the route, we'll be hard-pressed to find much in the way of natural beauty and grace. But I intend to persevere, and I think the farther north and west we go, the more likely it is we'll find something to please us.

By the time we're finished, we'll have acquainted ourselves, at least in passing, with much of what is characteristic and memorable in the landscape: the special places, the seasonal events and the notable species of plants and animals. Also the human element, part of the essential mix in these valleys for many thousands of years.

With a little luck, you'll come away with a vivid sense of having been there, in person, to experience this remarkable and engaging piece of countryside for yourself.

Time will tell, I suppose.

Forth, pilgrim, forth.

—David Pitt-Brooke
Hat Creek, British Columbia

The spectacle of nature is in the heart of a man; to see it,
he must feel it.
—Jean-Jacques Rousseau, *Émile, ou De l'education*

Of the gladest [sic] moments in human life methinks is the
departure upon a distant journey into unknown lands.
—Sir Richard Francis Burton (journal entry)

Breathless, we flung us on the windy hill,
Laughed in the sun, and kissed the lovely grass.
—Rupert Brooke, "The Hill"

1

Hot as Hades—Summer in the Similkameen

Bunchgrass campsite above the Similkameen River

DAY ONE
Thursday, August 2: Crater Mountain

Got to make this quick.

It's been a long day. I'm dog-tired and cold enough to be shivering, which is ironic, considering how close I came to heatstroke earlier this afternoon on the long climb out of the Ashnola River valley, southwest of the village of Keremeos. I'm wearing every scrap of clothing I packed up the mountain, including the down sweater I was sure I'd never use, but nothing seems to help. My fingers are clumsy and numb, white as marble. It's all I can do to hold this pencil. Putting up the tent is going to be a challenge.

Part of the problem, doubtless, is that I've had no proper meal since lunchtime. It's now almost nine o'clock in the evening and getting quite dark. Only six weeks past the solstice but already the days are closing in. The sunset is long gone. The western sky has faded to a pale aquamarine. Glowing twilight still bathes the summit but the night-tide is rising from the east, pooling in deep gorges far below. The meadows around me have taken on that luminous, numinous quality that dusk always imparts to ordinary beauty. In such clear air, the first stars seem very close. As I watch, a meteor blazes across the sky from northeast to southwest, bonus, no extra charge. A night under heaven, the first of many, or so I hope.

The southern interior of the province of British Columbia is mostly a great expanse of rolling forested upland between 1,200 and 1,500 metres in elevation, rising to modest summits of 1,800 to 2,200 metres.

But those forested uplands are deeply scored by a scattered, irregular network of narrow, relatively dry valleys, originating in the faults and weaknesses of a complex bedrock, further excavated and shaped by that dynamic duo of landscape architecture: glacial ice and running water.

The difference in elevation between forested uplands and the deeper valleys can be quite dramatic. Crater Mountain summits out at 2,293 metres. Keremeos, on the floor of the Similkameen River valley, practically in the shadow of the mountain, lies at an elevation of only 365 metres, a difference of almost 2,000 metres.

That difference in elevation yields a substantial difference in climate.

Winters on the high plateau are long and cold. Snow cover persists into May or June. Where native forests survive—mostly Engelmann spruce (*Picea engelmannii*), white spruce (*Picea glauca*) and subalpine fir (*Abies lasiocarpa*)—the climate is relatively cool and moist, even in summer.

Valley winters, on the other hand, are relatively brief and not nearly so cold as those in the high country. Temperatures are further moderated by the thermal mass of large lakes or rivers. Snow cover is limited and soon gone in the spring. Summers are hot and dry, despite the lakes and rivers. It is a landscape of open grassy meadows and forested parkland.

Two very different environments, then, upland and valley, sharing the same geographical space, coexisting, interlocking, inextricably intermeshed, but supporting radically different communities of plants and animals. An archipelago of semi-arid islands surrounded by the forested ocean of high plateau.

Takes me forever to fall asleep; I can't seem to get warm. And I've only just managed to drop off at last before I'm suddenly wide awake again, swimming out of dreams, to find the tent bright with light. Panicky, half dazed, I fumble with sleeping bag, tent, rain-fly, all those zippers. When I do finally get my head outside, I'm relieved to find that it's only the moon, nearly full, rising above the ridge behind my campsite, lovely image, another unexpected and unplanned bonus for my first night out. All around the tent and far into the dim distance the meadows are illuminated by the otherworldly, not-quite-daylight of moonshine. At such times I can almost fancy a presence in the landscape that goes beyond the ordinary, day-to-day fact of the thing, a shadowy awareness of the unseen world.

Back in the sleeping bag I realize, suddenly, that the chill is gone. I'm warm, at last, thank goodness, the bedtime snack having finally kicked in. I even shed a layer or two of insulation before drifting back into exhausted sleep.

DAY TWO
Friday, August 3: Crater Mountain to Ashnola River

When I wake again, it's broad daylight.

The top of Crater Mountain is mostly open ground, little tarns and heather meadows, with a modest summit ridge. There doesn't seem to be an actual crater, but the north side of the mountain is hollowed out into a great empty cirque enclosed by steep basalt cliffs. The open grassy meadows on the southern slopes, more typical of lower elevations, climb here to almost 1,800 metres, blending directly into the alpine vegetation. (Grassland and alpine in this part of the world are usually separated by kilometres of forest and many hundreds of metres of elevation.)

The daylight view from the summit turns out to be every bit as spectacular as I might have hoped. Far to the west, the horizon outlines the jagged forested peaks of the Skagit Range of the Cascade Mountains, just one of innumerable mountain ranges that crowd along the Pacific coast of British Columbia. To the south, across the Ashnola River valley, is a different extension of the northern Cascades, the Okanagan Range, comparatively rounded summits, with the alpine meadows of Cathedral Lakes Provincial Park and Snowy Mountain Provincial Park in the middle distance.

The Ashnola River itself drains off a height of land to the southwest. It courses through a deep valley along the south side of Crater Mountain before turning abruptly northward to pass below the mountain's eastern flank, tumbling toward the even more deeply excavated valley of the Similkameen River, north and east of my high perch.

Eastward beyond the Similkameen looms the extreme southern end of the South Thompson Highlands, Orofino Mountain and Mount Kobau. And somewhere out of sight beyond all that is the Okanagan Valley.

As always from the top of a mountain, I feel as if a few stout strides would take me to that far horizon. The long walk ahead seems practically accomplished. Nothing to it at all.

I love mountains and uplands, the world-striding view from the summit, but on this journey I'll mostly be following that network of valleys, home of the heart, with their odd and unique climate: too warm and too dry for such a northerly latitude, mimicking conditions ordinarily found much farther south in Washington, Oregon and Idaho, a curious northward extension of the Columbia Basin climate, thanks mostly to a powerful adiabatic effect in the lee of the Coast Mountains.

Consider a mass of air crossing those ranges from west to east. As the air flows up the windward side of the mountains, it decompresses and cools. If the air cools to the dew point, some of its moisture will condense and perhaps precipitate as rain or snow. If that happens, the air flowing down this lee side of the mountains will be drier and, being drier, will warm more quickly as it compresses with the loss of altitude. If that happens, air on the lee side of the mountains will be both drier and warmer than the more humid air at the same altitude on the windward side.

This is the adiabatic effect. Here, in these interior valleys, that adiabatic flow is the norm, the prevailing wind being from the west, day after day, week after week, year after year, a constant drying flow of air.

It does rain, of course, especially in the spring months. And it snows, too, in the winter months, so the soil is usually adequately charged with moisture at the beginning of the growing season. This isn't quite a desert. But the actual amount of precipitation is fairly modest. And through most of the summer and early autumn, moisture is lost from the soil more rapidly than it can be replenished by precipitation, a negative balance.

The whole living community is shaped and governed by that simple fact. Those species of plants and animals that can deal with the lopsided moisture regime—adequate moisture in the winter-spring, drought through the summer-fall—will survive and prosper. Those that can't, don't.

And here it is, the whole show, all nicely laid out for me, a living diorama.

Far away on the western horizon, the jagged peaks of the Skagit Range, crowned with puffy cloud caps. Beyond that, somewhere, rain forests, seashore, ocean, all moist and cool. On this side, blue skies, sunshine, grassy slopes. Down in the valley where the air is more compressed, a hot, dry climate, near-desert conditions. I can almost sense the countryside drying out as all that desiccated air flows off the mountains and down through the valleys toward me.

Late afternoon, now, and hot as hades. It's remarkable how much difference a bit of elevation can make. The air at the summit was cool and pleasant, but with every step down the trail I feel the heat building, not just with the warmth of the sun on the rocks and vegetation around me, but also with my descent into denser, warmer air. The track toward the foot of the mountain is very steep, with tight switchbacks carved into the rock. The hillsides across the valley loom abruptly across a gulf of shimmering air.

I'm suffering the first stages of heatstroke, a slight but noticeable confusion and headache. I've read somewhere that body temperatures above 40°C can be life-threatening (one's brain begins to poach inside one's overheated skull), and I know it's hotter than that here today on the rocky lower slopes of Crater Mountain.

In fact, the only thing keeping me alive is the river of sweat running over my face, neck and torso, cooling me by evaporation. There are strict physiological limits to that. Eventually my body will reach some ultimate point of dehydration and turn off the taps. Both water bottles are empty and the question is: Which am I going to run out of first? Moisture or mountain?

Mountain, happily.

I manage to reach the woods and the river at the bottom of the slope without exhausting my bodily fluids. Heatstroke is ordinarily treated by getting the patient out of the sun and cooling their overheated body with a water bath. Rehydration is important. The Ashnola serves admirably on all accounts. It's a lovely clear-water stream tumbling over great rounded boulders, hardly more than a big creek this far up the valley, with sun-dappled shade and birdsong as added benefits.

Certainly I feel much better after a dip in the river, a cool drink of water and a bite to eat. I take time to bandage my feet and change my socks. (I blistered both feet on yesterday's climb, and the jolting hike back down the mountain has not done them any good.)

The shadows are already lengthening and the heat has begun to ease a little. In a while I'll go looking for a place to set up my tent.

> *Rest is not idleness, and to lie sometimes on the grass*
> *under trees on a summer's day, listening to the murmur of*
> *the water, or watching the clouds float across the sky, is by*
> *no means a waste of time.*
>
> —John Lubbock, *The Use of Life*

A pleasant little clearing beside the road just above the river. In the cooler air and growing darkness I can hear water splashing over rocks below. I can smell it, too, that slightly acrid scent of water in a dry land. Also I can smell the foliage around me as it begins to breathe again after a long hot day. Cottonwoods, alders, maples and willows along the stream. Pines and Douglas-fir on the slopes above. Water in a dry land. Today's bit of grace.

DAY THREE
Saturday, August 4: Ashnola River to Fairview Road

With towering walls of stone rising steeply from both sides of the water, the first few miles through the Ashnola River canyon are the highlight of the day, though the road is rough going, dust and gravel. The riparian vegetation near the water, green and lush, contrasts beautifully with the pale, arid slopes above.

Some of the nicest bits of Crater Mountain's natural habitat are on those steep east-facing slopes, protected by the formidable, relatively inaccessible terrain, too rugged for logging and livestock. The slopes are a pretty fair showcase for the whole mosaic of different habitat types so characteristic of these dry interior valleys, a living fabric that clothes the physical landscape, not a blanket so much as a quilt of vividly different patches: meadows of bluebunch wheatgrass (*Pseudoroegneria spicata*) or rough fescue (*Festuca scabrella*), maybe a few scattered Ponderosa pine (*Pinus ponderosa*). Little copses of trembling aspen (*Populus tremuloides*) with understories of herbs and shrubs: wild rose (*Rosa sp.*) or common snowberry (*Symphoricarpos albus*). Below the cliff faces above the road are great patches of tumbled stone, talus slopes wearing pendant necklaces of green shrubbery nourished by the reservoir of moisture accumulated under the rock. Higher on the slope, patches of open Douglas-fir forest (*Pseudotsuga menziesii*) carpeted by lawns of pinegrass (*Calamagrostis rubescens*). And down along the river, a riparian woodland of black cottonwood (*Populus balsamifera tricarpus*), mountain alder (*Alnus incana*), Douglas maple (*Acer glabrum*) and various willows (*Salix spp*).

If we had to choose one bit of habitat, one patch of that quilt, to represent the whole landscape, we'd almost certainly choose the bunchgrass meadows so characteristic of these dry interior valleys. It's not uncommon to hear the valleys of southern interior British Columbia referred to as "grasslands," though, of course, there's much more to them, ecologically, than grass.

Certainly bunchgrass will be the holy grail of this pilgrimage. Whenever I come across a meadow of healthy native grass I'll feel reassured that the whole surrounding landscape, the entire quilt, is also in relatively good condition. And, contrariwise, where the native grasses are shopworn and scanty (or gone altogether) I'll know that something is terribly wrong.

A young woman with a small baby in a child's car seat beside her pulls alongside to ask if I need a ride. The kindness of strangers always takes me by surprise. I decline the offer with thanks, trying, awkwardly, to explain in twenty words or less why it's important for me to do this on foot. She smiles, nods and drives away. I doubt I did much of a job of expressing myself, but I go on with a lighter heart.

It's evening and the road has just started to climb back out of the valley. Suddenly I'm conscious of great fatigue. I'm surrounded by this huge, fierce, gorgeous piece of scenery, the view back along the deep trench of the Similkameen valley, past Keremeos to where the Ashnola debouches from its canyon, and beyond that to where the Similkameen itself flows into view, from around a corner to the northwest, but I'm much too tired to enjoy it.

I positively ache for the end of the trail and my night's rest. When the starting point for tomorrow's hike up the north ridge of Mount Kobau comes into view, I am at first delighted. It seems the perfect wayside gypsy camping place, a nice little clearing with a stream flowing down through the woods, green and leafy, the whole bit.

But when I get closer I can see there's garbage (and worse) strewn everywhere, scattered across the clearing, tumbled back under the trees. It's clear and incontrovertible evidence that there are aliens among us. They may look like humans, but their thought processes are incomprehensible.

Even so, what kind of sentient being would do this to such a pretty spot? What were they thinking? That the garbage-fairy would come along and pick up after them?

There's way too much mess for me to even think of cleaning it up. And anyway, I can barely stay on my feet. I retreat, working my way farther and farther back into the sheltering forest, my natural habitat, leaving the last broken bottles and bits of toilet paper far behind.

DAY FOUR
Sunday, August 5: Fairview Road to Mount Kobau

L uck is a lady to start, though I have to go looking for her. There is no water at my campsite and I can't bring myself to hike all the way back to the little stream in the garbage-meadow. While exploring one of the deep ravines on the north side of the mountain, not too far from my tent, I stumble, almost literally, across a minor miracle: a perfect little spring of clear sweet water welling out of the ground and flowing for perhaps fifteen or twenty metres before disappearing again into the thirsty gravel. Just sufficient to fill my bottles. (I use a filter, naturally.)

There are wide views from both sides of the north ridge: westward into the deep trench of the Similkameen valley and eastward out across the broad basin of the Okanagan Valley, where, in the middle distance to the south, little white comets (powerboats and their wakes), chase each other around the dark blue of Osoyoos Lake.

But if I'd been hoping to find anything in the way of pristine natural habitat on Mount Kobau, I'm bound for disappointment. The native bunchgrass is gone. Weeds abound. The whole mountain seems to have been pasturized, grazed to death.

At the top of the ridge I come upon a sizeable herd of cattle sheltering from the midday sun under the spruces. The ground beneath the trees has been trampled to bare earth, no undergrowth left at all. There is manure everywhere. Flies buzz. It looks like some down-at-heels farmyard.

According to my map this is Crown land, land that belongs to all of us, our common property, our inheritance.

One sometimes hears the phrase "tragedy of the commons" applied to this kind of abuse of public land by its users, as if this were the inevitable outcome, a kind of natural law.

The expression comes from an article by Dr. Garrett Hardin, first published in 1968 in the journal *Science*, and it refers, more specifically, to a parable that Hardin advanced.[1] In brief, a group of herders share a pasture, a limited parcel of land, on which each is free to graze as many cattle as he (or she) can acquire. At some point, as the herd grows, the carrying capacity of the pasture is exceeded, so that additional animals diminish the common resource.

Hardin argued that the logic of self-interest favours the continued growth of the herd and eventual ruin of the pasture, since each herder receives 100 percent of the benefit from every additional animal that he can place on the common property, while the cost (the diminishment of the shared resource) is distributed among the whole community, including the conscientious herders who restrain their selfish impulse.

Hardin's parable and expression are sometimes used in a way he never intended: as a sort of shabby and transparent rationale for the transfer of public property into private hands.

The central issue of the article in *Science* was actually the growth of human populations. Hardin's chief concern was with showing the impossibility of unfettered human access to the limited resources of the world, and it was in this context that he raised the example of the herders, arguing the folly of relying on self-interest (the marketplace we might call it nowadays), enlightened or otherwise, to prevent ruination of this larger global commons.

Ironically, Hardin's concerns are supposed to have been addressed here on Mount Kobau. In British Columbia, access to grazing on public land is controlled by the provincial Ministry of Forests. Our whole system of grazing leases, licences and permits is intended to prevent the kind of free-for-all that Dr. Hardin was writing of.

Only a single rancher or a small, strictly limited, group of ranchers has access to grazing on a particular parcel of public land, and they enjoy the privilege of tenure. You'd think it would be very much in their interest to manage this public property to maintain the quality of the range over the long term. And if they don't, for whatever reason, well, there's always the Ministry of Forests, keeping a watchful eye.

Supposedly.

But *Quis custodiet ipsos custodes*? Who shall watch the watchers? I think this is the real tragedy of the commons: that those agencies we have appointed to safeguard the public's interest have failed us.

Hardin's parable notwithstanding, some of the most extreme examples of the harm that can arise through unfettered access to the world's resources are not on public land at all. Private property rights are an article of faith in this country. Landowners are commonly assumed to have the right to do absolutely as they please with land they own. This is unfettered access writ large and, consequently, it's not uncommon to see private ranges, grasslands on private property, in a terrible state of abuse and neglect. This is the "tragedy of private ownership" that's less often belaboured. All the good intentions, all the work and care invested by a whole line of dutiful and conscientious landowners, genuine stewards of the land, can be thrown away, irretrievably, in a year or two, by an owner who doesn't know any better or doesn't care. And all it takes is one.

DAY FIVE
Monday, August 6: Mount Kobau to Richter Pass

The South Okanagan Grasslands Protected Area, Mount Kobau Site, one of those keenly anticipated green patches on my map, is a disappointment. Mount Kobau's south-facing slopes, like those on Crater Mountain, are mostly wide areas of open ground, set off by little stands of Douglas-fir forest or riparian woodland in the deeper gullies. All that open ground should be covered in bunchgrass. It isn't.

Instead it mostly supports a close-packed mass of big sagebrush (*Artemisia tridentata*), a sure indication of intense, chronic overgrazing and a badge of shame for range managers in this part of the world.

Big sagebrush is a large, greyish-green, highly aromatic native shrub. Older branches are covered in shredding bark; younger twigs are hairy, as are the leaves, one to three centimetres long, wedge-shaped, terminating in three lobes or teeth (hence the "tridentata"). The leaves persist through the winter. The plant blooms in late summer, with small, yellowish, inconspicuous flowers. Big sagebrush is widespread and common from low to mid-elevations in these arid valleys.

When livestock are loosed on a piece of rangeland, they tend to graze various species of plants preferentially, the tastiest ones first.

Under continued pressure, those species diminish and ultimately disappear from the ecosystem. Range managers call them "decreasers." The bunchgrasses are right at the head of that list.

Other species, presumably less tasty, will be more or less ignored by livestock until everything more palatable has been eaten. These species, the "increasers," will proliferate to occupy the niches formerly occupied by the decreasers. Big sage, cheatgrass (*Bromus tectorum*), balsamroot (*Balsamorhiza sagittata*), diffuse, spotted and Russian knapweeds (*Centaurea diffusa*, *C. maculosa* and *C. repens*) are increasers. Some increasers are native plants. Big sage and balsamroot, for instance, have always been part of these grassland ecosystems. Others, like cheatgrass and the knapweeds, are introduced species.

Not far from the summit of Mount Kobau, there's a parking lot from which a road leads off down the mountain. There are picnic tables, sanitary facilities and a little interpretive display. The interpretive display grandly proclaims "South Okanagan Grasslands Protected Area."

On this morning a little herd of twelve or fifteen cows eyes me suspiciously from the parking lot beyond the sign. Beyond the cows and the parking lot, as far as the eye can see, lies a mass of big sage, sign and symbol of the damage that livestock do to native grasslands in this part of the world. I look at the cows. I look at the sage. I look at the sign. And I can't help wondering: *protected from what?*

When I was a kid, there was a popular American comedian by the name of Flip Wilson. He had these characters he would assume, various personae, and one of them, the gorgeous Geraldine ("The devil made me do it"), had a saying: "A lie is as good as the truth if somebody'll believe it."

And we'd laugh! It was so outrageous, so preposterous.

Well, sadly, "a lie is as good as the truth if somebody'll believe it" seems to have become the standard and accepted way of doing business for corporations and governments. We don't even make a fuss anymore.

Call it a "grassland protected area," then. Make up a few maps with little green patches on them. Erect some signs. Somewhere there will be glossy brochures, produced and distributed at great expense.

What does it matter, really, that the actual ground has already been severely overgrazed and that grazing continues? As long as folks out there believe there's a protected area, believe that something is being done to preserve indigenous grasslands, what's the difference? The authorities will still get the credit. And it's much cheaper and less complicated than actually having to do something practical and tangible, like evicting those cows. Here we have words as a substitute for real action. As if proclaiming a protected area makes it a fact.

The really appalling thing is that it seems to work. I suppose there's a certain cold-blooded calculation involved. After all, how many people will ever make the drive up here to see for themselves. And how many of those will walk the trail back along the way I've come to see what conditions actually prevail on these public lands. The mass of people, even the most concerned and engaged citizens, live in urban areas and know only what they're told by their supposed servants, accepting it in good faith.

It's easy to get away with the deception.

End of rant.

I should perhaps make it clear that I've no quarrel with the livestock industry—cattlemen or ranchers. I live in that community; they are my friends and neighbours. I eat meat. I've been around livestock all my life. But it's evident that if we hope to preserve intact some remnant of the indigenous grassland ecosystems of southern interior British Columbia, or to rehabilitate grasslands already badly damaged by overgrazing, we're going to have to provide for reserves free from the grazing of domestic animals. That doesn't seem to be happening here in the South Okanagan Grasslands Protected Area—protected, it would appear, in name only.

At the summit a couple of young sharp-shinned hawks play in the thermal breeze off the sunward side of the mountain, dancing up there in the rising air, turning and dodging deftly with flaring wings and tails.

The view is to the south. The Okanagan Valley is on my left, and on my right, the Similkameen valley, running more or less parallel. Between the two valleys lies a tumbled mass of upland ground, the lower-elevation extension of the same Thompson Highlands that Mounts Kobau and Orofino, and the ridge I walked yesterday, are all part of.

The ground falls away steeply before my feet. Far below, at the very foot of the slope, is Richter Pass, a lower-elevation break in the uplands. I can see the slender line of Highway 3 snaking up from the Similkameen valley, threading the pass and dropping away, eastward, toward the little town of Osoyoos on the Okanagan side.

It's another scorching afternoon. On the way down the mountain I stop at every bit of shade (and there's precious little, believe me) for a rest and a few moments out of the sun, but there's no relief. By the time I reach the highway, I'm beat. And there's no river here to provide cooling.

I haven't the strength to go farther and, besides, it's getting on toward evening. Quitting time. There happens to be an old Douglas-fir, gnarled and lonely, standing on a little knoll not far from the pass. For lack of anything better to do, really, I haul my pack over there and lie down in the shade to wait for the shadows to grow a little longer. With a heavy growth of sage all around me I'm pretty well hidden, and my bivouac feels oddly private and secure, sheltered and safe, though the highway is not far away.

As respiration rate and heart rate and body temperature drop toward something approaching normal, I begin to experience an odd sort of contentment. It's a surprisingly peaceful place. Traffic on the highway is muted. I'm just living in the moment for now, kicked back, free of any responsibility to strive onward, watching the day drift by. I snuff in the smell of warm sage (a little too robust to be called a scent, I think) and the dry, hot air blowing up the valley, whispering across the sun-heated rock and through the desiccated grasses.

A little time later I hear chirps and rustlings from somewhere below me on the hill and a troupe of little brown birds comes swarming upslope through the scrub, foraging for seeds and small insects. I wonder if these might be Brewer's sparrows (*Spizella breweri*), not common, but one of the typical birds of sagebrush habitat. They work their way past and around me, intent on their business, diligent, going away up the hill, the sound of them diminishing to nothing. I feel flattered by their apparent acceptance of me, as if I were a regular part of the place, as if I belonged. A privilege extended to a favoured guest.

Eventually the sun sinks behind a shoulder of the mountain so that I'm finally out of direct light. It's still much too hot to do anything active, but little by little I hear the place coming alive as dusk deepens. Insects start singing. (Or whatever it is that insects do to make that sound.) A nighthawk flies by with its odd, undulating flight, strange pumping wingbeats, and buzzes at me. Pretty soon the sky is full of nighthawks, buzzing and booming, hunting the insects up there. And the scent of the desert grassland grows more and more intense as the air cools.

Nighthawks (*Chordeiles minor*) are robin-sized birds, though their wings are much longer than a robin's and more slender, more sharply pointed. Coloration is generally cryptic, in complicated patterns of dark grey, black and brown, but with striking white wing-patches across the primary feathers. Exceedingly awkward on the ground, they are supremely aerial, hunting and even drinking on the wing (swooping low over ponds to scoop up water in their oversized mouths).

The name, presumably, originates in the somewhat falcon-like appearance of the birds in flight, but it's inappropriate and unfortunate. Nighthawks have even been persecuted on occasion as raptors because of the name, though they are not hawks at all and, in fact, eat nothing but insects.

Nor are they creatures of the night. Strictly speaking they are "crepuscular" (delicious word), hunting in the twilight hours around sunrise and sunset. They have very large eyes and apparently hunt by sight. Their beaks are small for the size of the bird, but they have enormous mouths, which they use like a butterfly net to scoop up a great variety of flying insects, ants, beetles, grasshoppers, mosquitoes, moths and such-like. (The Louisiana Cajuns nicknamed nighthawks *crapau volans*, "flying toad," strange but apt.)

Nighthawks breed through much of North America, as far north as the southern Yukon and Northwest Territories, and south into parts of Central America. The males have a dramatic display flight, flying in great circles, eating the sky, diving repeatedly, and at the bottom of each dive holding their wings stiffly downward, so that the air rushing over the bird's primaries makes a hollow strumming sound, a booming, like air blown across the mouth of an empty bottle.

Nighthawks build no nest. The two eggs are laid directly onto the ground (or sometimes, in cities, onto flat tar and gravel roofs) at a site chosen by the female, usually quite open and free of vegetation. Only the female incubates, but the chicks are fed by both parents.

Young nighthawks are semi-precocial, independent of their parents and flying well just thirty days after hatching, fully grown and ready for migration by fifty days. Nighthawks are among the earliest migrants to depart in the autumn. They need to be where it's warm and there are lots of insects to eat. They gather in flocks for the journey and, doubtless, that's exactly what's happening in the sky above me. They have one of the longest migrations of any North American bird; some will go as far as Argentina.

It tickles me to think of those birds up there being on the threshold of departure for distant and exotic places. *¡Hola allí arriba! ¿Hablas español? ¿Quieres bailar el tango?*

It's almost dark before the temperature eases sufficiently to let me make camp. I pitch the tent, though I hardly know why (mostly, I think, to keep the night-critters from making themselves too familiar), and lay out my sleeping pad and bag. My bivouac is a little close to the highway for comfort, perhaps, but well concealed in a fold of the mountainside. I'm careful to avoid using any light. No point in attracting unnecessary and unwanted attention. Fly below the radar, that's my motto.

A revelation, then. Even in this less-than-pristine place I'm able to find a good bit of enjoyment and something of the grace and beauty I've been seeking. I might even begin to hear those great chords sounding, though distantly, from somewhere deep out of creation if I listen carefully enough.

It's been a long day and I have to say I'm having second thoughts about going on.

From here I had planned to follow the high ground south toward Black Mountain, Mount Kruger and the international boundary, with the idea of exploring two of the other separate units of the South Okanagan Grasslands Protected Area: Chopaka East and Kilpoola.

But my feet are in terrible shape. The strenuous efforts of the last four days have put blisters on my blisters. And the pack is starting to rub my hips and shoulders raw. I've padded the straps and belly belt with extra clothing, but that doesn't seem to help much. My whole body feels like it's breaking down, wearing out.

Also I'm worried about water. I filled the two bottles this morning from a spring near the top of the mountain, but even with the greatest care, just a mouthful every now and again to wet my whistle, I've only half a bottle left. And I have no idea where or even if I might be able to replenish my supply south of the highway. Certainly there's no water at this little bivouac spot.

Anyway, it's all daft. What was I thinking, starting my walk at this time of year? It's August, the hottest month. Not exactly the best time to be wandering around the arid landscapes of the south Okanagan, even if I had ample water.

I've been looking forward to doing summertime things on my way up the Okanagan Valley—swimming, working on the tan. But anywhere away from the water will be furnace hot these next few weeks. Not pleasant walking.

In September the weather will be cooler, not so good for swimming, but much better for walking. There'll be less traffic. The campsites will be less crowded. And there's something about autumn in the Okanagan that could be very nice: an echo of summer sunshine, birds migrating, the first hint of fall colours, fruit ripening on branch and vine.

Final decision in the morning.

DAY SIX
Tuesday, August 7: Richter Pass to Osoyoos

No decision needed, really. It would be plain madness to go up into those sun-baked hills with only half a bottle of water and me already badly dehydrated. The new plan takes me south to Osoyoos along Highway 3, a relatively straight run, about fifteen kilometres, downhill all the way, getting me there in plenty of time, I hope, to catch the one o'clock p.m. Greyhound, the day's only departure northbound. Exit, stage left.

Halfway to town I spot a tall rangy bush growing on the slope beside the road. Its general appearance and three-lobed greyish leaves are reminiscent of big sage, but it's clearly a different species. This is my first encounter with antelope-bush (*Purshia tridentata*) though I've been watching for it. Antelope-bush is one of the characteristic plants of lower elevations at this extreme southern end of the Canadian section of the Okanagan Valley. It's also characteristic of a whole community of plants and animals living here at the northern edge of their ranges, but really more typical of country farther south, the Columbia Basin of Washington State, Oregon and Idaho. It is thanks in large measure to this spilling across the international boundary of species more common and widespread on the other side of the border that the south Okanagan can claim to be one of the most biologically diverse places in Canada.

Descending off the mountain into this populated place, coming down that last long hill into Osoyoos, is like landing in an airplane. One minute you're way up there, high above the crowd; then it's down and down, back into the hive of humanity, the throng, to be immersed again in all the bustle.

First, naturally, a stop for cheeseburgers and an ice cream cone, washed down by many glasses of ice water. Heaven! Everybody should be required to suffer real thirst once in a while, if only so they can experience the timeless and exquisite relief of quenching it—one of life's great pleasures. Such a luxury it is, being able to drink all the water you want, not having to stop drinking before you're satisfied. It is customary in this part of the world to pay for the cheeseburgers and ice cream, while the water is complimentary, part of the service. It should almost be the other way around.

Osoyoos is evidently very much a tourist town, especially in the summer. Walking down Main Street (that's what it's called), threading my way through knots of nattily attired pleasure-seekers with my big pack, boots and all, I feel conspicuously grubby and dishevelled: Saint Jerome, or Jeremiah the prophet, fresh off the desert, in for a little rest and recreation.

If appearances don't mislead, most of these folks haven't been thirsty, not really thirsty, in quite a good long while, if ever. I have the impression that they are not so much unaware of all that heat and aridity back up in the hills, but, rather, that the heat and aridity are distant concepts to them. Unreal, somehow, down here in the town. Just part of the scenery or ambience, as in a theme park. There's a disconnect. In fact, the heat and aridity, the thirst, are already fading in my own mind, like a dream.

With a couple of hours to kill before departure, I make my way down to Gyro Park, a lovely leafy space on the edge of Osoyoos Lake. (It's another of the little green patches on my map.) I have a swim, change my clothing. Whoever has the seat next to me on the bus should thank me for that. Then I find a place in the blessed shade to sit for a while, just enjoying the cool breeze off the water and the *smell* of the lake. (Again, that slightly acrid scent of water in a dry land, reminding me of the Ashnola, only more so.) Another of life's great pleasures.

And there is so much water here compared to Crater Mountain or Mount Kobau or any of the other landscapes I've passed through these last few days. Oceans of the stuff! It seems unfair that there should be so little water up in the hills while down here, within sight, there is so much. But that contrast is part of the essence of these valleys. Water in a dry land.

The bus pulls away on schedule, rolling northward over ground I'd expected to spend days or weeks covering on foot. With every twenty or thirty minutes of effortless air-conditioned cruising I put another arduous day of hiking behind me. It's so easy. But I get no real sense of the countryside flying past, seen only through a glass, darkly.

Autumn is the mellower season, and what we lose in flowers we more than gain in fruits.
       —Samuel Butler, *The Way of All Flesh*

Though I am old with wandering
Through hollow lands and hilly lands,
I will find out where she has gone,
And kiss her lips and take her hands;
And walk among long dappled grass,
And pluck till time and times are done
The silver apples of the moon,
The golden apples of the sun.
  —William Butler Yeats, "The Song of Wandering Aengus"

The moment one gives close attention to anything, even a blade of grass, it becomes a mysterious, awesome, indescribably magnificent world in itself.
     —Henry Miller, *Henry Miller on Writing*[2]

2

Crossing Home Ground—Autumn in the Okanagan

Okanagan Lake, north of Penticton

Tuesday, September 25: Richter Pass to Black Mountain

Six weeks have passed since my last journal entry and the world has moved on. The flywheel of time spins forward. There's blue sky at Richter Pass this morning, but the air is chilly, which is more than a little ironic considering the oven-heat of this place when last I was here. The sun has lost much of its old strength and power, and there's a raw breeze from the north. I'm only lightly dressed for the walk and have to keep moving just to stay warm. Water is still a concern, but I have three full bottles in the pack—enough, I hope, to see me all the way to Osoyoos if need be, two long days of walking over the highlands to the south.

Some hours later I'm traversing a steep slope high above the Chopaka–Nighthawk border crossing when I flush a couple of mule deer (*Odocoileus hemionus*), a doe and her well-grown fawn. Away they go, bounding, or, rather, "stotting," the correct term for this strange-looking form of forward motion: all four feet come down together, then the animal bounces away, *boing*, as if mounted on a pogo stick. Soon the pair are gone, up and over a rusty barbed-wire stock fence and out of sight into the little gully beyond.

I half turn for a better look at the old fence running down the hill and am astonished to see that it lines up exactly with the highly visible international boundary markers at the border crossing on the floor of the valley, far below.

As far as I can tell, then, this old stock fence, a bit of neglected barb wire, marks the forty-ninth parallel and the international border, the line between this Dominion of Canada and those United States of America. A few feet farther to the south and I'd be an illegal alien. It's an interesting moment and nicely marks the southernmost extent of my travels. From this point on, it's northward all the way.

The Similkameen River does an odd thing just the other side of the international boundary. From the village of Cawston, in British Columbia, it flows more or less directly southward into Washington State. You might expect that it would continue to follow that deep-cloven valley, eventually draining into the Columbia River system somewhere much farther to the south. Instead, as if tired of waiting, it shies away suddenly to the left, like a horse bolting from the corral, doubles back on itself and flows away eastward, squeezing through a deep gap in the south end of the Thompson Highlands, making for a rendezvous with the Okanagan River at Oroville, Washington, not too far south of Osoyoos.

I spend the latter part of the afternoon walking the terraces high above the river, from west to east, enjoying the gorgeous views down into that deep gap and southward to where the Cascade Mountains give way to the Columbia Basin, a broad, rugged landscape.

The sun is already sinking toward the western horizon when I step off the track and begin to work my way out across the broken ground onto one of the rocky ridges above the river valley, hoping for an even better view and keeping my eyes peeled for a level spot where I might pitch my tent in the fading light.

The wind has been picking up and I know I'm going to pay a price for camping in such an exposed situation: a long, noisy, sleepless night. But I'm a sucker for the long view and I'm in luck. I could hardly hope for more spectacular scenery across the river valley and away to the south.

But as it turns out the really dramatic stuff is much closer, tucked in among the rocks at my feet: beautiful little patches of pristine bunchgrass meadow, much like those I saw on the east slopes of Crater Mountain (and probably protected, like those, by relative inaccessibility). But whereas those on Crater Mountain were perched high above the road, distant and unattainable, these are right up close and personal.

It happens that I'm carrying one of Tony Hillerman's novels along on this walk. His characters, including Navajo Tribal Police officers Jim Chee and Joe Leaphorn, often use the expression, or variations on the expression, "walking in beauty." I've never been quite sure if this represents authentic Navajo lore, but the words certainly resonate here this evening. Beauty, not just as an aesthetic quality or value, something on a scale of one to ten (though there is certainly plenty of that around me), but rather as a factor or outcome or extension of truth and *rightness*. We feel the rightness of pristine ecosystems as a sort of joy. And, for want of a better word, we call it beauty.

All the open hillsides in the Similkameen and Okanagan valleys should look like this. The Thompson, Nicola and Fraser valleys too. This is the garden from which we have strayed. Thank God there's some left. And thank God, also, that this is part of the South Okanagan Grasslands Protected Area: Chopaka East Site. Clearly this protected area is not all sham and spin (and thank God for that, too). I take back some of the harsh things I said at the summit of Mount Kobau.

Bunchgrass meadows have a distinctive pebbled, nubbly or tufted appearance from a distance, not unlike the pile in certain kinds of oriental carpet, very different from the uniform nap of your ordinary wall-to-wall or a lawn or pasture of domestic or native turf-forming grasses. The bunchgrasses grow in widely spaced clumps. The drier the ground, the wider the spacing of the clumps, very reminiscent of desert vegetation. And growing among the clumps of grass, especially at higher elevations or wherever the ground is more moist, are various species of flowering forbs, such as arrowleaf balsamroot (*Balsamorhiza sagittata*), silky lupine (*Lupinus sericeus*) and three-flowered avens (*Geum triflorum*).

At lower elevations, especially, where the climate is hotter and drier, there will be a scattered growth of shrubs: big sagebrush (*Artemisia tridentata*), antelope-bush (*Purshia tridentata*) and common rabbit-brush (*Chrysothamnus nauseosus*).

At first glance the individual clumps of grass appear to be separated by bare ground. But closer inspection reveals that the entire surface supports a vigorous living crust of mosses, lichens, little vascular plants and a whole fauna of tiny or microscopic animals, all desiccated and quiescent at this time of the year. This biological soil crust, or "cryptogamic crust," turns out to be a critical part of bunchgrass meadow ecosystems, conserving soil moisture and preventing erosion from rain and wind. It's incredibly fragile. Even my soft shoes make dents. Domestic livestock can destroy it very quickly, especially if the ground is soft. Cows and horses, goats and sheep are big, heavy animals and they have hard, sharp hooves.

There are bunchgrasses and there are bunchgrasses.

Depending on altitude and latitude we might expect to encounter twelve to fifteen quite different species between here and Williams Lake, including giant wildrye (*Elymus cinereus*), stiff and spreading needlegrass (*Stipa occidentalis* and *S. richardsonii*), needle and thread grass (*Stipa comata*), porcupine grass (*Stipa curtiseta*), red three-awn (*Aristida longiseta*), rough, Idaho, Rocky Mountain and western fescue (*Festuca scabrella, F. idahoensis, F. saximontana,* and *F. occidentalis*) and foxtail barley (*Hordeum jubatum*).

Following a thread of thought from earlier in my journey, if we had to choose a single bunchgrass species to represent them all (and, indeed, the whole mosaic of different habitats and ecosystems in these valleys), it would have to be bluebunch wheatgrass (*Pseudoroegneria spicata*), the king or queen of bunchgrasses, the single most widely distributed plant species in these arid valleys, from riverbank to high forested plateau, from the forty-ninth parallel to Williams Lake.

Bluebunch wheatgrass is a perennial bunchgrass, forming large clumps, with the tallest stalks reaching sixty to one hundred centimetres into the air. The leaves are bluish-green (as you might expect), the reproductive stems slim but erect with seeds disposed in a spike, awned or not, an awn being the little hair-like or bristle-like projection from one of the bracts enclosing the seed in some species of grass.

The plants are fairly deeply rooted, sometimes reaching almost two metres into the soil, and therefore are quite drought resistant. Also cold, shade and fire tolerant. But not tolerant of wet soils.

Bluebunch wheatgrass doesn't compete well with introduced grasses, partly because it is palatable to livestock and therefore one of the first native species to suffer from grazing.

Bluebunch wheatgrass is widely distributed, not just in the interior valleys of southern British Columbia, but from Alaska to California and east to Saskatchewan, Michigan and Texas. It is one of the "cool season" or "C3" grasses, growing best in the spring and autumn, relatively dormant in the heat and dryness of summer, and therefore perfectly adapted to the climate of these interior valleys.

Pitching the tent is a desperate battle with the wind unrelenting. By six-thirty the sun has gone behind the mountains, which makes for a short day and a long night to come. All through the early part of the evening, while I eat my little supper, make up notes, read, prepare for bed, the wind continues to blow fierce and strong around the tent, which flaps and shakes and snaps like a living thing.

Then, suddenly, everything goes quiet. It's uncanny, almost unnerving. I sit there waiting for the blast to resume. In the space of a few moments the wind dwindles to nothing, so calm I can hear night birds calling. Naturally I have to check it out. I extricate myself from the sleeping bag, unzip the tent and tent-fly (déjà vu, déjà vu) and crawl outside for a look around.

What a moment it is! By now there is only the faintest breath of air out of the north whispering through the bunchgrasses around the tent. As on Crater Mountain, back at the beginning of August, sunset has faded to a faint rim of blue-green sky along the western horizon. Also as on Crater Mountain, the near-full moon is rising into the eastern sky, shining through a diaphanous haze of high, thin overcast. A harvest moon. Another first-night-out surprise, blessing and grace. I couldn't have planned it any better, though I'm thinking I should pay more attention to phases of the moon on future sections of my journey. This sort of thing is just too good to leave to chance.

Deep down in the valley of the Similkameen, a few scattered lights punctuate the darkness. The farms along the river. That's America down there. Howdy neighbours! Much farther off to the southeast, many more lights: the town of Oroville, Washington. And from some-where, maybe out of the rocks, maybe out of the grass, maybe out of the night sky (or maybe from somewhere inside, from heart and mind, softly) the great chords begin to sound. Walking in beauty.

Happily may I walk
May it be beautiful before me,

May it be beautiful behind me,
May it be beautiful below me,
May it be beautiful above me,
May it be beautiful all around me.
In beauty it is finished.

—Navajo traditional night chant

DAY EIGHT
Wednesday, September 26:
Black Mountain to Haynes Point Provincial Park, Osoyoos

The beautiful bunchgrass meadows around my tent turn out to be rather the exception, and I spend much of the morning and afternoon fighting my way through the heavy growth of sage that covers the flanks of Kruger Mountain in the South Okanagan Grasslands Protected Area: Kilpoola Site. My efforts are rewarded with some nice views from the crest of the ridge down into the Okanagan Valley: the little town of Oliver to the north, Osoyoos and Osoyoos Lake far below, and the wider, more open valley south of the border.

By the time I reach Osoyoos it's late afternoon and I decide to head for the British Columbia Visitor Centre, hoping to get some advice on where to camp and how best to proceed northward in the morning. The advice they're able to give me is a bit meagre. Those folks seem to be mostly in the business of promoting the higher end of the hospitality industry. But it proves to be an interesting and thought-provoking visit nonetheless, because of what I encounter on the plaza outside: a monumental piece of metal sculpture, Indian warrior, feather bonnet, lance and shield, mounted on a rearing horse.

Very dramatic.

But *wrong*.

This is from the "give the folks what they want" school of heritage interpretation and I know it bothers me, but why? What does it matter? If somebody, First Nations or non-First Nations, wants to indulge themselves in this more glamorous version of the indigenous culture rather than something less spectacular but more authentic, why not? What harm is there in that?

It's this:

Falsifying the past destroys any value it might have had as a guide to the future.

For many thousands of years before the arrival of comers-from-afar in the early nineteenth century, these arid valleys of southern interior British Columbia were inhabited by various Salishan-speaking peoples: the Lillooet, the Nlaka'pamux (Thompson), the Secwepemc (Shuswap) and the Okanagan.

These Interior Salish peoples shared not only variations on a common language, but also their whole culture or way of life. They were mostly small groups of people living in tiny semi-permanent villages along the major rivers and lakes, but travelling to other locations to take advantage of various seasonal resources: alpine root and berry crops, upland game (deer, some elk, mountain sheep) and, most especially, Pacific salmon migrating up the rivers and streams to spawn.

One might even think of the pre-contact Interior Salish as "people of the salmon," prospering whenever and wherever migrating salmon were plentiful, struggling when the runs failed. In fact, it's thought that Salishan-speaking peoples may have been originally drawn from coastal British Columbia to the interior of the province sometime around 3550 B.C. by the lure of burgeoning salmon runs associated with the onset of a cooler, wetter, more maritime climate. And even many thousands of years later, there were still echoes of northwest coast culture in the technologies and life-ways of the Interior Salish. In a sense the distant coast came yearly to visit in the form of migrating salmon.

With a lifestyle based on the highly seasonal abundance of various resources, a great deal of effort had to be invested, not simply in the gathering of those resources, but also in the preparation and storage of large quantities of durable food, sufficient to carry the people through the leaner months of the year. Summertime shelters were usually temporary structures of matting, hide, bark, brush, even grass. But winter villages were characterized by more substantial semi-subterranean lodges, so-called pit-houses or *kekuli*, excavated into the ground, roofed with poles and earth, and accessed through a central hole in the roof via notched pole ladder.

Interior Salish society seems to have been admirably egalitarian and burdened with remarkably little political structure. None of the four peoples—Lillooet, Nlaka'pamux, Shuswap or Okanagan—had any sort of formal "tribal" organization. Individual villages were the basic political unit, usually led by a head-man or chief acting more as a facilitator than an authority figure. Based on commonly accepted abilities and experience, other individuals might well have supervised specific tasks and enterprises. Essential decisions were largely based on informal consensus. Women led in their own areas of experience and ability. Order was mostly maintained by force of tradition, honour, various forms of informal persuasion.

But here's the thing.

Everywhere those people went, on land at least, and everything they did, for thousands upon thousands of years, hunting, gathering, trading, seasonal migrations, whatever, was all done on foot.

It was a pedestrian culture.

That's one of the reasons I wanted to do this journey on foot. Seems only appropriate, a nod in the direction of that immensely long tradition. Perhaps I can even claim to be a part of it now, if only in a very minor way.

And I can't help wondering if that pre-contact culture's essential longevity, enduring relatively unchanged through all those thousands of years, in some sort of delicate balance with its environment, wasn't due in some large measure to its being a very low-impact culture of pedestrian hunters and gatherers.

Think how much larger this countryside must have seemed when everybody had to walk everywhere, when everything had to be carried on a human being's back. Most of the landscape, especially the high-lands, all that natural capital, would simply have been beyond the reach of little groups camping along the rivers and lakes.

In light of all that, the arrival of horses in the early years of the eighteenth century was something of a catastrophe, the beginning of the end for many natural ecosystems and perhaps for the indigenous culture as well.

Horses, of course, proved irresistible to indigenous peoples, not simply as a status possession or as a means of transportation but as a war machine. It's no accident or coincidence that the metallic rider outside the centre is carrying a spear and shield, rather than, say, a fishing net or burden basket. And it's no accident, either, that he's dressed as a plains warrior, echoes of northwest coast culture gone, the interior Salish now looking east and southeast to their source of horses and equestrian culture.

Virtually overnight these First Nations went from pedestrian hunter-gatherers to herdsmen and mounted hunter-warriors. Horses became the new currency and status symbol. A profound cultural change and not for the better. Yet it's that twilight image, the last hundred years, maybe less, of an age-old culture, that gets memorialized on this plaza in front of the visitor centre.

Horses are famously hard on grass. They graze closer than cattle, sometimes even pulling plants up by the roots. And those early herds multiplied rapidly. By 1808, in the Kootenay valley at least, North West Company explorer David Thompson could report that horses had become "common and frequently seen in large groups." Much the same must have been true in the Okanagan. Even before the first herds of cattle were driven across the border in 1858, en route to the Fraser and Cariboo goldfields, some of the more accessible south-facing slopes above the valley and the grassy meadows down along the lake would already have been suffering some degree of overgrazing.

By the time I reach Haynes Point Provincial Park a little after six o'clock, the sun has gone behind the shoulder of Kruger Mountain and the lakeside air is already chilly. Haynes Point isn't much of a nature preserve, though it's a pretty enough spot. I remember, from my brief visit to Osoyoos in August, that intoxicating smell of water in a dry land. California quail run in and out of the brush along the shore, topknots bobbing, calling to each other: *Where are you? Where are you?* And there's a nice little marsh off to the right, just inside the entrance.

But mostly Haynes Point Provincial Park is a public beach and campground.

And not much of a campground, either, by my standards. There's only one tent in the whole place from what I can see, that of a young couple on a bicycle tour. All the other sites are occupied by recreational vehicles, evidently the market that this park caters to. Big sites. Water and power hookups. And it's expensive, the fees more appropriate to a commercial RV park. If you can afford a $100,000 motorhome, I suppose, expense is all relative.

Should public parks, British Columbia's provincial parks, be catering to that relatively slender part of the demographic able to purchase a big RV, even if they can afford to pay the higher fees and generate more revenue for provincial coffers?

I remember with great affection childhood family camping trips through various national and provincial parks. (VW beetle, big canvas tent, the whole bit.) Doubtless those trips contributed hugely to my own affection for the countryside, helping to make me the kind of person I am. And doubtless, too, one of the big attractions for my hard-pressed parents was that such trips offered a relatively inexpensive form of family vacation.

What kind of society runs its public parks, not to mention museums, art galleries and archives, as profit centres?

Important questions, but all pretty much moot just now, at least as far as I'm concerned, because I've discovered, to my astonishment and chagrin, that, even now in late September, Haynes Point campground is full. *Complet. No hay vacantes. Ausgebucht.*

I do the full circuit. Then I walk it again. *De nada.* I kick myself for making that side trip to the visitor centre. Should have come straight here, though perhaps I'd have been too late even then. It occurs to me that this is one of those provincial park campsites for which a reservation ("additional charge") is more or less required, even in September.

Fortunately, as it turns out, the site manager happens to be doing his rounds while I'm thus engaged and stops to ask if he can help me. I'm pretty sure this is a polite way of inquiring what I'm up to. Guy with a pack and tent wandering around a campsite. Suspicious behaviour.

I explain. He responds, somewhat brusquely I feel, by confirming what I've already guessed: that the campsite is full. And then, for good measure, he adds that I'll have to leave. By now, of course, the light is fading fast, fatigue has set in big time and I'm beginning to feel more than a little desperate. Not my usual courteous self.

So I explain further that I'm on a walking tour, that I have, in fact, walked all day to get here and that I am consequently pretty much knackered. That I just need a place to bivouac overnight and will be on my way first thing in the morning, I promise. Further, that I really don't have anywhere else to go, have no intention of leaving and that, sorry about this, he's pretty much stuck with me. Words to that effect.

I suppose I'm lucky he doesn't just call the cops. That might have lent a fine unexpected twist to my pilgrimage and taken care of the accommodation issue. But he takes pity, the kindness of strangers again, and somehow manages to squeeze me in. Bless him for that.

I throw up the tent in near darkness (getting to be a habit), push the gear inside and gratefully follow it in. As I eat my cold supper, straight from the bag, I can hear the night coming alive outside. There's the noise of traffic and, from somewhere not too far away, the sound of human voices. I'm almost never nervous camping in wilderness, but here, camping so close to town, I feel distinctly edgy. Oddly, I feel safer and cosier inside the tent, my sanctuary and shelter, the flimsy nylon protecting me from the world and its dangers. I know this is irrational, like the proverbial ostrich hiding its head in the sand, but there's no denying the effect. Even so, I've cranked my hearing up a few notches and I'm paying more attention than usual to what's going on outside.

The last flights of migrating waterfowl land on the marsh and lake. I can hear them gabbling and talking over there: *Did you see . . . ? Well, no, we came down . . . Terrible headwinds . . .* The quail are still calling from the brush along the lake, reassuring each other. Something scampers and rustles past the tent. I tell myself it's a squirrel.

DAY NINE
Thursday, September 27: Haynes Point to Gallagher Lake

I wake to an unexpected and dramatic change in the weather: heavily overcast skies threatening much worse to come. It's always harder to get moving on a cloudy day, but I'm up and away betimes, as promised, no lingering in the campsite. It's still very early as I make my way through the deserted streets of Osoyoos and onto Highway 97, eager to cover some ground, heading north.

But, first, a brief stop.

John Carmichael Haynes was an Irishman, born in 1831, native of County Cork.

He left Ireland in 1858, age 27, bound for the newly established colonies of Vancouver Island and British Columbia where he intended to join the colonial police force then being assembled by Charles Brew.

Haynes landed in Victoria on Christmas Day, 1858, and was almost immediately appointed a special constable to help keep the peace among the many thousands of miners who'd been streaming into the Fraser River canyon all through that spring, summer and autumn, chasing rumours of gold.

The rush attracted, in turn, a whole range of entrepreneurs willing to provide the necessary goods and services to miners, at a price, of course. The Fraser River rush of 1858 was just the latest in a series of gold rushes along the Pacific coast of North America, starting with the California rush of 1849. The business of gold rushing had become almost routine, a sort of travelling circus that would up sticks and move onward every few months at word of some fresh discovery. Fortunes could be made catering to the miners, and provisions were in special demand.

But time was of the essence in that business. By the autumn of 1858, just months after the arrival of the first miners on the Fraser River, herds of cattle from Washington and Oregon, beef on the hoof, were already crossing the international boundary at Osoyoos Lake.

Two years later, in December of 1860, Governor James Douglas imposed customs duties and tolls on imported animals. And in 1861, John Carmichael Haynes was sent to establish a customs post at Osoyoos.

The site of Haynes's original Osoyoos Customs House is now marked by a stone cairn in a peach orchard across from the Lakeview Cemetery on 176th Avenue, north of Osoyoos, just off Highway 97.

By 1861, the focus of the rush had already passed from the Fraser River north into the Cariboo district. That was the year Billy Barker made his fabulous find on Williams Creek, triggering a fresh frenzy. In 1862, eight hundred men and nine thousand animals passed through Haynes's station at Osoyoos, and he collected more than £2,200 worth of revenue.

Cattle were driven northward at a walking pace to give them plenty of opportunity to graze along the way. The whole long trail from Oregon to the goldfields might take months to cover. The herds stopped somewhere along the way for the winter, a sheltered place with adequate water and forage for the stock, then went on again in spring when beef prices in the mining camps would be highest. Not surprisingly, grasslands along the trail and in the favoured wintering spots were soon badly overgrazed.

The heavy traffic in animals continued into the mid-1860s, but by then miners were already abandoning the Cariboo goldfields in favour of new prospects in the Omineca and Cassiar districts, farther north. Demand for beef dwindled. Stock began to accumulate.

Herds soon numbered in the tens of thousands of animals. By the 1870s, cattle were being driven *out* of interior British Columbia. This was the era of open range. Cattle were simply turned loose to fend for themselves. There was no supplemental feeding, not even in winter. It was taken for granted that the range could provide.

But it didn't.

In bad winters, cattle perished by the thousands. And grasslands in these interior valleys were so badly damaged by chronic overgrazing that many areas have never really recovered, despite the advent of winter-feeding and modern improvements in range management.

By the end of the day I've covered almost forty kilometres, mostly along the attractive dike-top footpath that follows the Okanagan River upstream from Osoyoos Lake to the McAlpine Bridge, north of Oliver. The weather did brighten a little at midday, but it was only a respite. By late afternoon, dark clouds have gathered again and I'm dead tired. Two strenuous days in a row. Time to get horizontal.

But where?

Slipping off into the woods to camp is not an option. There are houses everywhere. And something I noticed earlier along the river, there's poison ivy everywhere too. Poison ivy is tricky at this time of the year. Mostly the leaves are still the usual glossy green, clear warning. ("Leaves in three, let it be.") But some have turned a vivid red, mimicking staghorn sumac or Virginia creeper. And sometimes there are no leaves at all, just the bare twigs and white berries, nondescript but just as poisonous as the leaves.

Commercial campsites are not much my style, but there doesn't seem to be any practical alternative. At least there should be hot water. Lots and lots of hot water.

I've just finished my shower and am lying at ease, much relaxed, in the darkness of the tent, wrinkled like a raisin, clean from head to toe, when I hear the first raindrops bouncing off the tent-fly. Soon a steady pitter-pat, then a drumming roar. Earplug time.

I'm fine and dry and warm and secure for the moment, but this slow progressive change in the weather doesn't bode well for the morning. I've a bad feeling. It's autumn now. A rainy spell could go on for days. I'm no hero and I want to see the country at its best. A fair-weather trekker, that's me. Tomorrow I'll check at the campground office for a forecast, and if it looks like we're in for a spell of foul weather, I'll call another timeout.

DAY TEN
Friday, September 28: Gallagher Lake

Beam me up, Scotty, I'm out of here!

It's not the Starship Enterprise but an English family touring western Canada in a big recreational vehicle who offer a lift to this bedraggled backpacker. Good on them.

DAY ELEVEN
Thursday, October 11:
Gallagher Lake to Okanagan Falls Provincial Park

I've lost almost two weeks to bad weather. The days are shorter and the countryside is showing the first real signs of fall. The aspens on the hillsides and the cottonwoods along the river have gone a beautiful yellow-gold, quite lovely, torrents of colour coursing down the gullies among the evergreens, a touch of brilliance in an autumn-drab landscape. There was even a bit of frost last night. But the weather seems to have come around, and it looks like I'm in for one of those mostly sunny fall days that make walking such a pleasure.

I start again from the very spot where I quit two weeks ago. And I've not gone more than a couple of hundred metres up the highway when I come to an unexpected parting of the ways. On my right, Highway 97, north to Vaseaux Lake and the little town of Okanagan Falls. On my left, perhaps half a kilometre away, the great looming bulk of McIntyre Bluff rising sheer-faced from the floor of the valley. Between me and the base of the bluff, a patch of weedy waste, guarded by the remains of an ancient fence, long since flattened to the ground.

I can't actually see the Okanagan River, but I know it's over there somewhere, tempting me. The question is: Should I carry on up Highway 97, as planned, or should I go exploring?

Fences have power over me, no question, but this one looks to be hardly any fence at all. And the prospect of trudging up the shoulder of Highway 97, dodging traffic, seems distinctly unattractive.

No contest.

Once I get past the weeds, the little piece of countryside along the river turns out to be the most spectacular bit of ground I've seen since that bunchgrass-covered ridge above the Similkameen. The Okanagan River, a clear-water stream, still runs its natural course along the foot of McIntyre Bluff and on down to the McAlpine Bridge. In fact, this is the only unmodified section of the Okanagan River in Canada. The far bank is a steep slope of broken talus overshadowed by almost three hundred metres of towering vertical rock face. Barely a kilometre separates McIntyre Bluff from an equally precipitous bluff, unnamed, on the east side of the valley. They are like the two great stone pillars of a vast gateway. The sumac and willows along the banks of the river are dressed, like the aspens and cottonwoods, in vivid autumn colours, the willows yellow-gold, the sumac a brilliant alizarin crimson set off against the deep green of ponderosa pine and Douglas-fir. It's a beautiful spot.

I realize quickly that the waste ground between the highway and the river must once have been part of the right-of-way for the south Okanagan spur of the old Kettle Valley Railway (KVR). The railbed is still there, long since stripped of rails and ties. This section of the KVR was built during the Second World War so that fruit could be shipped from Osoyoos and Oliver to the main line at Penticton. It was decommissioned in the 1980s. And now it seems to present an inviting opportunity. Rather than return to the highway I decide to follow the right-of-way north, at least a short distance, to see what might be seen.

Which quickly brings me to the end of the river's natural run: McIntyre Dam, stretching from bank to bank, ponding the water upstream into a different sort of river, deep and sluggish. To one side, a large irrigation ditch carries water south toward the orchards and vineyards of Oliver. Below the dam there is faster water, and in that water a small school of fair-sized fish, perhaps a couple dozen altogether, with brilliantly coloured scarlet bodies and green heads.

Sockeye salmon (*Oncorhynchus nerka*).

Apparently this is all that remains of the Okanagan River's once-bountiful runs. As I watch, one fish, then another, tries to leap into a little stream of water running from an overflow pipe in the concrete wall at my feet. How pathetic. Think of it. A male sockeye salmon in full spawning colours, glorious, trying to swim into a pipe. Still trying to work his way upstream to wherever his nose tells him he must go to finish his race. How sad, to have come so far and through so many perils to end up like this.

Sockeye salmon require a nursery lake in which to spend their first year. At one time the lakes of the Okanagan Valley (Osoyoos, Vaseaux, Skaha, Okanagan, Kalamalka, Wood) represented something like 40 percent of the potential sockeye rearing habitat in the entire Columbia River system.

But since the early 1950s, this dam, constructed as part of the south Okanagan's flood control and irrigation system, has been the end of the road for sockeye migrating up the Okanagan River. The only nursery left to them is Osoyoos Lake. And Osoyoos Lake, with its warm temperatures and low oxygen levels, is a less than ideal habitat.

There's worse. This pathetic little remnant is the last of more than a dozen different sockeye salmon stocks once supported by the Canadian portion of the Columbia River system. The others are extinct, thanks mostly to intensive and extensive hydroelectric, flood control and irrigation developments. The Columbia River, once upon a time fast flowing and high volume, is now one of the world's most thoroughly dammed river systems. And salmon stocks have suffered terribly in consequence.

It's estimated that ten to sixteen million salmon would once have returned annually to the Columbia system. By 1995 the number had fallen to less than a million and many stocks were extinct altogether. The Grand Coulee Dam (1942) and Chief Joseph Dam (1955), just upstream from the confluence of the Okanagan and Columbia rivers, were constructed with no provision at all for migrating fish. They present an absolute barrier to migrating salmon. The engineers and builders seem to have had utter disdain for anything except their electricity. Of all the stocks that the upper Columbia system once supported, from the Chief Joseph Dam to Lake Windermere in eastern British Columbia, not a single fish remains.

Even on the lower Columbia, hydroelectric developments represent a significant hazard to migrating salmon. Aside from the obvious physical dangers—turbine blades and such—the impoundments created by the dams have altered the river in unfriendly ways. The once fast-flowing Columbia, which could hardly have been designed more perfectly to flush salmon smolts out to sea, is now a series of sluggish artificial lakes. The journey to the sea is much longer now for little fish, much harder work and more time-consuming. The water is warmer than it should be. And smolts face a whole range of exotic predators favoured by the new conditions.

Even without all those additional hazards, the mere presence of these fish, the fact of these fish in the pool below me, would represent a more than minor miracle, a series of profound improbabilities. Four years ago, another little school of scarlet fish, parents to these fish, managed against all odds to spawn somewhere in this little stretch of river. The fish I'm watching today would have spent their first winter in the gravel of the riverbed. In the spring they would have journeyed to their nursery lake, Lake Osoyoos. Tiny, tiny fish, fry, travelling all the length of the river from here to the lake, forty or fifty kilometres. Imagine the hazards of that, the odds against them surviving. But even that adventure pales to insignificance beside the journey they would undertake in their second spring, all the way down the Okanagan and Columbia rivers, a thousand kilometres, these very fish, finger-sized smolts now, past all the hazards, natural and unnatural, turbines and predators, and on into the wide ocean for two years of wandering, perhaps halfway to Japan. Then the call, the sudden alarm, and the rush homeward.

These very fish, right there in the river before me, would have been schooling off the mouth of the Columbia just four or five weeks ago. These very fish—that one right there or that one over there—swam past Astoria, under the docks of Portland, past all the towns and villages, made their way metre by metre, kilometre by kilometre, up the mighty river and then up its tributary, the Okanagan. Each hazard along the way would have claimed a toll; very, very few individuals escape to continue to the end. An unbelievable physical accomplishment, a heroic effort, far beyond anything a human being might be capable of. Superhuman. And here they are, at last, unheralded, trying to swim up a pipe before they die.

The archeological record suggests that the fortunes of indigenous peoples in the southern interior of British Columbia were closely bound to the fortunes of Pacific salmon. When salmon were plentiful, the First Nations prospered; when salmon were scarce, the First Nations along the banks of empty rivers dwindled and starved. Nowadays, our fortunes seem less closely tied to what goes on in this river. Even so, I'd argue, we will all be, in some essential way, deeply diminished when the salmon stop coming.

Vaseaux Lake is a spectacular bit of scenery, blue sunlit water in sharp contrast to the rugged countryside, with McIntyre Bluff still looming picturesquely to the south, back along the way I've come. There's a nice little provincial park, Vaseaux Lake Provincial Park, complete with interpretive display and boardwalk trail to a lakeshore bird blind. The park itself is just a slender strip of ground along the northeast edge of the lake and upstream into the extensive wetlands along that section of the Okanagan River north of the lake. But Vaseaux Lake Provincial Park is just one small element in what turns out to be a whole complex of protected areas.

There's the White Lake Protected Area to the west and Vaseaux Protected Area to the east, both Province of British Columbia lands. There are sanctuaries administered by the Canadian Wildlife Service for migratory birds and for California bighorn sheep. Ducks Unlimited has a couple of parcels. The Nature Trust of BC and their various partners have extensive holdings including the Dr. Geoff Scudder South Okanagan Grasslands Research Field Station.

It's all very impressive when you see it laid out on a map, more than a step in the right direction, cause for hope, enthusiasm, celebration.

Okanagan Falls isn't much to get excited about.

I'm writing of the waterway now, not the town. In the early 1950s, a dam similar to the one at McIntyre Bluff, part of the same flood control project, was constructed below the falls, just downstream from Skaha Lake, leaving only a short stretch of feeble rapids still visible.

Okanagan Falls Provincial Park is right next door. It reminds me very much of Haynes Point Provincial Park back in Osoyoos, more campground than park, though pretty enough in its way, especially now, with the maples brilliant in red and orange. And to complete the resemblance, this park, too, turns out to be completely full, no vacancy, when I arrive at the end of the afternoon. Astonishing, so late in the season.

What's going on, I wonder? Are these snowbirds, already headed south for the winter? I do one circuit, then another, just as at Haynes Point. This time there's no campground manager to help me out. But a middle-aged couple parked in one of the riverside campsites beckon to me as I trudge past a second time. It turns out that they've just stopped for a bit of a break from a long day on the road. I can have their site when they're finished. They even pour me a glass of wine while we chat.

This is more than a holiday trip for them. They've been living at the coast but are contemplating a move to the interior, attracted by the sunshine and the prospect of a quieter life. At the same time, they have misgivings about being so far from the city. This place, they declare, would be ideal if only it were a little closer to town. (Of course it would be rather a different place if it were a little closer to the city, but I forbear to mention this. The wine has sealed my lips.)

Camping at Okanagan Falls has a long tradition behind it. My father, as a boy, spent a few nights under canvas here, down from Penticton with his father and brothers, a common recreation in those days. And for time out of mind before that, the falls were a prime gathering and salmon-harvesting site for First Nations, specifically the Okanagan (uknaqínx) peoples who traditionally inhabit the Okanagan Valley north to the head of Okanagan Lake, east to the traditional territories of the closely related Lakes peoples, west to Douglas Lake and the upper Nicola River, and southwest into the Similkameen River valley. It's odd, in fact, considering the importance of this place to First Nations, that there is no reserve here, a consequence, I'd guess, of some shabby nineteenth-century chicanery by the colonial, provincial and/or federal administrations.

Nowadays, Okanagan Falls lies midway between the reserves of the Osoyoos Band to the south, and the Penticton Band to the north. Maybe that's appropriate. The sharing of resources was an important part of traditional culture here. Perhaps this was one of those places not possessed by one group or family but open to all, a place where everyone was welcome.

There is something in me that delights at the thought of being part now of that story, not just of our family, but of an immensely more ancient human tradition stretching back four or five thousand years, maybe longer.

DAY TWELVE
Friday, October 12: Okanagan Falls to Naramata

Right off the bat there's an unhappy choice to be faced, route-wise, between Highway 97, running north through the countryside west of Skaha Lake (*Skaha* from a Syilx word meaning "dog"), or Eastside Road following the shoreline along the other side of the lake. Either way, I'm not much looking forward to the traffic, the noise, the exhaust.

While I stand there, dithering, trying to make up my mind, a young couple comes along with a pair of golden retrievers on leash. As usual with golden retrievers, it's difficult to tell just who is walking whom.

The whole crowd stops to say hello. I pet the dogs, pass the time of day with the people.

Earlier I'd noticed a walking path along the east bank of the river that seemed to connect with some sort of lakeshore trail via a trestle bridge near the river's mouth. It looked inviting.

Purely as a topic of conversation, I ask the couple how far along the lake the trail might go.

"Oh," they exclaim, almost in unison. "All the way to Penticton!"

Well, hurrah! Eureka!

This turns out to be another stretch of right-of-way for the old KVR, now serving as a recreational trail, easy walking or cycling, smooth and level, mostly right along the water.

What with the KVR trail from Okanagan Falls to Penticton *and* the walking trails along the beaches or river dikes in Penticton *and* the KVR trail again from Penticton north to Naramata up the east side of Okanagan Lake, I hardly need to set foot on a roadway all day. It gets to be kind of a game. I start fancying myself as an urban backpacker or trekker, a wasteland adventurer, seeking out the hidden routes, the little corridors of greenery through the concrete and asphalt, flying below the radar.

It's fun.

I experience some moments of uncertainty trying to relocate the KVR right-of-way on the far northeast edge of Penticton, where the old railbed disappears beneath a residential subdivision. But I persevere and eventually find myself back on track (so to speak), hiking northward through the orchards and vineyards atop the lofty clay bluffs that loom over the water at the south end of Okanagan Lake. The late-afternoon views from the trail are quite lovely: north toward the little community of Naramata, not too far away on this east side of the lake, or across the vast expanse of water to Summerland or to Peachland, farther up the lake. At Peachland, perhaps thirty kilometres away, the lake passes out of sight to the east, in the general direction of Kelowna, somewhere beyond the steep mass of Okanagan Mountain.

I always get a kick out of imagining a time not so very long ago in years, but from a very different age of the world nevertheless, when all of the valley's traffic and commerce came and went by water. A slower, more elegant time. I picture the SS *Okanagan* or the SS *Sicamous* down there, steaming northward, nosing into the shore at this or that little landing, docking at the larger settlements, Naramata, Summerland and Peachland. There would be passengers disembarking and embarking, bins and boxes of produce being loaded from the local packing plant, farm implements, maybe a handsome team of horses.

It was a combination of lake boats and the Canadian Pacific Railway (CPR) that made agricultural settlement of the Okanagan Valley possible. Made it an economic imperative in fact. The whole future success of the CPR was predicated on a simple plan: fill the countryside with productive people and charge them to move their goods and freight and kids and livestock and anything else for which they might require transportation.

Hiram F. Smith, a.k.a. "Okanagan Smith," planted the first fruit trees in the valley, sometime around 1857, at his farm just south of the international boundary. Oblate missionaries Fathers Charles Pandosy and Pierre Richard planted the first fruit trees in the Canadian portion of the Okanagan Valley at Okanagan Mission around 1862. An early rancher, Francis Xavier Richter (for whom the pass is named), planted the region's first commercial orchard at Keremeos in 1880. But these were all modest, experimental endeavours, almost whimsical. You can drive cattle over hundreds of miles of rough trails to market. But what can you do with a box of apples? Sell it to the neighbours, I suppose— but that was a limited market in those days.

Realistic transportation came to the north end of the valley in 1886 with the start of regular service on the CPR main line through Sicamous. By 1892 the Shuswap and Okanagan Railway was complete to Okanagan Landing. The new steel rails brought substantial numbers of agricultural settlers into the Okanagan and carried their produce away to world markets.

Almost overnight the era of the giant cattle ranch, certainly the day of open range, was past. Not that the ranches disappeared. Some of the earliest are still in operation today, but suddenly there was a very different view of the future. And the future was agricultural development. Not just a farm here and a farm there, but whole swaths of the Okanagan countryside subdivided, ploughed, planted, irrigated.

The first and perhaps most spectacular example of that conversion was the Coldstream Ranch, east of the city of Vernon at the north end of the valley.

In 1890, on a holiday trip to western Canada, John Hamilton-Gordon, the 7th Earl of Aberdeen, and his countess, Ishbel Maria, Lady Aberdeen, purchased, sight unseen, 480 acres near Kelowna—promptly renamed Guisachan, "place of the firs," after Lady Aberdeen's childhood home—as a cattle ranch for the lady's brother, the Honourable Coutts Marjoribanks.

In 1891 the couple came west again to have a look at their new property. By chance, that visit coincided with the first exhibition of the Okanagan and Spallumcheen Agricultural Society. Lord Aberdeen was prevailed upon to open the exhibition and this seems to have been the occasion that first stimulated the lord and lady's interest in promoting the development of fruit farming in the Okanagan Valley—not merely in terms of creating a single fruit farm but in encouraging the growth of a whole community of such farms.

In October of 1891 they purchased Forbes George Vernon's ranch, renamed it the Coldstream Ranch and left the countess's brother in charge, with instructions for planting apple, pear and cherry trees the following spring, along with hops and various sorts of berries, including strawberries, raspberries, and gooseberries, to provide cash crops until the fruit trees could begin to bear.

By the end of the following year, 1892, some one hundred acres had been planted to orchard, with 25,000 fruit trees in the ground. That same year the first subdivisions were surveyed and land advertisements appeared. Construction commenced on a jam factory, butcher shop, fruit market and the beginnings of an irrigation system.

By the autumn of 1893, when Lord Aberdeen received his

appointment as Governor General of Canada, construction on the Coldstream Ranch internal irrigation system was well under way and nine hundred acres of planted orchard had already been sold to prospective farmers. In the summer of 1894 the Aberdeens came west again on holiday, and for the next five years, until the earl relinquished his appointment in the autumn of 1898, the Coldstream Ranch was summer home to the lord and lady and all their many houseguests.

I know I'm inclined to an unreasonably rosy and romantic view of that whole era, susceptible to an odd sense of nostalgia for a time I never actually experienced. And, surely, on a lovely summer day in, say, 1896, the fourth year of the Aberdeens' ownership, when the new trees yielded their first real crop of apples, the Coldstream valley must have seemed very much like a paradise on earth.

But I'll not deny the story has a much darker side, with all the unrelenting vicissitudes of trying to run a brand-new agricultural enterprise under untried conditions. By 1903 the Aberdeens had had enough. They sold their Kelowna property and began looking for other investors to assume part of the financial burden of the Coldstream Ranch. It wasn't until 1921 that the lord and lady (now styled the Marquess and Marchioness of Aberdeen and Temair), thoroughly disillusioned, managed finally to extricate themselves from their misadventure.

Ironically, by then, much of what they had originally envisioned had come to pass, though at a much greater cost in time, money and effort than they could have imagined at the outset. By the end of 1906, an extraordinary irrigation system, model for developments elsewhere in the Okanagan, was in place, drawing water from reservoirs on the high southern plateau and distributing it to the entire Coldstream valley through a cunning system of ditches, canals, flumes and siphons. From the perspective of a century or more later, the number of lives that have been shaped and enhanced by the Aberdeens' original vision seems well-nigh incalculable.

But one thing is certain: Agricultural developments utterly transformed the valley's natural environment.

Thousands of acres were permanently stripped of their native vegetation and ploughed over. Wetlands were drained. Whole water-sheds were appropriated and redirected to serve the new developments. There's an interesting paper by Ted Lea in the journal *Davidsonia* that uses mapping to calculate that by 2005 many lower-elevation ecosystems had lost over 60 percent of their original areas to agricultural development and subsequent urbanization.[3] Certain kinds of riparian ecosystems and open grasslands were even harder hit, losing close to 90 percent of their original areas.

A handy patch of Crown land on the mountainside high above Naramata is my resting place at the end of the day. There's no water, but I still have something left from when I filled the bottles in Penticton, and I should be able to refill them at Naramata Creek, not too much farther north from here. Tomorrow, with a little luck, Okanagan Mountain Provincial Park.

DAY THIRTEEN
Saturday, October 13:
Naramata to Okanagan Mountain Provincial Park

I wake to a chilly morning but with that great dome of clear blue sky that promises a full day of good walking. The kind of day when one feels glad to be alive. But cold mornings make for reluctant starts, and by the time I've managed to extricate myself from a warm and comfortable sleeping bag the sun is already high in the sky, lighting the long view down through the vineyards and orchards to the lake far below.

It's a straightforward walk this morning, with a stop for water, as planned, at Naramata Creek, lovely in the sun, with the clear stream tumbling down out of the forest and the aspens shining golden all along the gully.

I follow the broad gravel path for kilometre after kilometre, ever upward, but gently. It feels a little like cheating, truth to tell, almost too easy, such a swift passage through such rugged country, with spectacular views out over the valley at every turn.

The Kettle Valley Railway trail is, of course, vastly over-engineered for a walking trail. I am more conscious today than I was yesterday of walking an abandoned railbed. Evidence of the navvies' work is everywhere: the right-of-way slicing through the granite bluffs, the masonry retaining walls, the long slow curves and that steady, almost imperceptible grade, climbing up and up, but so gently as to seem practically level at first. Hiking up a steady 2.2-percent grade is deceptive, like bicycling into a slight breeze. At first I take it for granted that I'm just a little extra tired from yesterday's long walk. It's not until my second or third unscheduled break (complete with feelings of surprise and disappointment at my apparent lack of physical conditioning) that I finally realize what's going on.

Having left the KVR trail behind, I am perhaps halfway up the steepest section of the Chute Lake Road, just south of Okanagan Mountain Provincial Park, when I come to the edge of the burn. One minute there's Douglas-fir forest, green and lovely; the next, a wasteland of blackened spars. And that edge also happens to mark, more or less, a different sort of boundary for me, less tangible, more psychological and emotional.

Up to this point I've been exploring countryside relatively new to me. Now I'm back on familiar ground. Okanagan Mountain Provincial Park was at the far limits of home territory for a kid with a newly acquired driver's licence, but I came here every chance I got, always a little astonished to find such a wild and beautiful landscape right on the southern edge of what was becoming, even then, the ferocious urban and suburban sprawl of Kelowna.

A Fire Review Summary published by the Ministry of Forests observes that the Okanagan Mountain fire was kindled at about 01:55, August 16, 2003, by a lightning strike into the scattered pines and grassy slopes of Okanagan Mountain Provincial Park above Rattlesnake Island, on the east side of Okanagan Lake, between Naramata and Kelowna. The weather had been unusually hot and dry that summer. Gusty southwest winds were forecast for later in the day.[4]

The strike, in plain view of Peachland residents across Okanagan Lake, was reported almost immediately. The summer of 2003 had been a season of fierce wildfire, and communities everywhere in British Columbia's southern interior were acutely aware of the potential for disaster. Even so, the first firefighting crews from the Ministry of Forests Wildfire Protection Branch were not deployed until well after daybreak. Evidently the countryside was considered too rugged for crews to operate safely in early-morning darkness. The actual time of deployment is not specified in the Fire Review Summary, but witnesses testifying before the 2003 Firestorm Provincial Review set the time at around seven o'clock in the morning, five hours after the lightning strike was first reported, by which time the fire had grown to involve about fifteen hectares of the mountainside. A helicopter began bucketing the fire shortly after six o'clock in the morning, and by ten o'clock three water-bombers were at work.[5]

According to witnesses, the fire, though still active, seemed to be coming under control when, at quarter past eleven, the bombers were withdrawn. By twelve-thirty in the afternoon the wind was rising and the fire began breaking out toward the north. Two helicopters continued to work the blaze but seemed unable to keep up. The water-bombers were back by 1:55 p.m., but by then the Okanagan Mountain fire was essentially out of control.

Over the following days, as the blaze raged north and east along the very edge of Kelowna, the urgent priority, quite rightly, was to protect life and property. Considering the awful potential—it's not out of the question that large parts of the city could have gone up in flames—the loss of property was remarkably limited. And not a single life was lost. All in all, a testament to the skill and bravery and backbreaking hard work of firefighters. But in the heat of that battle, the fire was pretty much left to have its way with Okanagan Mountain Provincial Park. A holocaust, a burnt offering, sacrificed to save the city.

> *O may she live like some green laurel,*
> *Rooted in one dear perpetual place.*
> —William Butler Yeats, "A Prayer for My Daughter"

Well, yes, exactly. And so may we all.

It's my belief that human beings are hard-wired to form a deep and abiding bond with a piece of countryside, a particular landscape, their home territory, in much the same way that we're hard-wired to seek an early bond with other human beings. If kids are given the opportunity, they will at some point imprint on a particular piece of ground, and ever afterward that ground will be "home" to them. Perhaps they even measure the "homeness" of other places by reference to that original home territory.

Okanagan Mountain Provincial Park was one of *my* dear perpetual places. Home ground. A beloved piece of countryside, always there to welcome me back, one of my roots, a sort of earth-anchor.

The great fire of 2003 destroyed that anchor for me, an irreplaceable loss, not covered by insurance. When it was over, amid all the hearty self-congratulations on a job well done, on having dodged the bullet, I felt like one of the 239 home owners who *did* get burnt out.

I hate wildfire.

This is the first time I've been back to the park since the catastrophe and I can hardly stand to see it so diminished: charred, blackened, desolate.

It's not uncommon nowadays to hear wildfire characterized as a fine and necessary process in nature. Well-meaning people will tell you that it renews the land, that it's an essential part of the way these arid-country ecosystems develop. They make it sound like a cheerful spring cleaning.

Of course, wildfire *is* a natural process, especially in hot, arid country. So, for that matter, are drought, disease, plagues of insects, the whole range of "natural" catastrophes that shape ecosystems. Crap happens. And if you're trying to sustain the integrity of indigenous ecosystems it's important, somehow, to make room for catastrophe along with all the other natural processes. There are going to be wildfires in this country. I'd best get used to it. But I don't have to like it.

North of Chute Creek, more blackened spars, still standing or scattered like jackstraws by windthrow. Fortunately it's a calm afternoon, not a breath of air. I wouldn't want to walk through this stuff on a breezy day. Initially the way ahead seems clear and easy. But as I work my way north from the creek and back onto the slopes above the lake, deeper into the heart of the burn, I find myself on much rougher ground, with the trail growing ever fainter and more confused.

Everywhere I look there is evidence of intense heat: not just the charred snags, but bizarre cavities in the earth where whole root systems have burnt away. The heat has cracked and bleached the very rocks, scorched them clean, every trace of lichen and moss gone. I find it deeply disturbing, like coming upon a charred skeleton.

Tired and dispirited, I reach Koosi Creek just after five o'clock and decide to quit for the day. The sun is sinking low, and finding a campsite this evening is going to be a little trickier than usual. If a wind should come up during the night, one of these snags could be the death of me. I don't fancy being squashed in my tent. I need to find a little patch of open ground absolutely out of reach of falling jackstraws.

And I do, at the top of a knoll above the creek. There are long views south down the valley toward Penticton (now quite some distance back along the way I've come) and east across the lake to Summerland and the Trout Creek valley.

It's a beautiful evening, almost dark, as I write, and colder by the moment. The western sky is still that faint robin's egg blue beyond the charred trunks of fire-killed trees. Reminds me of those famous

Lawren Harris paintings, similar scenes north of Lake Superior, austere and lonesome, with the night wind soughing gently. (So far, anyway, thank goodness.) The lights of Penticton are bright. And there are lights along both shores of Okanagan Lake, with the biggest, brightest clusters at Naramata and Summerland. But above the lake, still, the mountains are mostly black, wild, except for a few scattered incandescent sparks in the darkness.

> *For my part I know nothing with any certainty, but the sight of the stars makes me dream.*
>> —Vincent Van Gogh (in a letter to his brother, Theo)

DAY FOURTEEN
Sunday, October 14: Okanagan Mountain Provincial Park

'm exhausted before I start walking. It was a restless night and I woke unusually early. Doubtless my insomnia was stoked by some lingering anxiety over the possibility of windthrow. Even asleep I had half an ear cocked for the stirring of wind, the creaking and rending of dead timber. But there was more to my discomfort than that. It was like sleeping in a graveyard. The place is haunted. I dreamt of fire and woke wondering who actually made the catastrophic decision to withdraw the water bombers on the morning of August 16, 2003. And why? In fairness, it was a summer of unrelenting emergency, fire springing up everywhere, homes and lives endangered, insufficient resources to deal properly with every exigency. Unhappy choices had to be made. But please God they didn't send the bombers elsewhere because this was only a park and a beautiful place and not worth defending from the flames.

It's true, you know. Life goes on. The world is supposed to end in fire, but it hasn't, not yet anyway, at least not here in Okanagan Mountain Provincial Park. The trail north from Koosi Creek runs through a tangled growth of shrubbery: snowberry, willows, two species of ceanothus: redstem ceanothus (*Ceanothus sanguineus*) and snowbrush (*Ceanothus velutinus*).

Everywhere I look I see the remains of last spring's rich growth of herbs and flowers: three-flowered avens (*Geum triflorum*), yarrow (*Achillea millefolium*), fireweed (*Epilobium angustifolium*) and so on. Also dense patches of tiny lodgepole pine seedlings (*Pinus contorta* var. *latifolia*). Fire-adapted species all of them, gifted with qualities that allow plants to survive a wildfire or quickly colonize the burned ground afterward.

Lodgepole pine is a prime example. I've even heard it said that lodgepole pine *requires* fire to reseed. Not quite. The truth is more complicated and more interesting. It *is* true that some lodgepole pine cones require heat (something on the order of 45°C to 50°C) to melt a coating of resin and dry the woody interior of the cone sufficiently to open the scales and release the seeds. In the event of moderate fire, seeds from those resin-sealed cones (protected from extreme heat by the insulation of the cone itself) are shed after the fire has gone, and they can effectively colonize the burnt-over ground, helpfully stripped of duff and competitors by the fire, perhaps even briefly fertilized by the ashes, perfect growing conditions.

But it's tricky. Chancy. If there is too little fire, not enough heat, the resin-sealed cones won't open. Too much fire, flames in the forest crown, and the cones will be incinerated along with everything else.

Resin-sealed cones are said to be serotinous. Individual trees tend to produce either mostly serotinous cones or mostly non-serotinous cones. It's a genetic thing. And under normal circumstances, especially in the absence of fire, lodgepole pine depends mostly upon non-serotinous cones to sustain the continued survival of the species.

In fact, non-serotinous cone–bearing trees tend to predominate in most stands of lodgepole pine. But (this is the interesting bit) the proportion of serotinous cone–bearing trees is much higher in stands that germinate after a forest fire. It's a form of natural selection. Fire selects for serotinous cones. Fire favours the reproduction of trees with serotinous cones.

It's interesting to think that fire-spawned stands of lodgepole pine are, in a sense, locked into a fire cycle. They are creations of fire and, in turn, they create conditions hospitable to future fire. You could almost think of it as a symbiosis: fire and lodgepole pine. Or, only slightly more fanciful, a form of farming. Fire creates these stands of lodgepole pine so it can eat them later. The young seedlings come up very thick and dense after a fire (thick as hairs on a dog it is said), many more than can survive to maturity. Most will die as seedlings or saplings or young trees, so the stand will be choked with dead wood, good fuel, littering the ground or still standing (so-called ladder fuels because they allow flames to climb easily into the canopy), all perfect conditions for the next wildfire.

Different plants have different adaptations. Some species, like aspen or various grasses, will grow back from roots or rhizomes buried so deep that wildfire can't touch them.

Other species have seeds or reproductive structures that are "fire-proofed" in various ways. Ceanothus, for example, produces abundant, heat-resistant seeds that can lie dormant in soil for hundreds of years.

In some species, the plants themselves are fireproofed. Yesterday, walking down Chute Creek along the edge of the burn, I passed a number of big ponderosa pines and Douglas-firs that were badly charred but still very much alive, their cambium layers protected by thick, insulating bark, and all their delicate bits, needles and cones, held high out of reach of moderate flames, on tall, branch-free trunks.

Other species, like fireweed, simply produce great quantities of highly mobile seed, colonizing the empty ground of the burn from beyond the distant margins of the fire. These are fast-seeding, fast-growing, early-maturing, aggressive plants. In a word, weeds.

And that, I'm afraid, is what Okanagan Mountain Provincial Park has become. Eleven thousand and thirty-eight hectares of weeds.

But it's true, life goes on.

Cold comfort.

The charm of Okanagan Mountain Provincial Park, as I remember it, lay chiefly in the little private places. Everywhere you looked there was loveliness: a little forested glade; flowers set in the moss on a rock face, like a Japanese garden; a sudden deep, secret canyon or crevice; the pleasing contrast and textures of grey rock and green trees, clouds of Douglas-fir boughs, the sprays of long needles on ponderosa pine.

Big trees, too. I walked past a fire-killed snag today that might well have qualified as one of the largest ponderosa pines in the province of British Columbia when it was alive. A huge, tall tree. How long to make a tree like that? Growth is slow on these arid hillsides. Three hundred years? Four hundred? Five hundred? More?

Gone, all gone.

Perhaps someday Okanagan Mountain Provincial Park will again support growth like that, beauty and majesty like that, but not in my lifetime or yours.

It's late afternoon by the time I reach the south end of Wild Horse Canyon and the beginning of a clear track north toward Kelowna. I'm amazed to find living trees in the depths of the canyon. Maybe there was more moisture here. Also, perhaps, the heat wasn't quite so intense. This was close to where the fire started. Even so, it must have looked like the end of the world on August 16, 2003, with flames and burning debris riding the wind across the gap of sky above.

I go to ground, finally, at the north end of the canyon. Perhaps it's the rigours of the day, the emotional ups and downs. Or maybe it's simply that I'm on the north-facing side of the mountain now. But I'm particularly feeling the chill tonight, a cold drift of air flowing down off the high slopes in the deepening dusk. Won't be sorry to get inside the tent and sleeping bag.

DAY FIFTEEN
Monday, October 15:
Okanagan Mountain Provincial Park to
Mission Creek, Kelowna

I feel like Frodo Baggins gazing down into the vale of Mordor, with that same sense of hopelessness and despair, an impression that's heightened by the clanking of rock-breaking machinery in a quarry somewhere higher on the hill behind me, and all the frantic activity around the base of the ridge in the subdivisions still under construction. The whole view to the north has been consumed by a runaway sprawl of urban and suburban development.

Don't much care for Kelowna.

Can't think of another town quite so spectacularly successful at turning gold into lead.

The history of Kelowna begins with Okanagan Mission, the first permanent non-aboriginal settlement in the Okanagan Valley, which Fathers Charles Pandosy and Pierre Richard founded in 1860. The first townsite was laid out in 1892 and the City of Kelowna was incorporated on May 4, 1905. The first Regatta was held in 1906.

For the longest time it was just a little, little town on the shores of Okanagan Lake, growing ever so slowly, green and lovely. In 1941 the census set the population at 5,154. Ten years later, in 1951, there was a jump to 8,466. But there were still only 10,000 people in 1959.

In the 1950s my folks would drive us little kids down to see the Regatta parade. In those days, Kelowna ended more or less where the Capri Centre is now, nine or ten blocks from the lake. Beyond that, orchards and fields. Beyond the orchards and fields, grassy hillsides and forested slopes. Hard to believe now.

The point I'm trying to make is that for the first hundred years this was an extraordinarily charming and beautiful little town. In those early days the valley was relatively isolated, a cul-de-sac, a long arduous journey from the outside world. Until 1925, when the Canadian National Railway finally arrived in Kelowna, the only real access was by water, north to Vernon or south to Penticton, and from there to Vancouver or points east by rail. (After 1914, one could also climb up the side of the mountain to the McCulloch station on the Kettle Valley Railway.)

A real highway connection didn't exist until the Hope–Princeton section of Highway 3, the Crowsnest Highway, was completed in 1949. And even then you had to cross the lake on a ferry to reach it. The "Big Bend" section of the Trans-Canada Highway along the Columbia River from Revelstoke to Golden, completed in 1940, provided only the most rudimentary, dusty, hair-raising connection to the rest of Canada. A similarly rudimentary road through the Fraser Canyon had been in place since 1927 but wasn't upgraded to proper highway status until the 1960s.

Then, in 1952, the Central Okanagan's Social Credit Member of the Legislative Assembly, William Andrew Cecil Bennett, a local hardware merchant, became premier of British Columbia. It was a development-oriented government, and suddenly sleepy little Kelowna was the place to be if you were a player.

The Bennett government launched an ambitious program of road building and upgrading. Endless miles of pavement were laid. The seven Fraser Canyon highway tunnels were completed. The final section of the Trans-Canada Highway through Rogers Pass opened in 1962 to bypass the Big Bend.

And people flooded in. Of course they did. We are a mobile society. This was an extraordinarily beautiful place. People naturally wanted to move here. Unless the city fathers (and mothers) had wanted to seriously entertain some sort of legislative limit to growth (no more likely back in 1962 than it is now), Kelowna was bound to grow.

One has to accept that, I suppose.

But what I object to—and I think this is legitimate—is the way it happened or was allowed to happen. The way growth was managed or, rather, not managed. Here was a town gifted with one of the most beautiful situations on God's green earth. Kelowna should have ended up in the same world-class superstar landscape league as Provence or Tuscany or the Cotswolds or the Aegean islands or, well, name your own favourite National Geographic destination. Instead, what have we got? The worst sort of cluttered, concrete, overcrowded, clogged highway, packed subdivision, huge vulgar house, strip-mall development that you can imagine.

It was so beautiful.

What a shame to have wrecked it.

A genuine and verifiable instance of reverse alchemy.

Of course Kelowna is not alone in this "uglification" of paradise, just a little out ahead of the pack. Penticton to the south and Vernon to the north are only slightly less awful. (And not for lack of trying, I might add.) In fact, I can't think of a town in British Columbia that is more beautiful now than it was when I was a kid. We live in a province built by avarice, acquisitiveness, selfishness. Greed, as a former vice, has been rehabilitated, sanctified and elevated to the status of a virtue. For the last fifty or sixty years especially, our destiny and environments have been shaped by the worst sort of narrow-minded, bottom-line, Junior Chamber of Commerce thinking.

I cover the last few blocks along Lakeshore Road practically at a run, as if the devil himself were after me, a steady stream of traffic roaring past, inches from my right elbow. It's only just gone three o'clock when I reach the Mission Creek bridge.

I had hoped for a little relief where Mission Creek empties into Okanagan Lake. A little greenery perhaps. A park. Some civic space. After all, this is Okanagan Lake's largest tributary, more like a small river than a creek, despite the name. Certainly something worth recognizing, maybe even worth celebrating.

But, no, this is Kelowna. No park. No civic space that I can see. Private homes, houses, condos.

I should have known.

There is no possibility of camping, of course. There's no way I can play the urban backpacker here, it's far too risky. A shower and a bed for me tonight. (It's an ill wind and all that.)

DAY SIXTEEN
Tuesday, October 16: Kelowna to Winfield

Credit where credit is due.

After bad-mouthing Kelowna yesterday, I now feel obliged to observe that any community with such a lovely linear park—the Mission Creek Greenway—running clear across the main part of the city cannot be all bad. I still think it's disappointing that the Greenway doesn't begin where it should, right where Mission Creek empties into Okanagan Lake. And I wish I could have seen Mission Creek as it originally was, wandering down to the lake, rather than confined to a straight-line artificial channel, essentially a big ditch. But, for all that, I'm impressed by the Greenway: 16.5 kilometres from Lakeshore Drive all the way across town and up into Gallagher's canyon, with more to come, apparently, as the land can be assembled. Good on you, Kelowna.

At this time of year it should be called the "goldway," with all the leaves on the cottonwoods glowing brilliant orange-yellow against the blue sky. Where the water in the creek is open to the sky, the surface is quicksilver. In deep shade the stream is dark green, almost black, with golden leaves floating down. Quite lovely.

From the Greenway I exit onto Hollywood Road and thence onto Springfield Road and up the hill toward Highway 33 and East Kelowna.

Kelowna seems to rejoice in ironic names. I come across an "El Paso" Road, dead end, no exit. And "Springfield," I suppose, is one of those names like "Orchard View" or "Green Acres." True, perhaps, once upon a time. Before Mission Creek was forced into the straight and narrow there were, doubtless, springs all over these fields. Now "Springfield" is four very busy lanes of blacktop.

At least I don't lack for a direct route. A series of arrow-straight roads (Gibson, McKenzie, Old Vernon) hurry me northward toward

Highway 97. The weather has given me sunshine and blue skies all the way across town, but now, as if to emphasize the need for haste, it begins to deteriorate. Clouds gather, cutting off the light.

This is the worst thing so far.

A test of endurance.

Four lanes of traffic on Highway 97 screaming by in the gathering darkness along the west side of Duck Lake, the blast and buffet knocking me back as each tractor-trailer hurtles past. It's like wading into storm-surf, all grit and grunge and dirty spray. I walk with my head down, leaning into it, blinking the particles away.

Then—this is one of those glimpses you get—I glance to the left, up the hill above the highway. And there, high on those steep slopes, meadows of beautiful bunchgrass, almost pristine by the look of them, under the Douglas-firs. At the same moment, almost biblical, the sun manages to find a gap between the horizon out of sight to the west and the dark clouds above. The countryside floods with a swelling golden light, shooting through the drizzle, kindling the autumn cottonwoods across the lake so that for a moment they glow almost incandescent.

And this, it seems to me, is the lesson and hope of these last few days. That even here, in the midst of this awfulness, the worst part of the journey so far, there is still grace to be found, little fragments of natural beauty, surprisingly durable.

One of the strengths of these grassland ecosystems, compared to, say, the temperate rain forests of the Pacific Northwest or the tropical rain forests of the Amazon basin, is that they don't seem to need huge tracts of land to prosper. The great forests need whole valleys and watersheds to sustain long-term functioning ecosystems. Here, it seems, a hillside is sufficient. You could have the better part of a functioning ecosystem in a large backyard, certainly on any sort of hobby-farm. A nice patch of bunchgrass meadow, maybe two or three scattered ponderosa pine or Douglas-fir, a little copse of aspen, perhaps some ground squirrels. Maybe a set of ponds, some riparian habitat, and a badger or red-tailed hawk or coyote coming through every now and again. This place never had vast herds of megafauna or groves of megaflora. It's mostly little stuff here. That's part of the charm.

Presumably someone owns that hillside and for whatever reason has chosen not to develop it. (So far, anyway.) Maybe they've not developed it because they can't. It's just too steep for cattle, too noisy or unstable for houses. But let that pass. Wouldn't it be wonderful if we could get ourselves to a place where, in terms of social status, owning a pristine bunchgrass meadow trumped building a huge vulgar house any day of the week? In that world a landowner might make a conscious decision not to develop because a pristine bunch-grass meadow—or a riparian woodland or a patch of antelope-bush savannah or what have you—is a possession worth having. Like a great work of art.

Maybe that's part of the key to turning all this lead back into gold.

What if we could encourage a sort of popular connoisseurship of natural habitat in these arid interior valleys, so that real prestige would attach itself to owning property that supports a relatively intact ecosystem. (*Well, yes, Denise and I count ourselves very fortunate to have that lovely section of rough fescue meadow at the north end of the lot. And have you seen our family of badgers?*) And perhaps, contrariwise, oppro-brium, ridicule, for owning a piece of property that horses or cattle or other livestock have grazed to the dirt.

Why not? If people can be connoisseurs of wine or food or art, why not of the natural ecosystems that are the basic foundation of their daily lives. Even if we could get ourselves to a place where ordinary folks are able to *recognize* the good stuff, ecologically speaking, we'd be way ahead.

The sun drops behind the mountains, the light fades and the vision vanishes. The rest of the way into Winfield is a trudge through rain and growing darkness.

> *The poetry of the earth is never dead.*
> —John Keats, "On the Grasshopper and Cricket"

DAY SEVENTEEN
Thursday, October 25: Winfield to Vernon

> *Calligraphy of geese*
> *against the sky—*
> *the moon seals it.*
>
> —Yosa Buson

That gleam of light over Duck Lake turned out to be the last bit of sunshine I would see for many long days. I've lost another week to bad weather. Conditions are often unsettled at this time of year, that's to be expected, but I've had a hard time curbing my impatience. What a relief it was, then, to wake up this morning to blue skies and, as Annie Dillard put it, that "long slant of light that means good walking."[6]

A pleasant stroll through the orchards along the east side of Wood Lake is a reminder or memento of what this countryside used to be and of what it might still be, even now, had the place developed differently: a valley full of farms and orchards and gardens. Even the surviving residue has a country charm to it, especially after the bustle of downtown Kelowna. I wish I could have seen it in its heyday, perhaps at apple-blossom time in 1948 before the killing frosts of 1949 decimated the orchards.

These are autumn orchards, the leaves yellow and sere on the trees and littering the grassy ground together with the windfall and discarded culls. The air is ripe with the sweet vinegar smell of rotting fruit, not unpleasant to me. Perhaps it's just one of those pungent odours that call up childhood memories. Lime tea and Madeleine cakes for Proust, the cider smell of fermenting apples for me.

Kalamalka Lake Provincial Park comprises a sizeable parcel of land (4,209 hectares) bordering the northeast edge of Kalamalka Lake. It's another "must-see" destination for anyone interested in the native grasslands of southern interior British Columbia and represents a substantial proportion of the province's protected higher-elevation grasslands.

Unfortunately it is nowhere near pristine, having been both overgrazed and logged before being protected in 1975. The lower meadows are overrun with weeds. Big mature trees survive mostly where the ground was too precipitous for machinery to operate.

On the other hand, the very fact that Kalamalka Lake Park exists at all is remarkable and worth celebrating. The land was originally part of the Coldstream Ranch. When the parcel came up for sale in the mid-1970s, an enthusiastic local campaign developed, a grassroots conservation initiative, so to speak, led by members of the North Okanagan Naturalists Club and supported by the local MLA, Pat Jordan, and District of Coldstream Councillor Dennis Seymour, urging that the land be purchased by the Government of British Columbia and set aside as a park to preserve a unique and beautiful piece of landscape. And so it was done, a significant investment at a time when concern over "the ecology" was still something quite new. Without that local effort the park wouldn't exist. By now, doubtless, it would be resorts and condos and monster houses like much of the rest of the valley, with walls and locked gates, maybe a nice private golf course.

I'm running late. The sun is almost on the horizon by the time I reach the park and I still have a strenuous climb to make before the light fades, partly because I want to pay my respects to the best bits of natural habitat, which (I happen to know) are on the relatively inaccessible rocky ridge that runs east from Rattlesnake Point. And partly because, if my calculations are correct and if the clouds gathering along the eastern horizon don't spoil it, something really magical is about to happen up there.

Rattlesnake Point is an appropriate name, I might add, considering that Kalamalka Lake Provincial Park is home to a sizeable population of northern Pacific rattlesnakes (*Crotalus oreganus oreganus*), all safely back in their underground dens at this time of year.

By the time I crest the hill I'm breathing hard but, as always, the view is worth any effort. The end of the ridge falls away steeply to the park boundary and I have an unobstructed prospect eastward along the length of the Coldstream valley, out across what's left of Lord and Lady Aberdeen's Coldstream Ranch, with the little communities of Lavington and Lumby just lighting up in the twilight. Somewhere farther out, hidden in the dark folds of the land, another little community, Cherryville. And on the far eastern horizon, the pinnacle peaks of the Monashee Mountains, freshly snow-capped but fading to shadows in the growing darkness.

In fact, I have plenty of time to dump the pack, put on a jacket and find a comfortable rock. Several minutes of patient chilly waiting pass. Then I see the first little glimmer and soon the bright rim of a full moon rising beyond the Monashees and shining at me down the length of the valley, illuminating the fields and houses and orchards. The highway and railway. The dark hillsides.

Perfect timing.

It's another full moon rising to mark another special moment in this pilgrimage–journey.

And by God but it's beautiful.

A scene freighted with very mixed emotions and full of memories.

I was a child here.

I have climbed to this lookout many and many a time. I have lived a good part of my life down in that valley. Somewhere there, tucked out of sight toward Lavington, is the little cottage I rented just after I got out of school, my first real home away from home. And closer to the base of the ridge below me, a small farm (part of the original subdivision of the Coldstream Ranch) where I spent a couple of memorable winters. I can remember hiking up to this very viewpoint on a snowy winter night, also moonlit, with a special friend.

When I was a kid, the Coldstream Ranch was generous in allowing public access to its fields and ranges, the only quid pro quo being that visitors not disturb the stock, pick up after themselves and leave the gates as they found them. That kind of openness was relatively unremarkable at the time. It was simply the way things were done.

I spent much time there over the years, changed sprinklers one summer as a student, walked the ranges in all seasons, skied them in the winter. It was a home away from home and, like Okanagan Mountain Provincial Park, it was one of those places where I had an opportunity to fall in love with my "home and native land."

And my experience was by no means unusual. Most of the kids I grew up with spent at least some time exploring the countryside, which is to say land that was actually owned by somebody else (the Coldstream Ranch or the BX Ranch or the O'Keefe Ranch) but for which we came, nevertheless, to feel some sense of proprietorship and affection.

None of that is possible now.

Nearly all of the deeded ranchlands in the north Okanagan, including all the old familiar fields and pastures below me, are closed and posted. "Private Property." "No Trespassing." "Keep Out."

There are, unfortunately, some good and sound reasons why this should be so.

Liability was an issue we'd hardly heard of when I was a boy. The idea that the Coldstream Ranch might be legally responsible if somebody got themselves bitten by a rattlesnake or fell off a rock or drowned in the creek would have seemed ludicrous to us. But things have changed; these are litigious times.

Then there's the whole issue of vandalism. Also the dumping of garbage, including bits of plastic that will probably still be around, not that much the worse for wear, when the pyramids have crumbled to dust.

Then there are the nitwits on motorbikes and ATVs and four-wheel-drive whatsits, out there chewing up the ground. (And, what's more, taking a sort of loutish pride in their handiwork.)

And, of course, the simple pressure of numbers. There are so many more of us now.

On the other hand, there are some not very good reasons for this posting of private ranges. There is a sort of exclusive jealousy over private property rights, a territoriality among large landowners, that didn't seem to exist when I was a boy. And, I'm sure, a more general atmosphere of paranoia fostered by lawyers and accountants and insurers and such-like.

The point I'm trying to make is this: how are kids supposed to form any sort of attachment to their native countryside when they can't get at it?

I suppose there's always Kalamalka Lake Provincial Park and I thank God for it. But that hardly seems adequate or sufficient. It's just one little patch in the whole landscape and the effect, if anything, is of limited borders and boundaries, constraint, confinement, rather than the freedom to explore. Certainly there's nothing there to foster the sense that the whole countryside is yours.

And there is still Crown land, thank God again, public land that, in theory at least, belongs to us all. But the sad fact (especially in the more settled areas of the province) is that the most desirable and accessible bits of countryside were long ago alienated from the Crown. What public land remains tends to be less attractive and often hard to access, being tucked away behind a barrier of privately owned land.

And there is a dangerous trend for public land leaseholders to behave as if the Crown lands in which they have some interest (grazing, timber, water or mineral rights) are a form of private property, even to the extent of discouraging public access.

Who cares? What does it matter?

I've already expressed my belief that human beings are hard-wired to form a deep and abiding bond with their home ground. I believe also that human beings who fail to establish that bond with some sort of home landscape are almost as diminished by the lack of it as those sad souls who fail to bond with other human beings. It's hard enough, in our highly mobile, urban, solipsistic culture, to identify with a home-place. The increasing difficulty of access to the countryside is going to make it virtually impossible.

By the time I've scrambled back down to Cosens Bay Road, the sun has long since set and night has fallen. Fortunately it's not all that cold and I can see well enough by moonlight to get along. I could probably walk these familiar roads blindfolded.

And I like walking in the dark.

Darkness frees the other senses from the tyranny of sight and allows the imagination fuller rein. It's friendly. Sheltering. On this night there is a cool breeze out of the east and I can smell the sweet-sour odour of fresh silage drifting down the valley from the Coldstream Ranch, another beautiful evocative pungent odour, like windfall apples, that carries me back to childhood.

A flock of geese flies by overhead, calling. Rodgers and Hammerstein's famous geese had the moon on their wings and so must these but try as I might, I can't see them. It's just disembodied voices and the barely audible whisper of flight feathers whipping the wind.

I walk past Martha and Dave Hett's little ranch, as it was then. I walk past Verite Jackson's old place. I used to wonder if she had any sisters similarly named, perhaps a whole family of the virtues. (But no, just one sister, Daphne, and one brother, Norman, if I remember correctly.) I walk past the Coldstream Women's Institute Hall (established 1931), rather overshadowed now by a large new Municipal Building.

Darkness and moonlight hide the ugliness of the world. Flatter it. You think you can see everything, the lustre of midday, but you can't, not really. Maybe that's what I need more of on this trip, a little glamour. (Glamour [glam′er] n. 1. Orig., a magical spell or charm 2. Emanating mystery and fascination.)

I walk on. Cosens Bay Road. Coldstream Creek Road. Kalamalka Lake Road. Aberdeen Road. Highway 6. Dogs barking and night traffic. Colder and colder. Lights clustering more densely now, and the muted background breathing of the city. An hour and a half, give or take, to cover the last ten kilometres into Vernon. I step off the street into the driveway just before eight o'clock. None too soon. I'm beginning to feel the chill. Partly simple fatigue, I suppose. It's been a long day. But the air *is* cold and I've a feeling it's going to be much colder before morning with the moon shining out of a clear sky. One can almost feel the seasons changing this night. I'll be glad to get inside. Get a meal. Get a bath. Get to bed.

The porch light is on. I'm expected.

DAY EIGHTEEN
Friday, October 26: Vernon to Whiteman Creek

I sleep late and wake to the first hard frost of the year, minus five or minus six degrees Celsius. The yard outside the window is grey with fog when I sit down to breakfast, but before long the sun is bright through the mist. Glimpses of blue sky promise another fine day.

The big maple outside the window sheds a steady rain of golden leaves. Each tumbling leaf sets others in motion, one or two at first, then whole clusters avalanching down. It's almost eerie on such a calm morning, as if some unseen hand were touching that tree, brushing first one leaf, then another—*away you go, sweetie, you're on*—releasing a steady, busy cascade of autumn colours like a ballet, like a pageant, like fireworks in slow motion. It's lovely, each leaf glows with sunlight, but it's also poignant. You know that when those leaves are gone (and the foliage on that maple is looking scantier by the minute) they will be gone for a good long time. We'll have many months of bare branches to endure, a landscape in black and white before spring dresses it all in bright green again.

It's a no-going-back, batten-down-the-hatches, better-get-in-the-last-of-the-firewood-if-you've-left-it-this-late-you-fool kind of feeling. Not likely, of course, that we'll be snowed in tomorrow. Surely there will be days ahead that harken back to golden autumn or even lingering summer. But in the warmest sunshine on the nicest afternoon the perspiration will dry chilly in the small of my back and I will not be fooled. Winter, deep and cold, is on the way. Time to get this done.

The earthmovers are quiet this morning, bright metallic insects silhouetted against the skyline, but they've not been idle. Great sections of the hill across the valley—green fields and bunchgrass when I was a kid—are now covered by a dense matrix of close-crowded houses and businesses, with many more to come, evidently. All the necessary excavations are ready and waiting.

This seems to be the way things are done nowadays. Call it "gravel pit development." Great broad terraces gouged deep into the living hillside, huge avulsed wounds into which the new construction can be nakedly packed. There's no sense of respect for the existing landscape, for the unique nature of a particular place. To whoever is responsible—if that is the word—for this mess, it's all just dirt and rocks, and inconveniently shaped for the purpose.

I take the view that such callous, rapacious development, executed with so little respect for a beautiful indigenous landscape, is an outrage. And I say further that this sort of abuse—the gross uglification of a formerly beautiful place—is an offence, not only against that once-lovely piece of countryside and all the living fabrics that covered it, but also against everyone else in this community who must now endure that eyesore forever and ever, amen. It's an act of vandalism on a giant scale. It diminishes and impoverishes us all, bleeding away just that much more of this town's dwindling stock of beauty and wonder and grace.

Now one might say fair is fair. Give them a little time. It'll look less raw when the landscaping starts to take effect, when the trees start to grow up. But, you know, there aren't ever going to be any trees in that subdivision up there or in the commercial development down below. No stately evergreens, no maples shedding colour in the fall, no flowering chestnuts in the spring. No oasis. Indeed, very little greenery at all. There's no room. The houses are just too big and too close together. (Actually, in many such developments, I understand, trees are expressly forbidden. Interfere with "the view," don't you know.)

Materially and technologically, at least, we are part of the richest, most ingenious culture ever. We can fly remotely operated vehicles past the outer planets of the solar system. We can cram the contents of a fair-sized library into a chunk of metal and plastic the size of a pocket knife, dancing gigabytes of information on the head of a pin. We can replace decrepit living joints with constructions of plastic and titanium, literally raising cripples from their beds, a genuine biblical miracle. We build gorgeous family homes, large enough, some of them, to house a primary school or medical clinic, and jammed full of conveniences inconceivable to our great-grandparents.

But we seem, somehow, to have lost the knack of living. Our towns and cities are roadkill ugly, increasingly so. The buildings are crowded together. The traffic is fierce. There's not a moment's relief anywhere from the relentless noise and the stink of exhaust. There's no joy.

This community of Vernon used to be famously beautiful, like Kelowna, a leafy little town surrounded by orchards and lakes under grass-meadowed hills. I love to look at photos of the town as it was in the 1920s, 1930s and 1940s. It's a worthwhile exercise, important, almost a duty. *Je me souviens.* All those big trees shading the main street.

When I was a kid, the town woke up one morning to find that crews had spent the night cutting the last of those trees down. As far as I know, they weren't diseased or anything like that. They were just . . . well . . . *messy.* Leaves in the autumn and such. Problems with the drains. Cracked sidewalks. It was, you remember, an era that threw out the old oak dining table in favour of space-age chrome and Formica. *So much easier to clean.*

Now my hometown is an ugly concrete burg like all the rest.

I assert my right to be angry about this. I grew up in one of the world's truly lovely landscapes. And it's been trashed, an appalling waste, what the American humorist Garrison Keillor called "the bald-faced vandalism of men in suits."

Over the years a wave of developers, profiteers, people with bank accounts instead of hearts and minds, have robbed me of my home place as surely as an invading army. These are not things of small consequence—merely aesthetic, trivial, decorative issues—but something much closer to the essence of what life is all about. A good life, well lived.

Beauty is a real quality of the world, not some illusion or figment. "Unless all ages and races of men have been deluded by the same mass hypnotist . . . there seems to be such a thing as beauty, a grace wholly gratuitous," wrote Annie Dillard.[7]

And I agree.

Beauty, especially the beauty of one's home place, is not mere window dressing. It is a necessity, like food and water and air, like the love of one's family and the respect of one's friends, at the very core of a meaningful and worthy existence.

Everything else, the gigantic homes, the mod cons, that's all just fluff. Or, worse, some sort of dreadful booby prize, the handful of beads we get for having traded away what really matters. If we don't have beauty, especially the beauty of wherever it is we live, we don't have anything. Impoverished landscapes breed impoverished people. No matter what size house they own.

Of course people have to live. I recognize that. And people need a place to stay.

Much as my heart yearns for the leafy little town of my childhood, I understand that it's gone and can never come again. The pressures of time and population are against it. The Okanagan Valley enjoys Canada's closest approach to a Mediterranean climate. And the sheer beauty of the place was bound to attract growth. We live in a mobile society. People see a desirable place, a good experience, they naturally want to climb on board. And somebody is always there, ready and more than willing, to sell them a place on the ride.

But does it necessarily follow that the bigger a town gets, the uglier it has to be? Is ugliness an unavoidable consequence of population growth? More people, more ugly?

These are questions for the ages.

Surely, if we can land a robot vehicle on Mars, we should be able to build towns and cities that, despite their size and population, are not merely workable, but charming, beautiful places to live. Towns and cities that are an ornament and enhancement to the countryside rather than an abomination.

Is this just a technical problem do you think? A design flaw? Something we can safely delegate to the engineers, landscape architects, urban planners, city managers and other such technocrats who normally take care of these things for us?

Well, no.

This is a matter of the heart.

And it's rooted in the failure of that bond between human beings and their home places.

In three or four generations our countryside has gone from living entity—beloved and intimately familiar to practically everyone who inhabited it—to mere real estate, private property, a commodity to be divided up, bought and sold (often sight unseen), used as the owner dictates, used up, in fact, and ultimately discarded. That's what has made such hideous development possible. That's why our towns and cities are so ugly.

When you think about it, this whole idea of land, these beloved home places, diminished to mere commodity, packaged items of runaway speculation, is deeply disturbing. The buying and selling of land for profit is such common practice in our culture, so deeply ingrained, that few people give it more than a passing thought. But it fundamentally poisons our relationship with the countryside, the earth, the ground. All our handling of land, all our land-use decisions are made with an eye to maximum future profit rather than the benefit and well-being of the land itself. We cease to be stewards, caregivers, and become dealers.

Perhaps we need to reconsider. Maybe land should have legal rights, legal protection, some form of emancipation. Why not? If we can grant the privileges of a legal entity with rights in a court of law to a business corporation, then why not to a lovely hillside meadow of trembling aspen and bunchgrass. An old Douglas-fir. A stream.

What if we started to see land not as a possession but as a cherished responsibility, like a child or a spouse or an aging parent. What if we *married* land? Or formally adopted it. When you could no longer properly care for your land, you'd take steps to see that it was provided for. Perhaps your heirs would assume the responsibility. Or you might deliver it into somebody else's care, but only if you were persuaded that they could do a good, loving job of looking after it. Maybe someday we'll see people taking out life insurance policies with their bit of land as beneficiary.

It's a thought.

And all those real estate agents would have to find regular employment.

The end of the day catches me just short of Whiteman Creek, around the north end of Okanagan Lake and twenty kilometres down Westside Road. Not a bad effort. I could always come out again tomorrow morning to cover the remaining ten kilometres to the bridge at Shorts Creek, where I'd planned to wrap up my trek this fall. But I think I'll let it be. From here I have a choice of routes in the spring, following either the Whiteman Creek valley or the Shorts Creek valley up into the high country west of Okanagan Lake and over the height of land into the Nicola basin.

*There is a love of wild nature in everybody, an ancient
mother-love ever showing itself whether recognized or no,
and however covered by cares and duties.*

— John Muir (journals)

Curiosity does, no less than devotion, pilgrims make.

—Abraham Cowley, "Ode"

*Diffugere nives, redeunt iam gramina campis
Abori busque comae
[The snows have dispersed, now grass returns to the fields
and leaves to the trees.]*

—Horace

3

High, Wide and Handsome—Springtime in the Nicola

Nicola Country: Quilchena Creek

Saturday, June 14:
Whiteman Creek to Shorts Creek Canyon

Eleven o'clock in the morning. I hoist my pack from the very spot (near as I can remember) where I finished my walk last October. With a shrug and a twist to settle the shoulder straps, I'm off, heading south along the Westside Road toward Shorts Creek.

I've not gone more than a dozen paces before my shoulders, unaccustomed to the load, start complaining. Not good. I stop to readjust the straps, feeling resigned, knowing that the first day or two will be the worst.

I'm way behind schedule.

Temperatures have been unseasonably cool this spring. The high country snowpack has taken forever to melt. But at last the weather seems to have turned in my favour. It's a lovely morning, the first clear, blue-sky day in ages. Wild roses and elderberry bushes bloom promiscuously along the margins of the road, and the countryside is as green as green can be.

I've decided to go with the Shorts Creek route.

Shorts Creek canyon is one of southern interior British Columbia's most spectacular landforms, a deep fissure carved into the highlands west of Okanagan Lake, right under Terrace Mountain's looming bulk, the product, perhaps, of a late ice-age torrent or "jökulhlaup," a raging under-ice river of high-pressure water loaded with boulders. It's a remarkable piece of scenery, well worth going some distance out of the way to see.

And I have personal reasons for my choice. I want to see how another once-beloved place, now designated Fintry Provincial Park and Protected Area according to my map, has fared with the passage of years. Shorts Creek canyon was another home of the heart, like Okanagan Mountain Provincial Park, Kalamalka Lake Provincial Park and the Coldstream Ranch. As with Okanagan Mountain Provincial Park, especially, Shorts Creek canyon offered my younger self a taste of real wilderness not too far from home: fiercely rugged country, unroaded, not much travelled, unfarmed, unranched, inhabited by eagles and bighorn sheep and bears. I even saw a mountain goat there once.

This is also my chance to take care of some unfinished business, a long-delayed exploration. I can remember reading somewhere, years ago, of an old-time trail leading west up Shorts Creek and over the height of land into the Nicola country. It would have been used by indigenous peoples travelling between the Okanagan and Nicola valleys, then by comers-from-afar for trading and prospecting and, later, maybe even for moving cattle. I've never been right to the head of the canyon. This is my chance, at last, to check it out. I'm taking a bit of a risk. If the trail is overgrown, or doesn't exist, there'll be hell to pay. It's an awfully long hike from here to the Nicola, and rough country for bushwhacking.

Just north of the Westside Road bridge across Shorts Creek there's a little track leading off into the bush. Not a proper road, no sign, probably doesn't even have an official name. But as far as I'm concerned it could be called "Memory Lane." When I was a kid, this was the road to Fintry High Farm. It wasn't unusual in those days to come upon abandoned old homesteads back in the bush, relics of the more hopeful years just before or just after the First World War. There'd be a little field or meadow, still clear but rank with grass, young trees growing up around the edges, maybe an old barn or shack smelling of pack rat and decay, its logs and timbers grey with age.

Fintry High Farm was like that. Still private property, of course, but the boy was as welcome to his trespass as the coyotes and magpies so long as he observed the usual courtesies, leaving the gates as he found them, respecting whatever buildings or old gear might still be lying about the place. And who was to care?

Then one day I arrived to find the whole place posted: "Property For Sale." "Block Brothers Real Estate."

And a few visits later, fresh outrage, houses under construction! On *my* stomping grounds! How dare they! Well, forty years later, those folks (or whoever has succeeded them) are still on the High Farm and it has become *their* stomping grounds. I go, cap in hand, to ask for permission to cross the fields.

Fortunately they're good-natured about it. I suspect they value their privacy above all. One has a sense that High Farm is their retreat from the world and that they normally take a dim view of casual visitors. But perhaps there's something about the giant pack that compels sympathy. I explain my own attachment to the place. Perhaps that helps. At least they take no offence. And very likely this is the first time they've come across anybody crazy enough to try hiking all the way across to the Nicola. Maybe they just recognize a holy fool when they see one. Leave him alone, people. Let him pass by and be gone. Anyway, I give them whatever blessing I can bestow. I'm already very tired and could hardly face the alternative: retracing my steps back to Whiteman Creek.

The walk through High Farm is like going back in time. Apart from the scattered homes, nothing much has changed except for Shorts Creek itself, still high water at this time of year. In my memory of this place the stream seemed well-settled between established banks. But it seems to have gone crazy, leaving braided gravel channels all across the valley floor. When I mention this to the owners they blame the creek's erratic behaviour on more rapid runoff from clear-cut logging in the highlands above. I feel a little frisson of misgiving, a sudden chill in my happy anticipation of the next few days, but haven't the heart to inquire further.

Otherwise I pass through without incident and into the great canyon beyond. Here there are further signs that all is not well. The creek has no room to wander within the confines of the steep rocky walls, but the intermittent tributaries draining off the plateau above have gouged deep gullies, mostly dry at the moment, in the loose gravel of talus slopes. In several places the path has been washed away, forcing me into long detours and a good deal of scrambling. The creek's main channel, where I remember water falling from pool to pool, is now just a deep ditch of stone and gravel, with the water hurrying swiftly downhill.

But tomorrow's another day, as the man said (or was it Scarlett O'Hara?) No need to borrow grief on this lovely evening.

No eagles or bighorn sheep or bears. Nor any mountain goats. But there's a nice little western meadowlark (*Sturnella neglecta*), singing from the top of a saskatoon bush (*Amelanchier alnifolia*). And, in a way, oddly enough, this is a wildlife sighting as remarkable and significant as any. I've been astonished to learn that meadowlarks, once common as dirt, one of the most characteristic species of these semi-arid interior valleys, are in trouble.

Adult meadowlarks are a greyish buff-brown above, variously

streaked and spotted. The throat and breast are bright yellow, marked with a distinct black "V" across the upper breast, "like a cravat" according to the famous American ornithologist Arthur Cleveland Bent. The outer feathers of the short, broad tail are white, particularly conspicuous in flight. The bill is relatively slender and pointed, as befits a bird feeding mostly on insects, supplemented by various grains, seeds and berries.

It's impossible to tell from appearances if this particular bird is male or female; the two sexes look much alike. (At least to us. Presumably meadowlarks have no problem telling the difference.) But the very fact that it is singing—a territorial display—suggests maleness. Apparently the females take very little interest in territoriality, leaving all that to the boys. Indeed, it's usual for females to share a male's territory, typically two nesting females to each male.

Male meadowlarks are among the very earliest migrants to return in the spring, occupying their territories as much as a month before the females arrive. That lovely song is a welcome harbinger of warmer weather to come and it seems to convey something of the very soul and essence of grasslands, almost as if the countryside itself had inspired the little bird's song, as if the meadowlark, like any other gifted musician, Villa-Lobos or Grieg or Sibelius, had somehow managed to capture the flavour of a beloved home place in its music.

The females construct their nests directly on the ground in open grassy areas: native grasslands, pastures, cultivated croplands. The depression is lined with grass and hair, then sheltered and concealed by a domed cover of woven grass or bark. Three to seven eggs are laid, five being most common. Incubation, mostly by the females, lasts about fifteen days. Young meadowlarks leave the nest after about twelve days, long before they can fly. Adults tend the fledglings for another two weeks, then go to work on the second brood of the year. It's fortunate for their species that meadowlarks are so fecund. Like mice and voles, they're pursued and eaten by almost every predator that crawls or walks or flies.

Western meadowlarks are—or have been—widely distributed in North America from southern Canada to northern Mexico and from the Great Lakes to the Pacific. For many people they are the quintes-sential grassland bird ("The very spirit of the boundless prairie," as Bent puts it), sometimes so much a part of their environment and so common as to be taken almost for granted.

How ironic, then, to learn that their numbers are actually declining, especially in more developed areas like the Okanagan Valley. That's due in part to the loss of breeding and wintering habitat. And to inhospitable agricultural practices, sprinklers instead of ditch irri-gation. And to urban sprawl. And to the encroachment of forest or shrublands. Birds are lost to poisoned grains intended to control rodents. Domestic pets, particularly cats, are a scourge, disturbing the nesting females and preying on both adults and fledglings.

I manage to find a little terrace under the Douglas-firs above the creek, level ground and sufficient space to pitch my tent for the first time in eight months. This is all Crown land, public property, and I delight in the almost-forgotten freedom. No need to dodge private holdings. No need to worry about who might be offended by my passage. Here I can come and go as I please, camp where I choose, by right. What a blessing. What a luxury. It feels like coming home.

> *And this our life, exempt from public haunt, finds tongues*
> *in trees, books in the running brooks, sermons in stones,*
> *and good in everything.*
> —William Shakespeare, *As You Like It*

DAY TWENTY
Sunday, June 15: Shorts Creek Canyon

Daylight is fading fast. A pathetic 4.25 kilometres for the day, as the GPS flies, and I'm absolutely knackered. The terrain is so rugged and so overgrown that I can't even find space for my tent. In the end I'm forced to construct a little pad of brush and dirt and debris to perch on. Relieved of the giant pack I spend the last few minutes of twilight questing up and down through the bush, searching for any sign of the missing trail.

Nothing.

Feeling bone-weary and hopeless, I retreat to my shelter for a drink of water, a bit of food and some badly needed rest. By the time I'm horizontal, darkness has fallen. I'm too tired to worry about tomorrow. Maybe the dawn will bring some fresh insight.

A tough, tough day and discouraging.

But even half dead with fatigue I can accept that all this stress and strain is part of the price I must pay if I want to enjoy the genuine article. Wilderness is wild, harsh, often nasty. Access, by definition, is difficult, demanding, even dangerous. Accommodations are not provided.

I pay that price willingly, even on days like today, for a chance to experience some precious bit of the world's dwindling stock of wild country. For a chance to enjoy that ineffable something at the heart of things.

Certainly I have the sense that today's pathetic little hike, despite (or perhaps because of) all its trials and difficulties, provided me with a more authentic and significant and worthwhile experience than all the long miles spent trudging through the developed and populated Okanagan, dodging cars and trying to find a quiet place to rest.

All of which is a long-winded way of saying that I'm delighted to find a sizeable chunk of relatively inaccessible country still left in Shorts Creek canyon. It lends the protected area a kind of legitimacy. I approve. Hope it stays that way.

There has always been a fundamental dilemma in the way this country manages its parks and protected areas. Usually we begin with a strong mandate to protect and preserve the natural beauty (and, more latterly, the ecological integrity) of some particularly treasured piece of countryside, reserved for its own intrinsic value and for the appreciation of all people.

But almost as soon as an area is declared "protected" there are calls for improved access and more facilities to accommodate and encourage visitors.

Some of that is sheer self-interest: Local businessmen who hope to profit by increased economic activity. Recreationalists who misinterpret "for the use and enjoyment of all people" to mean any sort of use, any kind of enjoyment.

But often the impulse to open the countryside to visitors is well-intentioned, genuinely humane and generous. The enjoyment of nature is part of the very essence of what parks are about. Even wilderness enthusiasts, who should know better, can be zealous with the urge to share some bit of countryside they've fallen in love with. They ache to give as many people as possible an opportunity to enjoy that particular slice of splendour. And from the activist's point of view there is much to be said, politically, for getting citizens out where they'll have a chance to fall in love with the countryside and be moved to support its protection.

Of course, once visitor traffic reaches an appreciable level, certain facilities become necessary just to save wear and tear on the landscape itself. Nobody questions that.

But it's important to understand that there is a price to be paid. Easy access and facilities fundamentally change and diminish a piece of countryside forever. It is, in fact, no longer really wild.

Many jurisdictions make some provision within their overall protected areas strategy for dedicated nature reserves or wilderness areas where development is minimized or prohibited. Here I make a nod in the direction of America's National Wilderness Preservation System, representing, at present, 762 wilderness areas including enormous reserves like Death Valley in California (more than 1.25 million hectares), Denali in Alaska (almost 900,000 hectares) or, one of the earliest, the Bob Marshall Wilderness in Montana (over 400,000 hectares). Credit where credit is due, kudos to them. Even back in 1964 when the Bob Marshall Wilderness was established, no roads or structures were to be built, vehicles and other mechanical equipment were not to be used. How enlightened! How farsighted!

It *is* unfortunate that many people, the elderly and infirm, many of whom, doubtless, have a great and sincere affection for the countryside, will never be able to visit those wild places, unfortunate that such places should be beyond their physical capacity. Doubtless, someday, access to the little section of Shorts Creek canyon I hiked today will be beyond *my* physical capacity. (It already is, very nearly.) Even now, I'm sure, there are any number of lovely places I haven't the strength or skill to visit. I accept that without complaint, with equanimity, almost with rejoicing, as long as I can know those places are still out there, relatively untouched, pristine and wild.

God save us from the "Mount Everest Gondola" or whatever similar abominations you can imagine. The "South Polar Express." Don't laugh. Even now the proliferation of companies offering helicopter and ATV access to the backcountry brings us uncomfortably close to the day when anyone with sufficient cash will be able to get themselves to pretty much any place on the planet they care to go. There's a double irony in that: a world where access to wild country is no longer limited by physical ability or endurance, but rather by one's ability to pay. A world where you can go any place you want, if you have the money, only to find there's no place worth going.

> *Something will have gone out of us as a people if we ever*
> *let the remaining wilderness be destroyed . . . We simply*
> *need that wild country available to us, even if we never do*
> *more than drive to its edge and look in.*
> —Wallace Stegner, *The Sound of Mountain Water*[8]

DAY TWENTY-ONE
Monday, June 16: Shorts Creek Canyon to Sandberg Lake

Early sunshine creeps down the basalt wall on the other side of Shorts Creek and illuminates the bright green of springtime aspens and cottonwoods along the floor of the canyon. The disembodied voice of a Swainson's thrush (*Catharus ustulatus*), liquid notes, spiraling upward, echoes from the stone. The snowbrush is in bloom, pyramidal clusters of tiny white flowers with glossy evergreen leaves. In the cooler shadows there are clusters of mountain lady's slipper (*Cypripedium montanum*), an elegant orchid in white and purple. Fragrant.

I feel like a different person this morning, much improved. Still a little stiff and sore, naturally, but ready to go on. This is an amazing thing about the human body: given half a chance it can recuperate. Repair itself. If you park a wrecked car in the garage overnight, it will still be a wreck in the morning. But lay your exhausted, strained, abused body down in sleep and by morning (with luck) you're halfway to recovery. All without any conscious effort on your part. It's magic.

It would be foolish to even think of attempting to follow Shorts Creek any farther upstream through the canyon, which is only going to get narrower and more rugged. If there was a trail, once upon a time, it's long gone, grown over or fallen into the restless stream. And another day of scrambling through the brush with my heavy pack would kill me.

So what are my options?

I could quit the walk, the whole project, which seemed a reasonable and attractive alternative yesterday evening, but now strikes me as a little drastic. I've come too far to give up so easily.

Or I could retreat back down the valley and try to find another route over into the Nicola. I know of a road up the Whiteman Creek valley that might serve.

Or I could venture a third possibility, which might save me a long tiresome scramble back down the canyon.

According to my map there's some sort of track, a little dotted line, running along the north rim of the canyon, high above my camp. In fact, the map shows a network of such lines all the way to the confluence of Beak Creek and the Nicola River, which is where I want to go. I've enough experience with maps to know that those little lines may represent nothing more than some cartographer's wishful thinking. But there's only one way to find out.

The slope is steep and slippery. I'm in constant danger of losing my footing. The mutinous backpack waits for a chance to overbalance and topple me backwards. (And I'm only too well aware that once I start to tumble there'll be no way to stop.) I thread my way nervously through outcrops of bare rock above sheer drops, and cling to clumps of grass and bits of shrubbery for precarious purchase, managing only a step or two upward at a time.

I'm far too anxious and winded to enjoy my surroundings, a spacious forest of Douglas-fir on this south-facing slope, carpeted with pinegrass. There are dramatic views back down into the canyon below, those weary kilometres travelled yesterday and the day before. The seasonal clock spins backward into spring as I climb, through blooming chokecherry (*Prunus virginiana*) and black or red hawthorne (*Crataegus douglasii* or *C. columbiana*), then earlier and earlier until, at the top of the slope, the hillside is still spangled with the golden sunflowers of balsamroot and white blossoms of saskatoon.

I find my track, no problem.

It's funny how the brain works. Of course I should have guessed what all those little lines on the map implied. But sometimes the spark doesn't jump. One and one don't make two. Sometimes you just don't want to know.

In every direction huge patches of the high plateau, north and south of the canyon and up onto the height of land to the west, many thousands of hectares, have been stripped of trees. I'm stunned at the extent of it. I had no idea. Small wonder that the creek has gone berserk.

In places the clear-cuts run right to the rim of Shorts Creek canyon, this spectacular bit of landscape, this treasure. In fact, I can see places farther up the canyon where some of the cutblocks actually dive over the rim onto the steep slopes below.

I think that's criminal.

Are we so poor (or so greedy) that we need to harvest our resources right to the limit of what is physically possible? Is there no allowance to be made for beauty and grace? When I was young and naive, I used to think that the best bits of the countryside would be left unmolested simply because they were too beautiful to wreck. Common decency would protect them.

More the fool, me.

I sometimes think that this kind of thing doesn't even have much to do with maximizing resource extraction. It's all about power. About proving who's in charge. In British Columbia the resource industries have always had the power and influence to do pretty much as they pleased. And sometimes, as in this instance, they seem to go out of their way to remind us just who's running the show.

It's a further fracturing of the bond between human beings and our home landscapes, well beyond even the excesses of urban and suburban development. Here the entire countryside has been industrialized. The landscape and living fabric have become pure commodity to be consumed down to the last atom. I see a feller-buncher working on a distant slope. They mean to take it all, don't they? Every last tree.

Seldom have I felt less rewarded by a long climb. I just want to catch my breath and get the hell gone. Westward ho.

> *Having to squeeze the last drop of utility out of the land has the same desperate finality as having to chop up the furniture to keep warm.*
>
> —Aldo Leopold, *A Sand County Almanac*

The rest of the day is a long walk through clear-cuts separated by bits of remaining forest. This is high-altitude forest now, mostly Engelmann spruce and subalpine fir. The difference in microclimate between the clear-cuts and the forest is striking. Under the trees, the air is cool and moist: yellow violets (*Viola orbiculata*) compared to white violets (*Viola canadensis*) down in the canyon, bunchberry (*Cornus canadensis*), and tiger lilies (*Lilium columbianum*) with their curling, dark-spotted, orange petals. I think the snow must just have gone, there's still that sharp cool smell of early spring in the air.

The cutblocks, by contrast, are hot and dry, a gravel pit climate, even though real summer is still weeks away. Considering the extent of these clear-cuts (deforestation isn't just something that happens in Third World countries) I can't help wondering how much they affect the regional climate. Maybe this is where the Okanagan's chronic water shortages are rooted.

Eventually I come to a tiny creek tumbling down off the higher forested ground to the right. It spills through a culvert under the road and hurries away toward the head of the canyon, somewhere out of sight to my left. This is the baby Shorts Creek, just getting started.

Then, less than half a kilometre along the road, I glimpse a little mountain lake just off to the left, still surrounded by a shelter belt of trees. Sandberg Lake, according to the map. The BC Forest Service maintains a small primitive campsite at the other end, but it turns out to be pretty awful, a prime example of the evils of easy access: the ground littered with smashed glass, beer cans and cigarette butts. I find a quiet private spot of my own, off in the trees, safe from prying eyes, where I can set up a little camp. I know it's a fool's paradise. There's another clear-cut just over the way. But I feel comforted to be back in the bush. The tent goes up, I eat a quick supper and am in bed before dark.

DAY TWENTY-TWO
Tuesday, June 17:
Sandberg Lake to Beak Creek and Nicola River

A short walk in the morning takes me up the road, around the corner and into a modest little valley, hardly more than a shallow depression between two hills. It's not much to look at, this little valley, but it represents a tremendous and magnificent thing. Here is the pass between two great river systems, the Columbia and the Fraser. Behind me, to the east, is Shorts Creek, the Okanagan Valley, the whole Columbia River system. Somewhere ahead, to the west, is Beak Creek, the Nicola River, the Thompson River and the whole Fraser River system.

Theoretically, at least, a raindrop falling at this end of the valley will end up as part of a vast tide of water flowing across northern

Oregon, past Portland and into the ocean off Astoria. A raindrop falling at that end will become part of a smaller but still impressive stream draining into the Pacific at Vancouver, British Columbia. The little valley itself is raggedly clear-cut, like much of the rest of the landscape.

The clear-cutting is so extensive you could almost imagine the whole landscape as open ground, not forested at all. There's some irony in that. It's very likely this little valley and, indeed, all the countryside I'm traversing from Okanagan Lake across to the Nicola River *would* have been open grassland at one time, long ago. The climate during the early Holocene, eight to ten thousand years ago, was much warmer and drier than at present. According to Dr. Richard Hebda, the Curator of Botany and Earth History at the Royal British Columbia Museum, the grasslands of southern interior British Columbia would have ranged to at least 1,300 metres above sea level and much higher on south-facing slopes. Hebda studies fossil pollen grains and other plant remains preserved in wetland and lake sediments. He reckons that grasslands might have occupied an area perhaps five times larger than they do nowadays. Even now there are still little grassy meadows on some of the steeper south-facing slopes at higher altitudes, a vestige or memento of that earlier time, perhaps.

There has been some speculation, with the anticipated warming of global climates, that grasslands in southern British Columbia might again extend their range into the highlands, reclaiming some of the ground lost to forest. But anyone who's hoping these clear-cuts might come back as grassland is going to be disappointed. Mostly they seem to come back as a scrubby tangle of shrubs, willows, alders and such, through which, presumably, eventually, seedling evergreens might find their way to sunshine and open air.

I come to Beak Creek, which drains higher ground to the south, a little wandering stream bordered by moose pasture and a narrow buffer strip of spruces. At this point the creek meanders deep and dark along the base of a north-facing slope, and it would seem that winter has only recently retreated from this place. The willows haven't yet lost their catkins, they're just now budding into leaf, and some of last winter's snowdrift still lingers in the deepest patches of forest shade on the other side of the stream.

Evening now, and much farther down the valley I come to a broader block of uncut forest. After a couple of kilometres the trees begin to thin. I see light ahead. Then I pass through a final fringe of aspens and out onto a wide natural meadow of bunchgrass, bright with spring flowers, sloping steeply upward to a high ridge on my right. Compared to the dreary scenery of these last two days, it's dreamland.

I stand there for a moment, dazed.

Without a doubt this is the nicest bit of countryside I've seen so far, better than anything I saw in the Okanagan or the Similkameen, barring those bits on Crater Mountain or on the ridge above the Similkameen River (but far more extensive than either) or along that little stretch beside the Okanagan River. Maybe not as wild as Shorts Creek canyon, but richer.

As always when I come across the good stuff, I find myself thinking that this is what all the valleys of southern interior British Columbia should look like. What they *would* have looked like before horses and cattle came along. Before ATVs and developers and exotic weeds and excavators and monster houses. This is the treasure we've been robbed of.

Till now I've mostly been taking comfort in little pocket grasslands, the tiny remnants of what used to be, the surviving scraps and fragments. Worth cherishing, all of them, but small potatoes compared to this.

I can't resist climbing the ridge for a better view, lugging my pack up the slope through a garden of yellow balsamroot flowers and blue lupine bedded in a luxuriant growth of bluebunch wheatgrass. A rich, high-elevation grassland. From the top I can look down into the wooded valley of the Nicola River, just below me now, and then out across the broad expanse of the Nicola basin, a vast shallow bowl, ridge upon ridge into the west, grassland seemingly without end.

I can also look back the way I've come.

And I realize that I've seen that view before, once, long ago. It was very different back then. The Beak Creek valley was uninterrupted forest all the way to the skyline. Now it's raw clear-cuts. So, too, with the headwaters of the Nicola River to the south: clear-cuts to the horizon. It's enough to sour the moment.

At least the view to the west hasn't changed. Not that I can see, anyway.

It's getting late, the sun is edging toward the horizon. And there's a change in the weather coming, a high thin overcast moving fast from the west. The sky overhead is full of disc-shaped lenticular clouds. Some sort of violence is happening up there. The wind across the ridge is picking up from the southwest. I'd love to linger; I could sit here for hours. But clearly it's time to be moving on.

I hasten back down the slope, through the grass and flowers, heading for the confluence of Beak Creek and the Nicola River where I hope to find a place to camp tonight. On the way down I flush a white-tailed deer (*Odocoileus virginianus*) out of the grass. It goes bounding away (rather than stotting like a mule deer) with that great white tail raised and flagging from side to side.

Farther on, almost at the bottom of the hill, I come upon a pair of black bears (*Ursus americanus*) still some distance ahead, both very black. Because of the disparity in size—one is noticeably larger than the other—I take them at first for a mother and her one- or two-year-old cub. But they don't behave like a mother and cub. As I watch they forage together for a while, then drift casually apart, ending up quite some distance from one another. Much too nonchalant. Eventually the little light bulb goes on in my head. It's a mating pair. I've read of mating behaviour in bears but have never seen it in progress. I go wide, giving them all the privacy I'm sure they desire.

DAY TWENTY-THREE
Wednesday, June 18: Beak Creek to Chapperon Creek

I wake to overcast skies and light rain. Moisture drips from the trees onto the tent. Even from my sleeping bag I can smell wet earth and vegetation.

To continue or not to continue? That is the question.

I hate to get my gear wet. Life is so much more complicated when the gear is wet. And I'm not crazy about getting myself wet either.

On the other hand, there's no possibility of shirking here. It's not like the Okanagan. I can't call time out, catch a bus, take a week or two off while this spell of bad weather blows itself out. My only option is to go on.

But maybe not just yet.

While I'm trying to decide, there are other issues to think about. Even without this unsettled weather, the next few days are going to be tricky. For all their relatively untouched and empty appearance, the open grasslands of the Nicola basin are mostly private property, divvied up among the region's great historic ranches as long ago as the 1880s and 1890s.

I'm camped on the very threshold of the biggest and most famous of them all, the Douglas Lake Ranch, Canada's largest working cattle ranch, half a million deeded acres starting somewhere just down the valley.

I think.

It's not easy to tell where Crown land ends and deeded land begins. When I was last here it hardly mattered. Those were the days when the dusty road up from Westwold boasted a huge sign: "Howdy Neighbour! Welcome to the Douglas Lake Ranch!"

This was another beloved place, home of the heart. The Douglas Lake Ranch was far away from town, hard to get to. Each visit was a major expedition and that, of course, lent it a special attraction. This particular piece of countryside has always seemed exotic to me. Romantic. High, wide and handsome.

Naturally I came here every chance I got.

Of course, even in those days, one always asked permission to go walking, only proper, a mandatory and civil courtesy, but in full confidence that permission would be forthcoming, perhaps with some slight caveat: "Best if you could stay away from such-and-such a place, we'll be moving cattle through there today."

Times have changed. I hear that the management now discourages casual visitors, though arrangements can be made for those willing to pay. Ecotourism I think it's called. Natural beauty as a commodity to be packaged, bought and sold.

I can't pay. And I don't want any hassle. So I'm going to try skirting the big ranch. I'll trace a great arc around the rim of the Nicola basin, then head down toward the lake at its heart.

But first a little side trip.

In the old days there was one spot I made a point of visiting pretty much every time I came this way, a gorgeous bunchgrass meadow that seemed to epitomize all that was best about the Douglas Lake Ranch country. Nowadays it's on the other side of the fence, out of bounds, so to speak. But I'm damned if I'll come this close and not make some sort of effort to pay my respects one last time, for *auld lang syne*. Today I'll get into position. And tomorrow a lightning visit, in and out, flying under the radar.

The drizzle has tapered off to nothing. I can see patches of blue sky when I poke my head from the tent. Evidently I've been spared a decision. It's just after noon when I finally get away, up the trail and through the aspens into the open. It *is* lovely, waves of grass rolling up the hill before the wind, lush and green, springtime at its best. It's as if I've managed to turn back the clock not just a few days or weeks, but years. Here the countryside seems more or less as it was when I was a kid. Nice to come back to a favourite place and find it relatively unaltered for a change. This is what I've been chasing all these miles and days. *Les temps perdu.* That lost grace and beauty.

(And what about all those clear-cuts up in the high country, all that mayhem I've left behind? From down here in the valley, not a glimpse or sign of them. Perfectly hidden. They're tricksy up there, my precious, aye, tricksy.)

A red-tailed hawk soars by, wings set, silhouetted against the blue sky. I hear a pair of kestrels calling from somewhere: *Killikillikilli.* The weather improves steadily, a perfect day for walking with mild sunshine and a bit of a breeze.

> *I have need of the sky.*
> *I have business with the grass.*
> *I will up and get me away where the hawk is wheeling,*
> *Lone and high,*
> *And the slow clouds go by.*
> *I will get me away to the waters that glass*
> *The clouds as they pass . . .*
> *I will get me away to the woods.*
>
> —Richard Hovey, "Spring"

For a long time I seem to have the countryside to myself. At first I feel mildly anxious, straying onto ground where I may not be welcome. But after a while, with sunshine and quiet, I begin to relax and enjoy the scenery. Then I top a little rise and come upon a couple of guys building a fence. The sign on their truck reads "Douglas Lake Ranch."

Merde.

There's no retreating. They've surely seen me. The monster pack is about as inconspicuous as a water buffalo. I go forward, fearing the worst.

But there's no problem. We chat for a bit. They ask me where I've come from, express polite amazement at my having walked all the way from Okanagan Lake, shake their heads in commiseration over the clear-cuts. In the end they give me a couple of apples out of the truck and wish me luck.

I go on with a lighter heart, making good time. The sun is still high when I reach my intended destination, a little meadow on Crown land (as I hope and believe) near Chapperon Creek.

I even have time to explore. The grass here is in great shape, lush and thick. Interestingly, it's a species of bunchgrass I can't remember having seen before on this journey: rough fescue. Rough fescue lives up to its common name in a couple of ways. The leaves, if you slide them between your fingers, have a rough, sticky feel to them. And older plants develop large dense clumps, which make for rough walking. You wouldn't want to hike cross-country very far through a thick growth of rough fescue. I expect to see more of it as I work my way northward.

I get the tent up, finish supper and there's still time to sit and enjoy the last of a golden evening, warm sunlight across the waving grass. The woods around the meadow are alive with birdsong. A woodpecker drums from somewhere farther back. Blackbirds call from out of the rushes around the pond at the bottom of the slope, and there are ducks on the sun-glinting water. The grass at my feet boasts a profusion of spring wildflowers. Blue-purple silky lupine. Three-flowered avens, with its downy pink flowers in (as you've guessed) clusters of three. And another little flower, deep indigo, that I take at first for self-heal (*Prunella vulgaris*) but which turns out to be small-flowered penstemon (*Penstemon procerus*).

This is how the world was meant to be. This is what I fell in love with as a youngster, expected to enjoy as an adult and presumed to grow old loving. Wedded to the countryside all my life.

So to bed, the tent suffused with evening glow long after the sun has gone beyond the distant hills. And later a different light on the tent. Another full moon in a special place, rising late, full and clear, shining out across the grasslands of the Douglas Lake Ranch. Perfect timing.

The earth laughs in flowers.
—Ralph Waldo Emerson, "Hamatreya"

DAY TWENTY-FOUR
Thursday, June 19: Chapperon Creek to Nicola River Valley

When last I visited this place, the bunchgrass was tall and thick and lush. The ground between bunches was undisturbed, well-protected by a nice growth of mosses and lichens, the biological soil crust. If there were weeds, there can't have been many; I don't remember seeing any at all. The meadow was pristine, a prime example of southern interior British Columbia's bunchgrass ecosystems. I remember thinking that it looked like it had never been grazed. I wondered how and why it had been spared.

Well, that was then. This is now.

Somebody must have decided that all that good grass was just going to waste and turned the horses loose on it. (Exhibit A: horsebuns everywhere.) The clumps of bunchgrass have been much reduced and some are evidently dead, grazed right down to the ground with no fresh spring growth showing. Worse, the crust between the bunches has been broken up, quite badly in places, exposing the bare soil. I can still see hoofmarks (Exhibit B). Must have been wet and soft when the animals were in here.

In fairness, I have to say that compared to some of the rangelands I've seen since I started at Crater Mountain this meadow is still in pretty fair condition.

But it's not what it was.

It has become, instead, a prime example of something else entirely: the unavoidable limitations of ranching and range management as an approach to the maintenance and conservation of indigenous grasslands.

The term "range management" implies the management of uncultivated ground as pasture for domestic livestock. Most of southern interior British Columbia's "indigenous" or "natural" or "wild" or "native" grasslands have long since been converted to "range."

I think of it as pasturization.

In theory, at least, "range" can revert to more or less natural grassland if left unmolested long enough, though, in practice, some of the invasive plants that proliferate under continued heavy grazing, such as Kentucky bluegrass (*Poa pratensis*) and cheatgrass, are extremely tenacious once they get established.

I should probably note at this point that, as far as I'm concerned, the Douglas Lake Ranch represents the very acme of range management. I can't think of another outfit in British Columbia that does a better job. Somehow they've managed to maintain this huge piece of countryside in a pretty good semblance of native grassland. (And also, not incidentally, prevented it from being converted to hobby-farms and golf courses and subdivisions.) Recognizing all that, I say, most sincerely, "God bless the Douglas Lake Cattle Company."

Even so, it's important to recognize the limitations. As rangeland goes, it's very good. But it's hardly what you might call pristine. And there are some unavoidable reasons why that should be so.

All the evidence suggests that the bunchgrass meadows of southern interior British Columbia (in sharp contrast to, say, the grasslands of the Canadian prairies) evolved in the absence of sizeable herds of large grazing ungulates.

There were no great herds of bison here. Regarding elk, expert opinion seems divided, but my impression is that they were present through these arid valleys in relatively small numbers, more or less as at present, and mostly along forest edges. (The elk that are present now are descended from introduced stock.) There weren't any moose or white-tailed deer. Both those species have extended their ranges dramatically in modern times and, besides, both are primarily browsers (rather than grazers) feeding off twigs and leaves rather than grass. There would have been mule deer here. And mule deer do graze grass in the spring and early summer. But they, too, are primarily browsers in the autumn and winter. Bighorn sheep are grazers of grass, certainly, but the bands would have been small and scattered, confined to limited areas of suitable habitat.

So, really, until cattle and horses and other domestic livestock came along, the bulk of the grazing in the grasslands of southern interior British Columbia would have been done by little light-footed critters:

pocket gophers, mice, voles, ground squirrels, marmots and such-like. And insects, I suppose.

Think of the difference that would make.

No bunches of wheatgrass or fescue grazed wholesale down to the roots. No disturbance to the soil crust between bunches.

That lack of disturbance allowed the evolution of a spectacular and remarkable form of indigenous grassland, in the same way that the isolation of islands allows for the evolution of spectacular insular ecosystems, with unusual, remarkable and often quite fragile or vulnerable communities of flora and fauna.

Now imagine the arrival of horses and cattle. Think of what that must have done to these indigenous grasslands. Big herds of huge, heavy, sharp-hoofed, hungry animals. Certainly, as I've seen so far on this walk, pristine grassland ecosystems in southern interior British Columbia mostly survive on terrain that is too rugged or too arid or in some other way unsuitable for domestic livestock.

When I hear concerned ranchers talking about grassland conservation, I applaud their good intentions. The future of grasslands in southern interior British Columbia is largely in their hands. Any effort to base range management on the natural processes of indigenous ecosystems has got to be a step in the right direction. And the Douglas Lake Ranch is proof positive that it can be done.

On the other hand, there's just no getting around the basic contradiction: The primary goal and purpose of the rancher is to raise livestock. And domestic livestock seem to be fundamentally and unavoidably harmful to the indigenous grasslands of southern interior British Columbia.

Range managers talk about "stocking rates," the number of animals that an area of rangeland can supposedly support without deteriorating, as if a certain level of grazing was more or less harmless. I'd contend that, given the way grasslands in southern British Columbia have evolved, there is no such thing as a harmless level of grazing by domestic livestock. Turn one cow or one horse loose on a pristine meadow and that animal is going to do some damage.

So, really, the essential question for range managers is not "What number of cattle or horses or other livestock can a given area of rangeland support without deteriorating?" but, rather, "What level of trauma can a given area of rangeland sustain and still recover?" and "How long will it take to recover?"

I think the answers to those two questions are probably the key to the Douglas Lake Ranch's success in range or pasture management. With such a huge land base, the ranch's managers can afford to rest a particular pasture after grazing, for years if need be, until it's more or less (though never quite completely) healed.

It might be interesting to come back to this meadow in four or five (or ten or twenty) years to see how it's getting on. I'll be keeping my fingers crossed that it will have recovered, at least somewhat, but I suspect it's going to be a good long time before the grass will be anything like pristine again.

Still, there is cause for optimism. It's a pretty good bet that all of the Douglas Lake Ranch ranges, like most of the other ranges in southern British Columbia, would have been grazed almost to death in the second half of the nineteenth century, when huge herds of cattle were simply turned out to fend for themselves year-round. And yet, look at it now. Obviously the bunchgrass can come back if given a fair chance. It's something to look forward to.

For the time being, though, I've no desire to linger. My blue-sky morning has developed another high thin overcast and there's a bright halo around the sun that bodes ill. Time to hit the trail.

Now the sky is black. The first drops come spitting down as I hammer home the last peg. I barely have time to throw the pack and gear inside, climb in after them and zip the flap shut before the warning tattoo of droplets on the tent-fly deepens to a roar and the heavens open. A little too close for comfort.

Toward the end of the afternoon the rain eases off, then stops altogether. A little later the tent brightens and I poke my head out to find the sun peeking from beneath the western edge of the clouds. Blue sky to the west and a rainbow to the east. No, *two* rainbows. The ground and vegetation are very wet, but I stalk around cautiously, taking pictures and generally enjoying my temporary proprietorship of this place. Then it's back into the tent as the sun goes down and the mosquitoes return (with reinforcements) to claim the night.

DAY TWENTY-FIVE
Friday, June 20: Nicola River Valley to Mellin Creek

A little garden in which to walk, and immensity in which to dream.

—Victor Hugo, *Les Misérables*

That's the trouble with rain on a backpacking trip: it's never over when it's over. The consequences linger awkwardly. So here we are, a fine and lovely morning. I've risen early, well-rested, thanks to yesterday's forced time out, eager to be on my way. But the tent-fly is soaking wet. The ground is soaking wet. Every leaf and twig in the bush is soaking wet.

I do the necessary, sponge moisture off the fly, spread the wet gear in the warm sun to dry, pass the time as best I can, hoping that the landscape, too, will be drying out while I wait. By ten o'clock I've run out of patience. The tent-fly, still damp, gets rolled and bundled into the pack (fortunately I've brought a plastic bag for just such an occasion, God bless the petrochemical industry) and I'm away.

The going is slow and sometimes difficult. At one point I find myself clinging to the steep slope of a precipitous wooded ravine, quite baffled as to how I might best proceed.

But the views are magnificent, westward across the grassy slopes and ridges of the Nicola basin to forested mountains beyond, and beyond those mountains to a line of snow-capped peaks, presumably the Coast Mountains, a hundred kilometres or more to the west. The sense of expanse is quite literally breathtaking, heart-pounding, overwhelming and oddly reminiscent of similar views in the foothill country of Alberta or Montana. Ranching country, high, wide and handsome, like something out of a Charlie Russell painting. (Just kind of naturally makes you want to step onto a horse, round up those dogies and head 'em out. *Hutsa!*)

In fact, the Douglas Lake Cattle Company was established at much the same time as the Cochrane Ranche and other similar giant ranches in the foothills of Alberta, all around the mid-1880s, in anticipation of a burgeoning market for beef to be created by the construction and opening of the Canadian Pacific Railway.

I spend most of the day working my way across a series of high meadows at around 1,200 metres elevation. More vestiges, I suppose, of that time in the early Holocene when grasslands were more extensive in southern interior British Columbia. Nice grass here. And for some reason these particular meadows are an exceptional garden of spring wildflowers. The seasons are visibly compressed, which is often the case at higher elevations, as if nature were trying to make up for time lost under the slow-melting snow.

The yellow balsamroot is still in bloom here. And so is the pink three-flowered avens, an even earlier flower, though these are starting to go to seed, showing the feathery persistent styles that earn them the nickname "Old Man's Whiskers" or "Prairie Smoke." At the same time, in and around these early bloomers, there are some gorgeous displays of sky-blue silky lupine, usually more belated.

Here also are two different species of yellow-flowered legumes: field locoweed (*Oxytropis campestris*), famously poisonous, and another that I tentatively identify as yellow hedysarum (*Hedysarum sulphurescens*), famously food for bears. And here is another legume, with delicate violet-coloured blooms, also poisonous, timber milk-vetch (*Astragalus miser*).

Fine-leaved daisy (*Erigeron linearis*), bright orange blossoms.

Cut-leaved daisy (*Erigeron compositus*), stalks rising from a basal cluster of fern-like leaves, with misleading flowers: at first just little yellow buttons showing no hint of the white daisy-rays that will eventually develop.

Field chickweed (*Cerastium arvense*), white flowers, of the "pink" family, with five petals so deeply divided that each seems at first to be a pair of petals.

Death camas (*Zigadenus venenosus*), a lily, white and lovely, sinister.

And the prize, red columbine (*Aquilegia formosa*), gorgeous blossoms, red and yellow, nodding in the sun.

So it goes, on and on.

These meadows are also a visible reminder of an even earlier era, when all this countryside was burdened by a mass of glacial ice as much as a kilometre thick, oozing ponderously under its own enormous weight. Here in the Nicola basin, the drift seems to have been predominantly from northwest to southeast, and most of these high meadows show obvious signs of having been graded and scoured by moving ice: great linear gouges and broad terraces. And with the melting of all that ice, a scattering of giant glacial erratics deposited across the freshly abraded surface. (One of which affords me a nice warm perch for lunch and a bit of a snooze in the sunshine.)

As the afternoon wears on, another batch of clouds moves in and the sunshine becomes increasingly intermittent. I decide to quit early.

Good decision. I barely get the tent up before the first little squall comes through. Happily, this is not a steadily deepening storm like yesterday's. It turns out to be one of those afternoons where showers alternate with brilliant sunshine, puffy clouds, blue sky. I'm in and out of the tent, reading, enjoying the view, making up my notes, botanizing. I even get out my little paintbox (there's a creek handy for water) and mess about with the colours for a bit.

Summer solstice: 4:59 p.m. The northern hemisphere tilted as far as it will go toward the sun.

A beautiful warm evening. Great to be alive. But the sun goes down into hazy cloud banks far to the west. I don't know what that might portend for tomorrow, but this is one of those comfortable, homely campsites and I feel a certain insouciance, knowing that if the weather turns ugly I can always hunker down here for a bit.

DAY TWENTY-SIX
Saturday, June 21: Mellin Creek to Spahomin Creek

I wake to overcast and a light rain that soon eases off. This is what last night's cloud banks foreshadowed and it drops me straight onto the horns of a dilemma. The weather is not that bad, but it's not that great either. Should I stay or should I go? Waste a day or take a chance on getting soaked? In the end I decide to go on, but I've an uneasy feeling that I'm letting my impatience get the better of me.

At first events seem to justify the decision. I make good progress. The weather continues to brighten. There's even a taste of blue sky and sunshine. Then things start to drift in the other direction. The clouds gather and darken. The wind begins to rise. I feel a spit or two of moisture.

The moment comes when I step out of a small grove of aspens to find a solid curtain of rain bearing down on me from the other end of a long meadow. An honest-to-goodness cloudburst. I can even hear it coming, the hiss and roar of it. I've barely time to run for the half shelter of a big Douglas-fir, dig some rain gear out of the pack and climb into it before the downpour is upon me. I spend an hour crouched in the lee of that fir, relatively dry but feeling colder by the minute. I'm dressed for walking, not sitting.

Little by little it dawns on me that this is no passing shower. This is your genuine day-long soaker, a front going through. Reluctantly I make up my mind to continue. I need to get moving. I've started to shiver. Should have stayed in bed, as they say, but it's too late for that now.

This part of the country looks to be pretty much completely pasturized, native bunchgrasses long ago converted to Kentucky bluegrass and other domestic forage grasses, smooth brome (*Bromus inermis*) and such-like. Another unavoidable limitation to ranching as an approach to the conservation of indigenous grasslands.

Kentucky bluegrass differs from the native bunchgrasses in a number of important ways. It can reproduce itself through seeding like the native bunchgrasses, but it mostly spreads by sending out long creeping rhizomes. Instead of growing in widely separated clumps, Kentucky bluegrass forms a dense mat of turf. One has the sense that here is a grass that evolved in the company of large herbivores. It's far more resistant than the native bunchgrasses to overgrazing and trampling. And it's decent forage.

What if it actually makes economic sense for a rancher to replace the native bunchgrasses with a mixture of bluegrass and other domestic forage species. Where does that leave indigenous ecosystems?

Rain gear is not designed for hiking, especially strenuous hiking. And most especially strenuous hiking under the weight and encumbrance of my monster pack. After a while it's a question of which has me wetter, the rain or my own perspiration. I'm not happy, but at least I'm warm.

And I have to say that even on such a miserable day there is grace and beauty in the world. Spahomin Creek turns out to be quite lovely, flowing through groves of Engelmann spruce. Clear, dark water spangled with spreading ripple-rings from the rain. It's deep and placid, much larger than I anticipated, almost a little river. I'm glad there's a bridge, otherwise I'd have to swim.

By now the light is fading and time is of the essence. It takes some searching but eventually I find a relatively dry spot under a big spruce. A pretty location, too, right beside the creek. Altogether one of the nicest campsites of the whole trip. Somebody is looking after me.

By the time I get the tent up, darkness has fallen and the rain is still pelting down. I work by headlamp, carefully extracting all of my still dry gear from the soaking wet pack and plastic wrappings. The only real failure of woodcraft is my sleeping pad, which I somehow neglected to cover properly. It is, accordingly, a little damp at one end. The clothes I'm wearing are, of course, sodden. When all is ready I shed the whole soaking mass in front of the tent—to be sorted tomorrow or the next day, whenever the rain stops (there's nothing I can't deal with, given time)—and hustle my wet, goosebumped, naked butt into the blessed dryness of the tent.

It's surprisingly cozy once I've had something to eat and have warmed up a little. I even read for a bit before lights out, seeking escape in Rivendell with Frodo and Strider, other pilgrims on other journeys, while I listen to the steady rain outside.

DAY TWENTY-SEVEN
Sunday, June 22: Spahomin Creek to Wasley Creek

An unexpectedly pleasant day, blue sky and sunshine, a nice surprise. Yesterday might be just a bad dream, except for the pile of wet gear lying in front of the tent. I get to work right after breakfast, sorting the mess. While I'm at it, stringing an improvised clothesline, hanging the wet clothing in the sun, sponging down the tent, I'm surprised to hear a truck grinding down the track toward the bridge, four-wheel drive, low range, low gear. A slippery ride this morning I should think, with all that wet clay. Wonder what the driver will make of my footprints from last night? Maybe he or she will be too busy keeping the vehicle on the road to notice.

Anyway, it's a lovely place to hang out for a bit, both literally and figuratively, with the stream running by and the sun shining down through the spruces. Calypso orchids (*Calypso bulbosa*) in the shade. Bear scat everywhere. I'd best not linger any longer than I have to.

Sizeable meadow with pond and wetland. A large dark shape in the middle distance sends me fumbling for the binoculars. Is it a bear?

Do they have grizzlies here? Maybe yes, maybe no. But this is a young moose (*Alces alces*).

Some things are so ordinary as to pass largely unremarked. This, it seems to me, is one of the flaws of conservation biology: with all the emphasis on "biodiversity," overmuch attention is devoted to the rare and the transient, the marginal, the endangered, while the commonplace is scorned or ignored. Enthusiasts will travel hundreds of miles to view an accidental species, something blown in from half a world away, while ignoring the chickadees around their back door.

And yet very often it is the commonplace that embodies the essence of an ecosystem: those chickadees, well adapted to their environment, able to tough it out through summer's heat and drought or the bitter cold of winter.

On practically any given day through this section of the journey and at this time of the year, if I were paying proper attention, I might hear a sharp whistle and catch a glimpse of yellow-brown fur, a smallish animal (the size of a domestic cat, two to five kilograms, but definitely not cat shaped), rather squat and short-legged and round, galloping for the safety of rock pile or burrow.

This is the rather endearing yellow-bellied marmot (*Marmota flaviventris*), brown above, buff-yellow below, basically a giant ground squirrel and largest of the local rodent tribe except for the beavers (*Castor canadensis*) down along the creek.

To my way of thinking, marmots and other ground squirrels are the quintessential animals of southern British Columbia's arid grassland valleys.

The vast grasslands of the Canadian prairies east of the Rocky Mountains boasted great herds of American bison (*Bison bison*), awesome, massive, shaggy-haired animals. Or, in the foothills, big herds of long-antlered elk (*Cervus canadensis*), equally impressive.

The valleys of what is now southern interior British Columbia had nothing to compare with that. Our herds of herbivores were mostly little guys, shy and not at all impressive: yellow-bellied marmots, Columbian ground squirrels, red squirrels, yellow pine chipmunks, bushy-tailed wood rats, northern pocket gophers, mice species and vole species too numerous to mention.

Unimpressive. Commonplace. Ordinary.

But absolutely the essence of the ecosystem: no trampling of fragile soils, no heavy grazing, just the delicate pitter-patter of little feet.

Yellow-bellied marmots are creatures of open ground, although they prefer rocky habitat for denning sites. Open ground means safety and security, plenty of room to see danger coming, sufficient time to warn the rest of the colony. (These are social animals, enjoying company, living in groups of ten to twenty animals, getting safety in numbers.) And open ground offers a lot to eat: grasses, sedges, forbs (especially dandelions and clover), seeds and roots.

Like any good farmer, marmots rise with the dawn and retire shortly after sunset. But they're rather too indolent to be good farmers, spending most of the day feeding, sunbathing and generally hanging out, keeping a wary eye out for predators.

And they don't put anything by for the winter.

They've got a better strategy.

Yellow-bellied marmots spend something like two-thirds of their lives in hibernation. It's the perfect adaptation for an environment where most of the year's productivity is crammed into those three or four months of spring and early summer when the soil has sufficient moisture to support a vigorous growth of plants.

Marmots emerge from their burrows in April, mate almost immediately (males defend a harem of up to four females) and the young of the year are born a month later in May. Litter size averages four or five (and ranges from three to eight). Kits are born blind, naked and helpless, but they emerge from the burrows within a month and are weaned at about six weeks of age.

With reproduction taken care of, the rest of the marmots' waking time is devoted to the serious business of eating and putting on weight, laying in sufficient fat to see them through those eight months when they will neither eat nor drink. Then, in August, they retire to grass-lined hibernacula for that long, long winter's nap.

Let me repeat that phrase in case you missed it: "eight months when they will neither eat nor drink." Think of that! Human beings can last something like seven to ten weeks without eating. And then we die. Just a few days without water and we're finished. Eight months! And no harm done. How do they do it? Metabolism slows tremendously. Body temperature drops to near-ambient, sometimes within a degree or two of freezing in winter. Respiration and heart-beat are barely perceptible. Even so, it's a miraculous thing, like science fiction. Surviving in suspended animation while the world creeps slowly toward another spring.

The breeze has strengthened all afternoon. Now there's a brisk, chilly wind blowing out of the southwest, though the sky is still clear. It's cold work getting the tent up in a little patch of rough fescue perched above Wasley Creek. By the time I'm finished my hands are numb, fingers white, and I'm looking forward very much to getting inside. Makes me uneasy, all this wind. What does it portend? More rain?

DAY TWENTY-EIGHT
Monday, June 23: Wasley Creek to Quilchena Creek

I rejoice in yet another blue-sky morning, notwithstanding the wind ablowing all night long and still blowing hard, stirring the fescue, old man's whiskers and silky lupines, sunshine-bright, that grow just outside the tent. My own little garden, if only for a few hours.

Walking southwest now, straight into the wind, across wide-open grassy slopes. I seem to be out of the woods at last, though not very far out of the woods. In fact, the transition is amazingly abrupt. On the north side of Wasley Creek there are south-facing slopes, wide-open bunchgrass meadows, the beginning of all the Nicola basin's hundreds of thousands of hectares of grassland. On the south side of the creek, by contrast, steep north-facing slopes, dense forest.

"Aspect" is a term ecologists use to describe the physical orientation of a piece of ground. Is the ground level or sloping? In what direction does it slope? And to what degree?

Aspect and altitude have an enormous influence on local climate: soil-moisture, air and soil temperatures, exposure, insolation, degree days and so on. North-facing slopes are cooler and wetter than south-facing slopes. Higher altitudes are cooler and wetter than lower altitudes. High-altitude, north-facing slopes are the coolest and wettest of all. Low-altitude, south-facing slopes are warmest and driest.

(Significantly, high-altitude south-facing slopes and low-altitude north-facing slopes may have quite similar local climates.)

And local climate plays an enormous role in shaping the biological community that develops on a particular piece of ground.

There are other factors, of course, especially the nature of the soil and even the bedrock under a given piece of ground. Is the soil well drained or not? Is it well provided with minerals and nutrients or is it relatively sterile?

The sum total of all these physical factors, what might be called "the growing conditions," is subject to a bewildering complexity of balance and change and variation across the landscape. It's almost impossible to map and measure and quantify technically.

But there is another way to get a handle on it.

Two pieces of ground with more or less similar growing conditions, a sort of ecological equivalence, will tend to support similar communities or "associations" of plants and animals. The grassy meadows on the high south-facing slopes of Crater Mountain, for example, will support a combination of species quite similar to meadows on north-facing slopes far down in the valley because growing conditions are more or less equivalent in both situations.

Let me put that another way. Equivalent growing conditions are indicated by equivalent and characteristic communities of plants and animals.

If you were to spend any amount of time hiking around out here, you would soon notice that plants are not randomly distributed across the landscape.

They tend to occur in fairly typical, easily recognizable combinations or associations or communities. Partnerships. And those plant associations are a reliable indicator of growing conditions. Bunchgrass and big sage suggest warmer, drier conditions and well-drained soil. Douglas-fir and pinegrass suggests cooler conditions and more moisture. A growth of trembling aspen and saskatoon bushes cascading down through a gully suggests even more moisture. And so on.

Ecologists call these recognizable combinations or associations of various plant species: vegetation units, plant associations, site associations or habitat types. Site associations are named according to their dominant species. So we might speak of a "Ponderosa Pine–Bluebunch Wheatgrass–Fescue" association or a "Big Sage–Bluebunch Wheatgrass" association.

Once you begin to recognize the various plant associations or habitat types, a walk through the countryside becomes a stroll through the neighbourhood, recognizing and greeting old friends as you go along. In fact, once you begin to understand which species *should* be associated with which in a given habitat type (and in what proportions), you become a bit of a connoisseur.

I surprise another mating pair of black bears, much closer than before. This time one of the pair is a beautiful cinnamon brown. (I wonder how many people catching a glimpse of this animal would mistakenly identify it as a grizzly. It's certainly got that grizzly bear colour.) The black one spots me, stands up for a better look, then drops to all fours and begins to retreat hesitantly upslope. It's clearly anxious to get away but doesn't want to abandon its partner. Brown continues to graze for a time but eventually notices me, thereby resolving black's dilemma: they gallop off together, heading for cover.

In the badly worn copy of *The Mammals of Canada* sitting on my bookshelf back home, A.W.F. Banfield suggests these two bears are probably *Ursus americanus cinnamomum*, the typical subspecies of southern interior British Columbia, a race of largish black bears in which the brown colour phase is almost as common as black.[9]

Females come into estrus in late June or early July, but implantation of fertilized eggs is delayed until October or November. Cubs are born in their mother's winter den between mid-January and early February. They are very small when born, about the size of a squirrel, naked and blind. Cubs are weaned at about five months and are self-sufficient at six to eight months. But they stay with their mother through a second winter, dispersing in the spring when she mates again. (Females with young cubs do not come into estrus.) Juvenile females reach sexual maturity at four to five years, males a year later. According to my old *Mammals of Canada*, black bears have survived to twenty-three years in captivity, but that record has long since been surpassed. In 2013 the Minnesota Department of Natural Resources reported a wild bear that had perished of simple old age at thirty-nine and a half years.

The winter hibernation of bears is relatively shallow. A hibernating bear's metabolism does slow and body temperature drops by four to seven degrees but not nearly so dramatically as with the deep hibernators—marmots and ground squirrels and so on—whose body temperatures may fall to near-ambient. And winter-lethargic bears can be roused, even by loud noises. Bears have relatively poor eyesight (about like ours) but fair hearing and an excellent sense of smell. (Presumably smelling salts or a nice juicy cheeseburger would bring them wide-awake in a moment from their winter's napping.)

Even though I've caught these two in the open, perhaps eating flowers, which are highly nutritious, they are not really grassland animals. Black bears are creatures of forest and forest-margin, semi-arboreal, climbing trees readily for food and security (using their sharp curved claws, non-retractile).

I like bears. I always get a fellow feeling when I encounter them. Apparently I'm not alone in this. Various indigenous cultures have folk tales of human mothers raising bear cubs (very painful nursing I understand) and vice versa. Both species walk flat-footed. Human beings, too, come from semi-arboreal stock, climbing trees at need. Both species are omnivorous, mostly eating plants—black bears graze grasses and sedges, sprouts of forbs, tree buds and shoots, roots, berries and fruits—but not eschewing meat when we can get it, though neither bears nor human beings have the teeth to do a very good job of chewing raw flesh. Our flat-topped molars have evolved for crushing rather than cutting.

I've read that skinned bears look disturbingly like men.

Young cubs will cry when afraid, hum when contented.

But I'm not foolish about my sympathies either. According to *The Mammals of Canada*, male black bears average 169 kilograms, with a range of 115 to 270 kilograms, and females average 136 kilograms, with a range of 92 to 140 kilograms. The weight of individual animals varies 25 to 40 percent over the course of a year. Black bears are fattest in August and thinnest in spring, naturally, when food is scarce after they emerge from their winter dens. They are formidable animals by any measure, muscular, intelligent and well-armed. Most are shy, quick to flee, but on rare occasions, according to Dr. Stephen Herrero, black bears have attacked and eaten human beings.[10] Best to keep one's distance.

Here is another young moose, very close this time, moving away through a little grove of dead lodgepole pines, half blown down, tossed this way and that. He, or she, puts me in mind of a deer on stilts picking its way through a maze, stepping high and deliberate, first one leg, then another. In a surprisingly short time the animal works its way through the tangle and is gone.

My camp above Quilchena Creek is graced by a cluster of ponderosa pines, so beautiful, like a Japanese print, with sprays of long green needles gathered in groups of three. I wish these trees luck and a long life, hoping against hope in this era of climate change and mountain pine beetle epidemic.

That wind is still blowing hard out of the southwest and now there's a gathering overcast.

DAY TWENTY-NINE
Tuesday, June 24:
Quilchena Creek to Hamilton Commonage

I was expecting rain for sure this morning, but no, I wake to another blue-sky day, though the air is a little hazy. Like everyone else these days, I've grown accustomed to knowing what the weather will be like this morning, this afternoon, tomorrow. It feels strangely unsettling to live with uncertainty out here, simply having to accept whatever arrives, minute by minute. This unceasing, inexplicable wind is getting on my nerves. I feel vulnerable. What does it mean?

Quilchena Creek (like Wasley Creek) seems to mark the very boundary of the Nicola grasslands, the edge of the basin, with forests on the left bank, wide-open rangeland on the right. On my map, Quilchena Creek flows west to southwest until it reaches Quilchena Falls, then dekes sharply to the right, heading northwest toward Nicola Lake.

Quilchena Falls turns out to be a long cataract or series of cascades rather than a free waterfall. Even so, it's quite impressive. The creek, which has been meandering across a broad terraced upland, suddenly tumbles into a much deeper valley, almost a trench, running at right angles. This is evidently an ancient watercourse excavated in some forgotten age of the world by a much larger stream, long vanished. Quilchena Creek, thus captured, has little option but to follow the old watercourse down toward Nicola Lake, perhaps twenty-five kilometres away to the north.

I elect to stay high, seeking some sort of path across the uplands above the creek, hoping for a view. I am not disappointed. Here is the most spectacular piece of grassland scenery so far, a broad vista all the way down along the deep valley of Quilchena Creek to Nicola Lake in the distance. And north of the lake a further expanse of open country toward Kamloops, my route for the next three or four days at a glance.

It's a day for wandering. Since I'm not following any kind of fixed route I go where fancy takes me, through an endless series of grassy meadows, scattered groves of ponderosa pine, little copses of trembling aspen, from one viewpoint to the next. I feel more like a genuine gypsy or nomad than ever before on this journey. That freedom to roam is one of the things I craved when I started. Going where I please, here and there, but always northward.

Some fine grassland here, some not so fine, but on the whole quite satisfactory. As if to attest to the quality of the habitat, a pair of sharp-tailed grouse (*Tympanuchus phasianellus*) flush from beneath my feet, rocketing up and away at high speed, gone in seconds out of sight over the ridge. These will be "Columbian" sharp-tailed grouse (*Tympanuchus phasianellus columbianus*), one of six subspecies of sharp-tail found in North America.

Sharp-tails are medium-sized grouse. Big males weigh about a kilo. With both sexes showing pale cryptic coloration, brown and buff above, lighter below and on the tail, they are well equipped to blend with their surroundings. The tail is wedge-shaped and the two centre tail feathers are elongated, giving the species its name. Sharp-tails are birds of open country, one of the characteristic species of British

Columbia's grasslands. And they are distinguished from all other species of grouse in the province by their habit of dancing.

In the spring and fall, males stake out territories at traditional dancing grounds called "leks," with dominant individuals at the centre of the lek, younger males around the periphery. With wings spread and drooping, brilliant yellow fleshy comb prominent over each eye, pale violet air sacs (one on either side of their necks) inflating and deflating, the boys display by rapidly stamping their feet, rattling their tail feathers, confronting one another across invisible boundary lines.

The ladies visit briefly in spring to mate—usually with dominant males near the centre of the lek—then depart to nest. The hens are grassland connoisseurs, preferring bluebunch wheatgrass and rough fescue for cover. They incubate their eggs (twelve per clutch, on average) and raise the chicks, all without any help from the males. Timing varies widely, depending on the weather, but chicks in this part of the country usually hatch in late May or early June. They're extremely precocious, able to stand and run shortly after hatching and to fly (sort of) within a week to ten days.

If there are any chicks on these meadows they should be getting around pretty well by now, eating mostly insects and other invertebrates at this time of year; shifting to berries and green vegetation in the fall; then to dried berries, hips, leaves, twigs, buds and catkins in the winter.

Sharp-tailed grouse are widely distributed in North America, from Alaska and the Yukon south to northern Utah and Colorado, and east to Quebec.

But within that vast area they inhabit only a fraction of their former ranges. Many populations, especially of "Columbian" sharp-tails, have declined to the point of extinction. They have become, like meadowlarks, a symbol of vanishing grasslands.

Sharp-tailed grouse prefer relatively undisturbed habitat. There must be adequate cover for nests and growing chicks. Riparian ecosystems are essential for cover and forage in the winter. Sharp-tails are particularly vulnerable at their leks, and females avoid disturbed leks altogether.

Unfortunately, in recent decades, same old story: various forms of disturbance (urban and agricultural land development, heavy livestock grazing, biocides, direct interference from people and pets, forest ingrowth, fire) have resulted in widespread fragmentation, deterioration and loss of habitat.

I walk obsessively. I walk and walk and walk, devouring countryside until sundown puts an end to my walking. Then I drop the tent on the first bit of level ground I come to, nicely sheltered by a bit of bunchgrass. No water, of course, just an overnight bivouac. The wind is still blowing out of the south. There's a lovely view west across the deep gulf of the Quilchena Creek valley to the high ground of the Lundbom Commonage on the far side.

And here's some more of that yellow-flowered legume I've been calling hedysarum. Actually I'm not at all sure of my identification. It's been years since I last saw yellow hedysarum in the foothills of Alberta. I'm not even sure it grows this far west. The main thing I remember about hedysarum is that the roots are important food for grizzly bears, especially in the early spring when there isn't much else to eat. There are no grizzly bears here I'm pretty sure, though it looks like grizzly country. Very much an open-ground species, the grizzly bear, like sharp-tails. They should be here but aren't.

That serves to point out yet another of the unavoidable limitations of ranching as a strategy for conserving indigenous grasslands. Ranchers as a class, even the most enlightened, are not sympathetic to predators. Many are actively hostile. The only good bear, wolf, coyote, cougar is a dead bear, wolf, coyote, cougar.

In fact, any species considered inimical to grazing livestock is not welcome, and that even includes critters as innocuous as badgers, say, which supposedly dig holes that livestock can step into.

Consequently, even if a piece of rangeland shows a nice growth of grass, it's still only a facsimile of the original ecosystem because it will be lacking many of the keystone native animal species that the rancher has decided might interfere with or complicate the raising of cattle.

All of which is to say that we need some sort of balance. The future of grassland conservation in British Columbia is very much in the hands of ranchers, as it has been for the last 150 years. And ranchers are among the most passionate advocates for grassland conservation. Of course they are; their futures depend on it and they love the country. But given the nature of their business they labour under unavoidable limitations. If we're serious about preserving indigenous grasslands we're going to have to make room for live-stock-free reserves.

DAY THIRTY
Wednesday, June 25:
Hamilton Commonage to Quilchena Hotel, Nicola Lake

At last, the overcast I've been expecting. A little cooler this morning too, but no rain just yet. That uncanny wind is still blowing hard from the south. And here's a new experience for me, something I've never noticed before: the subtle scent of silky lupines, growing thickly across the hillside above the tent, vivid blue blossoms at their very peak.

If I read the map correctly, the land immediately above and behind me is part of a large publicly owned parcel of range, the Hamilton Commonage. And there's a second more or less matching parcel, the Lundbom Commonage, away on the other side of the Quilchena Creek valley.

The idea of commonage is much out of fashion nowadays. And I doubt that either the Lundbom or Hamilton Commonage is used as originally intended: to provide rangeland access for smaller ranchers in an area of the province where most of the open grassland had been appropriated early on by the large cattle companies. I'd guess that, nowadays, most of the grazing on these two commonages is leased out to some of the same few large ranches that own most of the rest of the landscape.

Even so, the effort may not have been in vain. In an age when ranchers are increasingly jealous of their private property rights, increasingly reluctant to allow access to their deeded lands, these two commonages may well become the last sizeable areas of grassland in the Nicola basin accessible to ordinary people; the last places where ordinary people can still fall in love with the beauty and grace of their own countryside.

The Lundbom Commonage especially is already being used not simply as a recreation area but as an open-air classroom, a place where people, especially youngsters, can learn more about the ecology and biology of native grasslands, an undertaking, I might add, led and promoted in part by local ranchers, especially the late Laurie Guichon. Credit where credit is due.

Perhaps eventually, if enlightened viewpoints prevail, we might even see these commonages serving as a sort of conservation ark, defined areas of the countryside devoted to the conservation of indigenous grassland ecosystems, rather than the economics of the livestock industry. "De-pasturized," you might say.

Back to sunny skies. I don't get it.

And here's a track leading down into the Quilchena Creek valley, gently at first, then more steeply. Much of the bedrock along this section of the trail is overlain by a deep layer of fine silt. At the end of the last ice age, when the escape of meltwater from what is now the Nicola valley was hampered by ice dams, the whole area would have been inundated by a series of temporary glacial lakes much larger and deeper and muddier than the present lake. I wonder if, in fact,

I'm descending now below the surface of the largest and deepest of those lakes.

The vegetation is changing, too, as I move down off the uplands into the valley. Last night's camp had common rabbit-brush (*Chrysothamnus nauseosus*), a suggestion of drier, warmer conditions at slightly higher elevations. A little farther down the hill, on the last terrace above the creek, I start to see a scattered growth of big sagebrush. At the fenceline just above the creek itself, I dodge a bit of prickly pear cactus (*Opuntia fragilis*). And the wild roses are in full bloom in the woods along the creek, their scent replacing that of silky lupine higher on the hill, the seasons fast-forwarding again as I lose altitude.

To sit in the shade on a fine day, and look upon verdure is the most perfect refreshment.
—Jane Austen, *Mansfield Park*

I take lunch in the leafy shade beside the creek, with the sweet scent of wild roses and greenery in the air. I can smell the water, too. And the susurration of the creek is like a narcotic. I can barely keep my eyes open. All in all, a delight to the senses.

I note, with interest, how comfortable I feel in this place compared to the wide-open spaces up the hill. At last night's camp, though the view may have been spectacular, I felt vaguely uneasy much of the time. A little too exposed. Vulnerable to wind and weather. At the mercy of unfriendly eyes.

But down here, beside the creek, I'm perfectly at ease. I could fall asleep in a moment.

I've been tempted to compare human beings to sharp-tailed grouse and grizzly bears and meadowlarks. Grassland species, all of us. Creatures of the open ground. But that's not quite right. I think human beings, like black bears, perhaps, are more properly creatures of the edge, of sheltered meadowlands rather than wide-open prairie. For all the millions of years it took our species to evolve, surely our most characteristic situation has been the very one I'm now enjoying: looking out at the grasslands from under the cover of trees along the edge of a stream. This is our natural habitat, our heritage.

I decide not to refill my bottles just yet. I don't trust the water here. I'm headed for the Quilchena Hotel down by the lake and I can top up there. Not too far now, I think.

Ha! Famous last words. Farther than I thought. But it's a pleasant enough walk through the fields along the lower creek, part of the Triangle Ranch, which is itself part of the historic Quilchena Ranch. The men are just taking off the first crop of alfalfa hay, huge cylindrical bales that have replaced the little square bales of my youth (which themselves replaced the huge loaf-like loose haystacks of an earlier generation).

By the time I reach the hotel I'm desperately thirsty. I settle myself, pack and all, on the veranda (in deference to my disreputable state it seems best to stay outdoors) and wait for the server to bring me my double cheeseburger and pint of ale. I can only guess what I must look and smell like after twelve days of arduous walking. But she is the soul of courtesy and I appreciate her restraint. *I am not an animal.* Perhaps compared to some of the cowboys who stop in, rough and ready, fresh from branding or whatever, I'm not so bad as all that.

This is a major leap, psychologically, from the lonesome prairie above Quilchena Creek back into the world of traffic, noise and cheeseburgers. I suppose I can congratulate myself now that I've actually made it all the way from Okanagan Lake to Nicola Lake. But I'm not out of the woods yet. Just like up there on the lonesome prairie, the most pressing question (after water) is "where am I going to spend the night?"

Sadly, the hotel is beyond my budget. Besides, I'm quite used to my little tent and I rather like it. So, no, I'm just looking for a safe, quiet, inexpensive place to camp. The waitress at the pub can't help but suggests I walk across the lane and talk to the people at the golf course, another part of the establishment. Apparently they can accommodate guests who arrive in Winnebagos and such. Maybe they can find a place for me.

On this journey I have deliberately shied away from human contact. It's not that I'm anti-social, not by any means. It's just that I've wanted to focus my attention and awareness on the countryside, the landscape, the terrain, and I find that difficult to do if there are other people around, commanding my attention. But more than once along the trail I've been astonished by the kindnesses that have reached out and found me, despite my reticence.

And this is one of those times. I tell my story to Carolyn and Laurie at the golf course. Their standard reply is that I can't pitch my tent in the RV park. There's a rule against it. But, scarcely missing a beat, they add that, if I'd like, I'd be welcome to camp in their backyard. Me, a perfect stranger. How could I turn down an offer like that? I even get a hot shower. Clothing laundered. And coffee in the morning! It's so heartening. There are, doubtless, bad people in the world. How reassuring to find that there are also good and kindly folk to make up the balance.

And so to bed, feeling clean and civilized.

DAY THIRTY-ONE
Thursday, June 26: Nicola Lake to Trapp Lake

The wind is blowing more fiercely than ever from the south in the morning, ruffling the surface of Nicola Lake into whitecaps. But the sun is out and it's another shining day. Traffic on Highway 5A is heavier than I'd expected, a steady stream of big eighteen-wheelers, avoiding the steep grades of the multi-lane Coquihalla Highway between Merritt and Kamloops, or perhaps dodging the freight scales east of Kamloops. Highway 5A is definitely a secondary road, two narrow lanes and minimal shoulders, so I take the full blast of each truck as it roars past. I've barely started, have a long day ahead and already I feel worn out.

I have to say that, given the conditions, most of the drivers seem to be going out of their way to be courteous, slowing down, swinging across the centre line when they can. Much appreciated. I give them a wave and they return it. Right back at you, friend. Best to stay alert, though. Every now and then there's a guy who evidently feels some need to assert his right to the road, barrelling past straight down the white margin line, just inches away.

There are compensations.

On the steep slopes above the highway toward the north end of the lake are some of the best-looking pocket grasslands I've seen anywhere. Part of the Nicola Lake IR #1, Upper Nicola Indian Band, I think. Kudos to them.

And birds.

At the very north end of the lake a pair of black terns (*Chlidonias niger*) are kiting around in the wind, so buoyant on their wings, so nimble. They dip to the surface of the lake, then back into the air, with no effort at all. Farther along a pair of western kingbirds (*Tyrannus verticalis*) are living up to both their Latin and common names, defending territory beside a pond. And one Bullock's oriole (*Icterus bullockii*) rejoices in brilliant orange and black against this pale landscape.

The Guichon Ranch has teamed up with Ducks Unlimited to create and enhance an extensive area of wetland north of Nicola Lake. Wonderful riparian habitat, alive with waterfowl. Kudos to them as well.

And everywhere this morning the air is perfumed by the sweet scent of wild roses.

Ten kilometres north of Nicola Lake I leave the highway for a gravel road branching off to the right, Old Kamloops Road. According to the map, it will take me north along the east side of Stump Lake, affording me a few kilometres of relief from the traffic. (The highway swings west at this point to pass up the other side of the lake.)

The Stump Lake Ranch is one of the early ones, dating back to an 1879 Crown grant, 160 acres pre-empted by former Nova Scotian Peter Fraser and enlarged by subsequent owners to a very respectable sixty thousand acres. In 1998, Derek Trethewey purchased the ranch with the idea of developing some of that real estate, especially the waterfront properties along the lake. Trethewey's efforts to escape or minimize restrictions imposed by British Columbia's Agricultural Land Reserve Commission generated a good deal of controversy. Conservationists pointed to the Stump Lake Ranch as a prime example of the threat that unchecked urban and suburban development posed to grasslands.

You'll know, by now, that I'm no great fan of development. It's all a curse.

But my walk up the east side of the lake provokes some interesting thought. Ten years along, the subdivision is well advanced. There are paved roads, houses, yards, fencing. One or two of the properties, clearly purchased with the idea of creating some sort of equestrian establishment, look to be pretty much bereft of whatever natural habitat might have been there in the beginning. On the other hand, some of the others, with no horses or livestock in sight, are not bad, habitat-wise. Not bad at all. These are big parcels, the buildings are well-spaced and some of the more elegant homes are clearly designed to blend with and complement their natural surroundings.

I suppose the point I'm trying to make is that it's not so much the conversion of ranchlands to residential developments that's appalling. It's the way in which it's done. If such properties were developed in a loving and respectful way, they might actually be an asset to the countryside, an ornament. A nicely spaced residential development, done with a view to minimal impact and the preservation of natural habitat, might be a reasonable approach to conserving indigenous ecosystems. At least it would free some of the countryside from the pressing need to graze livestock.

Perhaps someday we'll get to the point where folk will be buying properties like these not because they want to play cowboy or even because they want to build a big luxurious home in a beautiful place, but because they've recognized an exceptional bit of grassland habitat and want to devote themselves to it, cherish it and sustain it in the same way that somebody else might purchase an elegant heritage home or a beautiful garden and give it all they have because it pleases them to possess and maintain something of such intrinsic value and beauty.

Nobody in their right mind, I hope, would purchase a fine heritage home or a beautifully landscaped garden only to demolish it in favour of a parking lot or a playing field or some other banality.

It seems similarly daft, to my way of thinking, to purchase a beautiful bunchgrass meadow or a pristine wetland only to turn it into a horse pasture. Or a set of condos, for that matter. There are other places, less precious, where those condos or that horse pasture could go.

Some conservationists would argue that the development of a beautiful bunchgrass meadow simply shouldn't be allowed under any circumstances. And in many instances I would agree. Really exceptional bits of grassland habitat are now so scarce in the valleys of southern British Columbia that the development of such jewels should not be permitted. They shouldn't be treated as tempting real estate. They're too valuable.

But given the ferocious growth rate of grassland cities like Kamloops, Kelowna, Vernon, Penticton and the other population centres in these interior valleys, it seems inevitable that some rangelands will have to be developed. Does it necessarily follow that they will have to be trashed? Perhaps. But then again, perhaps not. The two enterprises, residential development and the conservation of indigenous grassland ecosystems, could coexist. What's needed is a strong, ingrained social ethic to guide that inevitable development.

As a society we need to foster and reward an appreciation of life's finer things: the undisturbed stretch of riparian habitat along a creek. A rich and vigorous meadow of bluebunch wheatgrass. A stand of old Douglas-firs. We need to encourage a sort of connoisseurship that could recognize and cherish exceptional bits of natural habitat. And to back it up with a powerful inhibition against destroying those bits.

In 1972 a madman with a hammer attacked one of the world's finest artworks, Michelangelo's *Pietà* in Saint Peter's Basilica, Vatican City, badly damaging it. The world reacted with shock, horror, outrage, that something of such beauty and refinement could be so wantonly diminished. Painstaking restoration was immediately undertaken at great expense.

Perhaps someday we'll see that same sort of outrage at any wanton destruction of nature's finest works. I think that the threat of outrage plus the sense that a piece of land is worth far more to connoisseurs, so to speak, with the indigenous ecosystems intact and flourishing, might well guide the kind of development that is an asset and ornament to the countryside, rather than a curse.

I filled my water bottles this morning, of course. But it's been a long, warm day and I've been walking pretty steadily. By the time I reach the home-ranch at the head of Stump Lake, I've long since emptied both bottles and am very thirsty. Also I've a feeling that drinking water will be hard to come by on this last stretch into Kamloops, and I'm anxious to refill the bottles while I can.

I'm always reluctant to go knocking on doors, asking for help. I know what I must look like. It's the times we live in. Folk are wary of opening their homes to disreputable-looking strangers, quite rightly. And I'm not anxious to court trouble.

But I'm desperate.

Down in the yard I'm greeted by a young woman, Jolene, who makes me welcome, gives me a cold drink of water (several actually) and cheerfully fills my water bottles.

Evidently she's done a good deal of backpacking herself,

understands my situation. It strikes me that there's something almost biblical about the act of offering a thirsty traveller a drink of cooling water—the kindness of strangers again—and I bestow blessings as I hike back up the lane to rejoin Highway 5A.

The highway climbs steadily, passes through a narrow stony gap at the head of the Stump Lake valley and descends abruptly into the Campbell Creek valley on the far side.

This is the very rim of the Nicola basin. To the south, surface water drains toward Nicola Lake and then down the Nicola River into the Thompson River at Spences Bridge. Northward, the ridge drops steeply forty or fifty metres to a stagnant-looking pond. Water from that pond drains into Campbell Creek and then into the South Thompson River, just east of Kamloops.

I've a feeling that at some point in the chaotic times toward the end of the last ice age, a much larger Nicola Lake filled its basin and drained northward through this gap. That stagnant pond down there would have been the plunge pool for a substantial waterfall, a river of meltwater tumbling through the gap and flowing away northward through what is now the Campbell Creek valley.

I walk on through the evening looking for potential camping sites, casually at first, then with increasing desperation. On past Napier Lake, Richie Lake, Trapp Lake, all slender little linear lakes reflecting the blue of the sky, like beads on a string, occupying the bed of that long-vanished river. As anticipated, the countryside is increasingly built up. Darkness has almost fallen before I come across a reasonably private spot near Trapp Lake, not in sight of any dwellings and well hidden from the highway. Notwithstanding the kindness of strangers, there are wicked people in the world and it doesn't do for the solitary pilgrim to forget that or get careless.

DAY THIRTY-TWO
Friday, June 27: Trapp Lake to Kamloops

Takes me a few moments in the morning to realize that there's no wind. None at all. It's perfectly calm, a little eerie, actually, after days and days of constant breeze. What does it mean? Time will tell.

Otherwise, it's another lovely blue-sky day, though a bit hazy.

Trapp Lake, a long, skinny, finger lake, shining in the morning sun, reminds me very much of prairie rivers I've seen, winding their way along the bottom of deep coulees excavated from the surrounding uplands, working their way deeper and deeper into the earth as the water runs downhill toward a distant sea. My elevated perspective affords me a view of the surrounding countryside that few others get to enjoy. Travelling down Highway 5A beside the lake is like driving along the bottom of a ditch—all you can see are open slopes above the lake, reaching for the sky.

From up here, though, the ditch seems relatively insignificant. What catches the eye instead are the great expanses of rangeland running away in all directions. A grassland bridge between the Nicola basin and the Thompson River valley.

Now I understand what that wind was all about.

It was blowing summer into the country.

Even this early in the morning the day is almost too warm, and it's going to be a scorcher by the time I get to Kamloops. On Shumway Lake, a young woman in a canoe, solo paddler: another sign that summer is icumen in.

This is hobby-farm country, where old ranches and farms are gradually being divided into smaller and smaller holdings with larger and larger houses, ostentatiously sporting the full range of amenities. Back in the day these uplands would have been far enough out of Kamloops to support a whole series of little communities, represented now by surviving place names—Beresford, Knutsford, Aberdeen and (my favourite) Blackloam—plus an occasional aging community hall.

Nowadays, of course, it's all just part of the city, far enough out to afford a taste of rural living, more stars at night and a little quiet, but close enough that the mall or junior's soccer games are still only minutes away.

I wish I could have seen it when it was all just bunchgrass. Wouldn't that have been something? A piece of the big sky country, a great expanse of high grassland falling away steeply into the deep valleys of the North and South Thompson rivers.

The City of Kamloops occupies a naturally dramatic location at the confluence of the two rivers, the North Thompson arriving from the north, the South Thompson from the east, and the two rivers, united, rolling away westward to join the Fraser River at Lytton.

I'm now coming into the traditional territory of the second of four Interior Salish peoples of southern interior British Columbia: the Shuswap or Secwepemc people. Originally they comprised something like twenty-five local bands in seven separate divisions spread over an enormous area of countryside from Soda Creek in the northwest, down both banks of the Fraser River to Pavilion, east to Spallumcheen (not far from the head of Okanagan Lake) and east again to Windermere in the Columbia River valley, then north to Tête Jaune Cache and even beyond in the upper reaches of the Fraser River. Here at the junction of the North and South Thompson rivers we would have had the *Tk'emlúpsemx*, "People of the Confluence," in the Kamloops Division of the Secwepemc people.

Historical Kamloops dates back to November 1811, when David Stuart of the Pacific Fur Company turned up to spend the winter of 1811 to 1812 trading with the Secwepemc people at this natural meeting place. Stuart returned during the spring of 1812 to establish a more permanent post, and that same year North West Company trader Joseph Laroque established a rival post. In 1813 the North West Company purchased the assets of the Pacific Fur Company and eight years later, in 1821, merged with the Hudson's Bay Company (HBC).

HBC Fort Kamloops served as trading post and way station for annual brigade trips from New Caledonia (Fort George, Fort St. James, Fort Fraser) to tidewater, at first via the Okanagan and Columbia rivers to Fort Vancouver near the mouth of the Columbia, and then, after 1847, via various routes to Fort Langley near the mouth of the Fraser River.

But Kamloops, as a city, really dates from the 1880s and the construction of the Canadian Pacific Railway. For many decades the CPR and the Canadian National Railway were the city's chief economic engines, along with ranching of course.

If Kelowna's culture hero might be the gentleman-orchardist, Kamloops's would be the gentleman-rancher. When I was a kid, the best hotel in town was called "The Stockman." But things were changing even then. The pulp mill opened in 1965 and Kamloops became more mill town than anything else, perhaps a little rougher than Kelowna, with giant pickup trucks rather than high-end cars as the status vehicles of choice.

Partway down the hill, a truck honks as it goes past. I wave back automatically before I do a double take and recognize Jolene from the Stump Lake Ranch. A few minutes later, Carolyn and Laurie from Nicola Lake pull over to say hi and offer me a lift. Thanks, but no thanks, I tell them and wave as they pull away. Nice to see them again, and Jolene, too. I'm pretty sure they're all just heading into town to do their regular Friday-afternoon business, but it's good to think they were keeping an eye out for me.

And so down into Kamloops, the intersection of Highway 5A and Highway 1, the maze of streets, the blaze and blare of traffic and the heat. Kamloops is an oven in the summer; this afternoon is just a foretaste. Drifting in from somewhere is a whiff of Russian olive in bloom.

I reach the bus depot with almost an hour to spare. Too hot for a cheeseburger, I have ice cream and cola instead. And water. I'm pleased with my timing. It will be good to be off the road this July long weekend. Already the traffic is ramping up. I'll use the break to resupply and regroup so I can be ready to hit the trail again after the holiday.

Come forth into the light of things. Let Nature be your teacher.
　　　　　　　　　　—William Wordsworth, "The Tables Turned"

The soul that sees beauty may sometimes walk alone.
　　　　　　　　—Johann Wolfgang von Goethe, *Italian Journey*

The grass so little has to do,—
A sphere of simple green,
With only butterflies to brood,
And bees to entertain,
And stir all day to pretty tunes
The breezes fetch along,
And hold the sunshine in its lap
And bow to everything.
　　　　　—Emily Dickinson, "The Grass So Little Has to Do—"

4

Grasslands on the Doorstep— Lac du Bois Grasslands

Lac du Bois Grasslands

DAY THIRTY-THREE
Sunday, July 6:
Kamloops to Batchelor Ridge

Raindrops spatter the big windshield as my bus rolls into Kamloops on the return trip. But it's just a passing shower. In a moment the sun is shining again. Seems I've lucked into one of those beautiful vivid days, blue skies and sunshine one moment, billowing dark-shadowed cumulous clouds the next. It's a fine day for walking—as long as the rain holds off—and still relatively cool.

Last week's hot spell barely made it through the long weekend: a false start to summer's heat. Doubtless the real thing will turn up any day now. Every cool morning is a blessing.

The Kamloops bus depot is in Southgate, on the south side of town, well above the river. The view from that neighbourhood is northward, across the city and across the deep valley to a broad expanse of open, grass-covered hills, rising steeply from the valley floor at first, then sloping back more gradually to higher-elevation forests in the distance. The grassland extends for kilometre after kilometre, all miraculously undeveloped and much of it protected as part of the Lac du Bois Grasslands Protected Area (15,712 hectares), established April 1996, another one of those sanctified green spaces on my map, another required stop on the pilgrimage.

Friends who know about such things have implied that any tour of the grassland valleys of southern interior British Columbia would be sadly incomplete without an extended visit to Lac du Bois Grasslands Protected Area. I think I'll take the next three or four days and make a loop, north across the grasslands to the margin of the forests at the north edge of the protected area, then west to Lac du Bois itself, and then back down into town.

The long steep climb up Batchelor Drive is not particularly encouraging, with new subdivisions all around reminding me of the Okanagan, and I prepare myself for all the usual disappointments.

But then, one of those moments you get, I pass through an open gate, over a cattle guard and into a different world. The little hill on my left (this is on the very edge of the city of Kamloops, mind you) is covered with as lovely a growth of mature native bunchgrass as I've seen anywhere. The ground must still be damp from an earlier shower because I can smell wet earth and vegetation. It's every bit as good and beautiful as my friends have hinted and for a moment my spirits soar.

But then I take another couple of steps and discover that somebody on a motorcycle has clawed their way straight up that steep slope, creating a scar that is going to take decades to heal, assuming it ever gets a chance. Already an erosion-gully is forming where rainwater runs down. Weeds are moving in around the edges of the exposed and disturbed soil.

And there's worse to come. Much worse. Pretty soon every little slope I pass has been chewed up by motorcycle and quad tracks. I can hardly stand it.

These great crosshatched gouges across the grassy slopes are wounds, plain and simple, wounds deliberately inflicted. I feel both sad and angry, as if some beloved other had suffered a terrible beating.

The people of Kamloops should be angry too. This makes the whole town look bad. I'm sure Kamloops is full of intelligent, thoughtful people who are as appalled by this sort of ecological vandalism as I am. So why should the tone and flavour of the city be set by a bunch of clowns mounted on two-cycle engines? This is the irony of our times anywhere and everywhere: that the appearance of a community is not determined by its best people but by its nitwits.

And it's doubly irritating that this kind of vandalism, which wouldn't be tolerated for a moment in a more urban setting, is winked at out in the country, like this was still the Wild West. Imagine if these cowboys took their motorcycles across the lawns and flowerbeds of Riverside Park in downtown Kamloops. The Mounties would be there in a moment, sirens going and lights flashing, ready to kick butt and take down names.

But out here? No problem. Fill your boots. Go crazy. Whatever turns you on.

And yet, I tell you, the finest public garden in Kamloops is clumsy and primitive beside the elegance and complexity of these natural gardens, which have thousands of years of development behind them and are perfectly adapted and in balance with their environment.

It turns out that this section of the grasslands south of the actual protected area has been designated an "All Terrain Vehicle Area." Presumably it represents some sort of trade-off: land-use planners sacrificing this part of the landscape to "motorsports" enthusiasts, partly in the hope of securing their cooperation in the park's establishment and partly in the hope, I suppose, that they might leave the park itself alone, provided they have somewhere else to trash.

Wishful thinking, I fear, doomed to disappointment.

It comes as no great surprise to find fresh motorcycle tracks going off through the grass just inside the park boundary (just past the sign asking riders to stay off the range) with the ground all chewed up by knobbly tires.

But on the whole I'm relieved to find that my worst fears haven't been realized. The park still looks surprisingly pristine, especially considering what's going on next door. My friends were right, this was well worth a few extra kilometres. And the farther north I go, the nicer it gets.

Some time later a posse of six dirtbikes comes screaming up behind me. This doesn't do much for my park experience, but they do slow down when they spot me, which is much appreciated. And they do stay on the trail as they roar past. Also much appreciated. Credit where credit is due.

The establishment of a new park is a complex and difficult process, especially nowadays in the face of so many outspoken, competing and often conflicting interests. That's particularly true for an area like the Lac du Bois Grasslands, which has had such a long and varied history of human use.

Parks are no longer created by government fiat. They require consensus, some level of approval from all the interested parties ("stakeholders" to use the current jargon). Even the most worthy proposal can be killed or derailed by adamant and vocal minority opposition. It's astonishing, really, that any park proposal at all comes to term. Especially considering that there are those in these communities who are adamantly opposed, on principle, to any sort of government conservation measure, park, protected area, ecological reserve, whatever.

It's an exceedingly tricky business, stickhandling a park proposal through due process, and park managers have become very accommodating, going out of their way to conciliate as many of the conflicting interests as possible, anxious to avoid stirring up opposition.

The irony of this political necessity is that the people most opposed to the park, the anti-park factions, attract the most concern and attention. And the most careful conciliation. Rather than a preservation or even conservation imperative, the emphasis seems to be on all the various human activities and uses that can still be enjoyed despite the change to park status.

The result is that we end up with very "soft" parks. In fact, I notice that the brochure I'm carrying avoids the term "Park" altogether. Instead the Lac du Bois Grasslands are designated a "Protected Area."

Ominous.

The term "Protected Area" seems to be a form of new-speak, a retreat from full park status to something, in fact, much less well "protected." Many activities that would be prohibited in British Columbia's provincial parks (as being inconsistent with the conservation or preservation ideals of a park) will be permitted here: continued grazing of livestock, hunting, motorcycle and ATV access, agricultural research and so on. About the only activities expressly prohibited are commercial logging (not a big factor in a grassland park), mining (the area has already been thoroughly prospected and there's nothing there) or energy exploration and development. All pre-existing land act tenures, special use permits, trapping licences and other legal tenures and rights are recognized. One hopes there will be no real estate development, but nowadays one never knows.

Even so, most conservationists would agree I'm sure: a soft park

143

is better than no park at all. We have to remember that this whole landscape could easily have gone the way of Beresford and Knutsford across the valley. Private land. Big houses. Hobby-farms and acreages and subdivisions. What a blessing, then, that this remarkable piece of ground is still here, still in surprisingly good natural condition and still accessible to all of us. In time, with a little luck, perhaps this landscape will earn the popular respect and love it merits. And that bond between people and their home places might help to protect it more in the long run than any regulation or designated status. Hurting it will become unthinkable.

Certainly it is a refined and marvellous thing to have such a significant protected natural area so near to a major urban centre, right on the threshold of the city, literally within walking distance. It's something the people of Kamloops should be very proud of. I hope they lift their eyes every so often to that expanse of grass, green in spring, golden in summer, pale in autumn, shining white in winter, and think: *Wow! Look at that! Isn't it great! Isn't it grand!*

The sweet rolling hills of home.

DAY THIRTY-FOUR
Monday, July 7: Batchelor Ridge to Lac du Bois

I wake to the hooting and chuckling of grouse, dress hurriedly and get myself outside. Naturally I'm thinking: *sharp-tail!* I know they occur in the park and of course I'd be glad to catch another glimpse of a species that is considered something of a rarity nowadays. Perhaps I've happened onto a lek, a dancing ground, wouldn't that be something. But when I crawl from the tent it's a dark dusky spruce grouse that flushes from the grass, whirring away through the Douglas-firs along the top of the ridge. A more ordinary species of loveliness.

It's a meandering day. I'm headed in a general way toward the north edge of the park through a rolling landscape of grassy hills and hollows, still green, not yet faded by summer heat, past a scattering of little ponds, all ringed with luxuriant fringes of shoreline vegetation—mostly great bulrush (*Scirpus lacustris*), as distinct from alkali bulrush (*S. maritimus*), Nevada bulrush (*S. nevadensis*), American bulrush (*S. americanus*) or cattail (*Typha latifolia*).

Lots of birdlife, too: yellow-headed blackbirds (*Xanthocephalus xanthocephalus*), ruddy ducks (*Oxyura jamaicensis*), blue-winged teal (*Anas discors*), buffleheads (*Bucephala albeola*), goldeneyes (*Bucephala clangula*), redheads (*Aythya americana*) and a single, lonely American coot (*Fulica americana*).

Some good grass, some not so good. Not all of the Lac du Bois Grasslands Protected Area is as pristine as I might, at first, have hoped. Back in the day when this part of the country was first being settled by comers-from-afar, these grasslands were divided into many separate private holdings. Different parts of the Lac du Bois Grasslands have very different histories, and some sections were evidently better managed than others. It's still a remarkable landscape, but clearly some parts of it are going to need a little extra loving care in restoration.

One of the park's permitted activities (which I failed to mention yesterday and of which, for a change, I wholeheartedly approve) is education. The Lac du Bois Grasslands are well on their way to becoming one of the finest outdoor classrooms anywhere. And I can hardly think of another bit of countryside that better illustrates the variety and diversity of British Columbia's indigenous grasslands.

This gets a little complicated, but it might give you a clearer view of things. Bear with me.

Grasslands in British Columbia are usually classified according to a system devised for this province's Ministry of Forests. They nearly all fall into three of the system's fourteen biogeoclimatic zones, arranged in layer-cake fashion from lower to higher elevations: the Bunchgrass zone, the Ponderosa Pine zone and the Interior Douglas-fir zone.

The Bunchgrass zone (BG) dominates the lowest portions of British Columbia's southern interior valleys, from valley floor to maximum elevations of about 1,000 metres. The BG zone is further divided into a couple of "variants," essentially subzones, sometimes called lower grasslands and middle grasslands.

Lower and middle grasslands in pristine condition are both dominated by bluebunch wheatgrass.

But in the lower grasslands, bluebunch wheatgrass grows relatively sparsely. There's a good deal of open ground crusted with mosses and lichens between clumps of grass. Big sage is often present. In fact, lower grasslands are reminiscent of desert ecosystems, with widely spaced plants and dry-ground species like prickly pear cactus, northern Pacific rattlesnake and poison ivy. It's a tricky zone to go camping in.

In the middle grasslands bunchgrass grows more thickly with less space between plants. Big sage becomes increasingly scarce at higher elevations and a greater variety of flowering forbs are present.

Next comes the Ponderosa Pine zone (PP) at elevations between 335 and 900 metres. The vegetation is similar in many ways to the Bunchgrass zone except for the presence of ponderosa pines, sometimes quite widely scattered. Bunchgrass grows more luxuriantly at these higher elevations, fescues as well as bluebunch wheatgrass. And there are more flowering forbs.

Similarly for the Interior Douglas-fir zone (IDF). Ponderosa pine gives way to interior Douglas-fir at higher elevations, between 350 and 1,450 metres, on valley slopes and the high plateau above. Bunchgrasses and flowering forbs grow more luxuriantly on drier sites at these higher elevations than at any lower-elevation site.

The Ministry of Forests classification system reflects a simple ecological truth: climate and growing conditions in these southern interior valleys vary along gradients of temperature and moisture from lower elevations to higher elevations.

The city of Kamloops, on the floor of the Thompson River valley, is much warmer and gets much less precipitation than Lac du Bois, up at the north end of the park.

Summers in Kamloops are long, hot and dry, but winters are relatively mild. Downtown Kamloops doesn't get much snow. Lac du Bois summers are much less severe. But winters up there are longer, colder and much snowier, and growing seasons are shorter.

Naturally the biological communities growing at different points on the slope between Kamloops and Lac du Bois reflect those gradients in climate and growing conditions.

But the system falters on the actual complexity of the landscape, which is far from a smooth, even slope from valley floor to mountaintop, and on the simple reality that many factors other than elevation can affect growing conditions: soil or substrate, slope, aspect of slope (north, south, east, west), groundwater and so on.

In fact, the whole biogeoclimatic classification system based on "zones" (suggesting broad, relatively uniform swatches of countryside) seems odd to me, an oversimplified and misleading way of looking at a complicated landscape.

Take the Bunchgrass zone, for example. Certainly there are open meadows dominated by bluebunch wheatgrass. But there are also many other natural habitats that have nothing whatever to do with bunchgrass: wetlands (marshes, ponds, rivers, streams), riparian habitats (cottonwood and willow thickets) bordering the wetlands, rocky cliffs and the tumbled talus slopes beneath them, aspen groves, dense shrubby patches of snowberry or wild rose and, yes, even some open groves of ponderosa pine or interior Douglas-fir growing on sheltered north-facing slopes way down in the Bunchgrass zone.

I find myself more inclined toward a school of thought exemplified by the work of American grassland ecologist Rex Daubenmire, professor of botany at Washington State University from 1946 to 1975. Daubenmire saw landscape as a patchwork or mosaic of distinct, recognizable plant communities grading into one another, sometimes gradually, sometimes abruptly—plant communities that could be assigned to fairly well-defined "habitat types" according to the characteristic mixture of species present.

Consider one particular "habitat type" as an example: aspen groves, let's say. No two aspen groves are going to be exactly alike. But it's easy to see that they both belong to a fairly well-defined and recognizable type of habitat that might be further specified or subdivided, perhaps according to whether a particular grove has an understory of wild rose or of snowberry.

The whole point of Daubenmire's work, if I understand it correctly, is that different sets of growing conditions support or yield different and *characteristic* communities of plants.

Or to put that another way, the community of plants or particular habitat type occupying a particular patch of ground accurately and specifically reflects the sum total of all the various ecological factors, the growing conditions, that operate on that patch of ground.

Or to put it yet another way, a recognizable community of plants provides a sensitive and specific indicator of growing conditions—the sum total of all those complex factors—in that particular patch.

So the difference in understory between those two aspen groves (wild rose versus snowberry) is no accident but suggests some subtle difference in the growing conditions. The two groves are related ecologically but are different.

Lac du Bois turns out to be a pretty little lake nestled into the forested slopes right on the edge of the grasslands. Ironically (and unfortunately) it isn't actually part of Lac du Bois Grasslands Protected Area. Pity. There's garbage everywhere. And to judge by the scars, Mad Max has been busy making his mark here as well.

The sun is westering. I retreat to the privacy of a little forested gully with a trickle of clear water sufficient to refill my bottles this evening and again in the morning. Finding a spot sufficiently level and open to pitch the tent turns out to be a bit of a challenge. I explore the near side of the ravine first, then jump the little creek and start to work my way up the far slope.

I'm just climbing toward the lip of the ravine when I hear an odd sound coming from somewhere above: *Tschic-Tschic.*

What the devil is that?

Then again. *Tschic-Tschic.* Repeated, *Tschic-Tschic.* I climb hastily (and probably unwisely) out of the ravine and onto the grassy meadow above to see what I can see.

And there, on the far side of the meadow, is a black bear trying to climb a largish Douglas-fir. She works by simultaneously bracing the claws of both back paws (*Tschic-Tschic*) before reaching up to embrace and grip the trunk with the claws of her front paws (*Tschic-Tschic*). Then she brings both back paws up, clawing for a new higher hold (*Tschic-Tschic*). Just like a lineman going up a pole with climbing spurs and belt.

Evidently she's heard me mucking around in the gully, an unknown threat, and has been trying to clamber to safety. Now she decides it's too late for that, drops to the ground and lumbers off into the forest. Then I see them. Two tiny black cubs, way up in the feathery top of the tree, swaying around like a couple of monkeys. I'd never imagined they could climb so well and so fearlessly. I retreat back across the gully and a good way further down the creek before finally pitching my tent.

DAY THIRTY-FIVE
Tuesday, July 8: Lac du Bois to Mara Mountain

No further sign of Mama Bear and her Two Little Bears . . .

I could simply have followed Lac du Bois Road all the way back down to Kamloops but elect instead to explore a more lightly travelled track south from the lake through the meadows beneath the darker forested slopes of Wheeler Mountain.

Good choice.

Not too far south of Lac du Bois I flush a pair of long-billed curlews (*Numenius americanus*) from the edge of a little pond.

Long-billed curlews always make an impressive show, being the world's largest sandpipers, weighing almost a kilogram (comparable to a sharp-tailed grouse) and measuring up to sixty-five centimetres from tail-tip to beak-tip. (I'm writing here of the females, which are quite a bit larger than males.) Buff-cinnamon in colour. Their call is loud and unmistakable: *Curlee Curlee Curlee*. Their silhouette is unmistakable too: fully one-third of the bird's length is beak, an enormous proboscis evolved, presumably, to extract little marine organisms from the mud during winters on the seashore, or to pick grasshoppers, beetles, earthworms and the like out of the turf during spring and summer nesting season.

It must be like eating with chopsticks all the time.

Curlews like to nest on gently sloping open ground, presumably so that the sitting birds can get an unobstructed view of any approaching danger. According to Dick Cannings in his monograph *Status of the Long-Billed Curlew in British Columbia*, long-billed curlews prefer habitats with very short grass for nesting, including grasslands that have been heavily grazed or burned, or those covered with invasive cheatgrass.[11]

Eggs are laid, typically, about the third week of April. Both sexes incubate and defend the nest vigorously. Eggs hatch in twenty-eight days and the young are precocious, able to move about almost immediately. (Again reminiscent of sharp-tailed grouse.) The nest is abandoned within twenty-four hours of the chicks' hatching. Females abandon the brood after two or three weeks, leaving the males to chaperon the young until they fledge. Chicks from a typical nest will be flying by early July, by which time the southward migration of adults will have begun. The young birds begin their own migration by late July or early August. Hurry, hurry, hurry. No time to lose.

Suddenly I'm into a heavy growth of big sage. Some of these plants are not so much bushes as small trees, perhaps the biggest sagebrushes I've ever seen. You remember what I wrote about "increasers" back at Mount Kobau. Evidently this part of the protected area would have been one of the less well-managed bits, subject to gross chronic overgrazing at some point in its history. And clearly it's going to need a large extra helping of Tender Loving Care if the indigenous grasslands are to be restored.

"Just living is not enough," he [the butterfly] said, "one must have sunshine, freedom, and a little flower."
—Hans Christian Andersen, "The Butterfly"

I can feel the heat of the day building as I make my way to lower elevations. Eventually I'm obliged to take shelter in the shade of two little Douglas-firs growing on a north slope, handy to the path. It's my first heat-of-the-day break of the summer. Call it a siesta, one of the pleasures of vagabonding. I snooze for a bit, watch and listen to birds, read for a while. Two tiger swallowtails (*Papilio canadensis*) flit through the shade of my little shelter. Maybe they're feeling the heat too.

I think about those cows and the overgrazed sections of the Lac du Bois Grasslands Protected Area and I think about that pair of curlews.

It could be pure coincidence that I've seen curlews on this tour of the Lac du Bois Grasslands but no sharp-tailed grouse. Even so, the coincidence, if that's what it is, leads to some interesting reflections.

All over the world the cry of the curlew is emblematic of wild and untamed country. But in fact, as Dick Cannings points out, our long-billed curlews tolerate overgrazed rangeland quite well, even preferring it during nesting season.

Sharp-tailed grouse, on the other hand, prefer a thick growth of grass and lots of ground cover. They don't do well on overgrazed range.

Politics, it's said, is the art of the possible. That's never more true than in the politics of ecosystem preservation. As long as the livestock industry has a sort of veto-vote over the establishment of protected grassland ecosystems, we may have to content ourselves with grass-land "protected areas" that continue to be grazed and overgrazed by livestock. And we may have curlews but perhaps not sharp-tailed grouse or, indeed, any of the other creatures reckoned incompatible with grazing livestock: the other competitive grazers (mainly micro-grazers, pocket gophers, ground squirrels, marmots, all the "varmints" traditionally unwelcome on rangeland), badgers (nature's rototillers, said to create holes dangerous to livestock, horse and rider) and, of course, all the various predators, coyotes, wolves, cougars, bears, which are the stockman's particular anathema.

I leave my shelter late in the afternoon. Soon I'm having difficulty forcing my way through the heavy growth of sage, which is almost impossibly dense in places. Always the way down seems more over-grown and difficult. Always the way up seems a little easier. I find myself herded higher and higher onto the slopes of Mara Mountain, an abrupt summit on the south edge of the park overlooking the Thompson River and Kamloops Lake. Not what I had in mind at all.

By the time I get free of the sage I'm way up among the rocks, the evening is far advanced and I'm pooped. But then, at last, a bit of luck. Somebody is looking out for me. At the end of a faint game trail I discover a little grassy shelf, almost level, cut into the side of the moun-tain, as snug a bivouac as I could want. No water of course, and only a precious little left from this morning, but there's enough space for the tent, and the views out across the city and down the river valley can't be beat.

Of course I still have no idea how I'm going to get down in the morning. There's a change in the weather coming too, a high thin over-cast moving in fast from the west, just like that first evening above the Nicola River. Perhaps the dawn will bring inspiration.

DAY THIRTY-SIX
Wednesday, July 9: Mara Mountain to Kamloops

B ut the morning just brings heavier overcast with curtains of rain along the horizon. I find myself a viewpoint from which to plot the path of least resistance down through the sage (*this line past the tree, that trail, left at the boulder*). That helps. Before long I'm through the worst of it and onto a little track that should take me to the bottom of the hill close to Agriculture Canada's Kamloops Range Research Unit on Ord Road.

It was the severely overgrazed condition of British Columbia's rangelands in the early part of the twentieth century that prompted the establishment of the Dominion Range Experimental Station back in 1935, with the Lac du Bois Grasslands as a study area. The present facility on Ord Road in North Kamloops was established in 1947. Some of the cows out on the grasslands wear radio collars and are presumably involved in one of the station's ongoing projects, another part of the deal made in establishing the protected area: that the station would be able to continue its research program.

I have tremendous respect for the work that's been done here at the research station. When first established in the 1930s, the dark days of the Great Depression, it was a very forward-looking enterprise. This is where much of the seminal research on British Columbia's indigenous grasslands was done. And the names associated with the station are an honour roll of grassland research in this province: Ed Tisdale, Alastair McLean, Victor Brink, Brian Wikeem, Al van Ryswyk, Rick Williams and others. These scientists are my heroes. In fact, it's a modest thrill, an honour, to think that I'm walking the same ground that the great ones would have trod in their daily work.

(You may think I'm being foolish, grandiloquent, but believe me, there is real respect. These were men steeped in grassland biology and ecology, scientists who lived in the field, knew the ground. There were no keyboard researchers in those days.)

But times change.

The research station was established with the idea of improving the management of rangelands: grasslands as productive economic units, a raw natural resource, the mainstay of a healthy livestock industry. Lord knows there's still a desperate need for all that. The future of grasslands in southern interior British Columbia is very much in the hands of the livestock industry and we need to support them in their conservation efforts. But surely in a protected area, one of the very few protected and relatively pristine grasslands in all of British Columbia, we could do without the cows.

Wouldn't it be great if the research station could take the next step forward, move beyond range research, morph into something more purely directed toward understanding the biology and ecology of these still not very well understood grassland ecosystems. A centre of research that could do for indigenous grasslands what the Scripps Institution of Oceanography or Woods Hole have done for oceanography.

The first drops of rain catch me as I step onto the paved road at the bottom of the hill. The weather has been deteriorating all morning. Typical warm front: slow moving, inexorable. First a hint of precipitation on the western horizon, then across some of the nearer hills, then edging down the valley toward me, one ridge after another fading behind the oncoming curtains of rain. A storm with all the time in the world. Even now just a spit or two. It's coming, it's coming. You cannot run, you cannot hide.

Decision time.

From here my route takes me back across town, then west along Highway 1. It's a route that is neither elegant nor satisfying, but I'm pretty sure it's the only way, at least until I can get clear of the city.

Rain changes everything, though. I really do hate to walk in the wet. Especially along the edge of the highway.

There's a man crossing the parking lot of the research station. I detour in through the gates to cop a drink of water and ask if he's heard a weather forecast. (Besides, how could I pass this close and not pay my respects to the holy mother church.)

"Rain," he says.

Then adds, "For the rest of the week."

No decision at all, really. Another weather break, another delay. Can't be helped.

The whole secret of the study of nature lies in learning
how to use one's eyes.

    —George Sand, *Nouvelles lettres d'un voyageur*

Yet a little while is the light with you. Walk while ye have
the light, lest darkness come upon you.

           —John 12:35

We say of the oak, "How grand of girth!"
Of the willow we say, "How slender!"
And yet to the soft grass clothing the earth
How slight is the praise we render.

        —Edgar Fawcett, "The Grass"

5

Going Down to the River— Early Summer in the Thompson Valley

Ashcroft and the Thompson River valley from Cornwall Hills

DAY THIRTY-SEVEN
Friday, July 11: Kamloops to Six Mile Point

'm back.

Over the next couple of weeks I'll be heading west down the lower Thompson valley from Kamloops to Ashcroft, up through the Cornwall Hills into the Hat Creek valley, over the Clear Ranges into the Fountain Valley, down into the Fraser valley and north to Lillooet.

That's the plan anyway.

I'd like to get it done before the real heat of summer rolls in, but that might be too much to hope for. Even now, it's warmer than I could wish.

From Kamloops west, the Thompson River follows a relatively narrow valley, deeply cut into the surrounding highlands. Just beyond city limits the river widens into Kamloops Lake, almost thirty kilometres long, completely filling the bottom of the valley.

Because of the lake and because of the extreme ruggedness of the surrounding uplands all of the traffic between east and west is squeezed into a relatively narrow corridor. The Canadian National Railway runs along the north shore of the lake and river. The Canadian Pacific Railway runs along the south shore. And Highway 1 runs south of the lake as well, threading its way through the hills above the CPR right-of-way.

I plan to get through it all as quickly as I can. That means taking a deep breath, gritting my teeth and marching off along the shoulder of the highway. It's going to be tedious, not exactly the scenic route, but it'll have to do.

What's to look at?

Well, there's the Afton Mine.

Here we have a huge hole just south of the highway west of Kamloops. And I do mean *huge*, almost a kilometre from lip to lip and probably 250 metres deep. How can something so big disappear so completely into the landscape? It's more or less hidden behind a low ridge. I'd bet that very few of the casual passersby on the Trans-Canada Highway even know it's there.

The mine's ore body is part of something called the Iron Mask Batholith, which is part of a geological structure called the Nicola island arc, which is part of a larger structure called the Quesnel Terrane (which is part of an even larger structure called the Intermontane Belt of British Columbia).

It's fairly common knowledge nowadays that much of British Columbia is made up of exotic bits of the earth's crust, "terranes," that were created elsewhere and carried here on moving plates of oceanic crust, before being plastered onto the western edge of the North American continent.

The Nicola island arc is thought to have originated as a chain of volcanic islands very similar to modern-day Japan but positioned on this side of the Pacific Ocean about three thousand kilometres south of here, and separated from North America by a small ocean basin.

An island arc begins life as a collision between two separate plates of oceanic crust. The older, denser plate subducts beneath the younger, sliding down into the heat of the earth's mantle. The subducting plate liquefies to magma. Giant globs of that magma work their way up and through the overriding crust, leaking through at the surface to create a chain of volcanoes. Not all the globs make it to the surface. Some solidify within the crust as "plutons" (little globs) or "batholiths" (big globs).

The Iron Mask Batholith is one such.

It's loaded with copper ore, mostly sulphides, though closer to the surface groundwater has oxidized the sulphides to yield metallic copper, something relatively rare in nature. And with the copper there's gold, the mine's most profitable product. In fact, though the original open-pit Afton Mine ceased operation in 1997, the rising price of gold has prompted an ambitious underground approach to the remaining ore body, now called the New Afton Mine.

The huge hole in the ground may be invisible from the highway, but the material that came out of that hole is not. Farther down the road, a gigantic fake hill comes into view, all carefully graded and nicely seeded with non-native grasses. I know from aerial photos that there's a big pond of tailings behind it.

Those were not dwarfish treasures down in that hole, with miners picking at glittering veins of yellow metal. In fact, the mineralization is very finely disseminated through the rock. The New Afton Mine is expected to yield just 0.69 grams of gold per tonne of ore. That's a scrap of gold the size of a Rice Krispie, a little one. It's easy to forget, in the warm, comforting glow of the word "gold," that the chief product of this mine, any mine, is waste.

When my father was a young man, before the modern highway was built out around Six Mile Point, all the road traffic between Kamloops and Ashcroft followed a little track up and over the ridge behind the point, then back down to the village of Savona at the west end of the lake. Six Mile Road is still there. It's my chance to get away from highway traffic for a bit and find a camping place for the night.

DAY THIRTY-EIGHT
Saturday, July 12: Six Mile Point to Garden Creek

In the morning the scenery surprises me. I'd pictured a simple pass, the road going up one side of the ridge, through some sort of gap, then down the other side. Instead I find an attractive little upland, rolling hills and hollows, a scattering of bulrush-ringed ponds, grassy meadows, open forest. A lovely landscape, though the range isn't much, weedy and shopworn.

That, at least, should come as no surprise. It wasn't just vehicle traffic passing through this gap in the old days. Given the lay of the land, every single cow on every single cattle drive between Kamloops and Savona over the last 150 years must have funnelled through these little meadows, starting with all the thousands of head of beef driven north and west toward the Fraser and Cariboo gold rushes of the 1850s and 1860s.

All this would hardly be worth mentioning except that on the far side of the pass, where Six Mile Road turns downhill into the Durand Creek valley, I decide to hop the roadside fence in search of a viewpoint from which to scout the route ahead. The grass on the other side of the fence is in beautiful shape. It's a classic meadow with healthy clumps of blue-bunch wheatgrass and a well-developed cryptogamic crust covering the ground between clumps of grass. The complete package, deluxe version.

Naturally I'm delighted. It's not simply that this piece of range is in great shape, though God knows that's always cause for celebration. It's that at some point, back in the day, this piece must have been as badly damaged as all the rest, but has managed to come back. Hurrah!

That's the thing about grassland ecosystems. Given half a chance they do come back. And it doesn't take centuries.

Evidently this piece of ground has been sheltered. Sheltered completely and for an extended period of time. It looks to me as though there haven't been any cattle or horses on these meadows for years. Even my lightweight, soft-soled shoes are shattering the protective crust between the bunches, leaving footprints in the light soil. I hardly know where to step. In fact, I don't bother with the viewpoint or the snack I've been looking forward to. I get myself back across that fence. Certainly if there had been any stock on that ground recently, I'd have seen lots of evidence.

Protection and lots of time. That's the key. There's hope for the future. Makes my day.

Kill-dee. Kill-dee. Deee deee deee.

Up it goes and away, flying strong and fast on long, slender, pointed wings, calling the whole time. That's the sound of spring and summer in the arid valleys of southern interior British Columbia.

Killdeers (*Charadrius vociferus*), aptly named, are robin-sized plovers (though longer legged and sharper winged than robins), handsomely marked and harlequin coloured. The adults are mostly brown above (wings, back and cap) but pale below with a white belly, breast, neck, throat and forehead. Two black bands on the breast, a dark line across the bill below the eye and a dark forehead give the impression of alternating black and white horizontal stripes when you're facing the bird. The lower back, rump and the base of the tail are rusty orange.

Undisturbed killdeers show typical plover behaviour, alternately running and standing. They can move quickly across the ground, only to stop abruptly, bobbing and teetering, looking and listening, perhaps pecking up a bit of food. Killdeers are considered shorebirds, but they're often found, as just now, some distance from water, foraging in grassland habitats: meadows, pastures and cultivated fields.

As a species they seem to be doing quite well, thank you, which makes a pleasant change. Evidently this is one of those species that can coexist happily with human beings. They're widespread and abundant in North America, breeding from Alaska to Mexico and from Newfoundland to the Pacific. They winter from northern South America to the southern half of the United States and even farther north along the Pacific and Atlantic coasts.

Here in the valleys of southern British Columbia, killdeers are among the first migrants to arrive in the spring, often turning up when there's still ice on the ponds and patches of melting snow on the ground. This is all the more remarkable when you consider that they feed almost exclusively on insects and other invertebrates.

Mating pairs get together on migration or shortly after arrival. The displaying males posture elaborately with drooping wings and tail spread to show the rusty coverts to best advantage. Pairs, male and female, both calling loudly, take to the air on highflying nuptial display flights.

Killdeers nest directly on the ground. They seem to like a good view: nests are always in the open, often on bare patches of gravel or soil. The nests are modest structures, little more than shallow scrapes sometimes decorated with pebbles or bits of vegetation. Female and male share nesting duties. The male excavates the nest. The female lays four, rarely five, buff or brownish eggs, pyriform (blunt and rounded at one end, somewhat pointed at the other) and well camouflaged with dark blotches. Both birds incubate. The killdeer's striking coloration, so vivid when the bird is in motion, provides surprisingly good camouflage when it is sitting on its eggs in the middle of a patch of gravel.

The young are extremely precocious. They abandon the nest as soon as they have dried after hatching. And they can feed themselves within a day. By the time they're fully fledged, late in June, they're virtually indistinguishable from adults. But that doesn't leave Mom and Dad off the hook. Even though the young are able to feed themselves from the beginning, the adults must chaperone them constantly, sheltering and brooding when necessary and trying to ward off danger.

What killdeers lack in architectural ability they more than make up for in acting skills. The broken-wing distraction display of both sexes is famous. When danger threatens, a warning note from the adults freezes the youngsters into well-camouflaged immobility. Both adults fly around calling loudly. If that doesn't distract or discourage the intruder, one parent or the other will crouch on the ground (on that side of the intruder away from the chicks) with wings drooping and tail spread, flopping and calling piteously to lure the threat away.

Now we come to one of the defining plants in these arid interior valleys, part of the essential flavour of the place: a fair-sized deciduous shrub, up to seven metres tall; small oval leaves, toothed at the tip; clusters of very dark purple berries, sweet but full of seeds (actually, strictly speaking, not berries at all but "pommes," like tiny juicy apples). The plant? *Amelanchier alnifolia*, serviceberry or saskatoon (from Blackfoot *mis-ask-a-tomina* or Cree *mis-ask-quah-toomin*).

For a few weeks in early spring—my favourite time of the year— the hillsides and ravines through these valleys are luminous with clouds of snowy white saskatoon blossoms, while all the surrounding meadows, just starting to blush green with the new growth of grass, are erupting with spectacular bouquets of bright yellow "sunflowers," arrowleaf balsamroot. It's a landscape-sized floral arrangement of brilliant blossoms, white and golden yellow, amid the fresh green of early spring foliage.

Amelanchier alnifolia was a significant plant for native people. Berries were eaten fresh or dried like raisins or mashed into cakes and then dried. The tough wood was used for everything from digging sticks to dip-net hoops.

A word to the wise though. As with other members of the rose family (including domestic apples and cherries), saskatoon twigs, leaves and seeds contain quantities of a cyanogenic glucoside, prunasin, sometimes sufficient to poison browsing deer or livestock. If you're looking for a stick to toast marshmallows or hotdogs with, it might be wise to steer clear of this species (though our bodies can handle small amounts of the toxin and cooking is said to destroy it).

Another wonder: a tiny pond full of tadpoles, hundreds of them. And they're huge. These will be young spadefoot toads, more correctly great basin spadefoot toads (*Spea intermontana*). Oddly, considering the size of the tadpoles, the adult toads will be quite small, just 4 to 6.5 centimetres from snout to vent.

Let them enjoy their pond. Once they leave it they're going to spend the rest of their lives battling desiccation. Inhabiting these dry grasslands and open forest, they will use the little black hardened blade of keratin at the base of the first toe on each hind foot (the "spade" in "spadefoot") to dig their way down out of the Thompson valley's hot dry air and into the relatively cool moist shelter of the earth, burying themselves alive.

Day's end. Garden Creek is just a little creek, but surprisingly pristine, back in the hills, protected from trampling by an ancient fence that's grown right through the middle of an old cedar tree. There's a woodpecker nest in the bole of the birch above me. I can hear the youngsters talking. I fill all the bottles, lovely water. Water is going to be an issue over the next couple of days. If Jimmies Creek and Brassy Creek are dry, I'm in trouble.

DAY THIRTY-NINE
Sunday, July 13: Garden Creek to Brassy Creek

I come to a trickle of water running down one of the minor gullies along my route. But it's no use to me. There's not enough liquid to cover the intake of my filter and both of my water bottles are still nearly full anyway from this morning's top-up.

Also, I can see that I'd have to wait in line. The waterhole is taken. There's a little snake, s-curved across a patch of mud beside the trickle, drinking and drinking. *Sip-sip. Sip-sip.* It's not a rattlesnake. This is one of the garter snakes, with a pale longitudinal dorsal stripe running the length of its back. More specifically, it's a common garter snake (*Thamnophis sirtalis*), lacking the speckling of dark spots characteristic of a western terrestrial garter snake (*Thamnophis elegans*), the other indigenous species.

This gully is good habitat. Doubtless, when finished drinking, the little snake will be off into the green shade, looking for something to eat. (Is it tasty, Precious? Is it scrumptiously crunchable?) A slug or a worm, perhaps. Or something a little larger. A frog or a toad or a salamander. Maybe even a mouse or a little fledgling bird, fallen from the nest and helpless. Such *isssss* life.

Lunch and siesta time under the generous shade of an old interior Douglas-fir, windswept and picturesque. The view is spectacular out across the valley. Even from this high perch I can hear the murmur of traffic along the highway and the throbbing of ganged locomotives pulling their huge loads up and down the two railways. Just can't get away from it in this tight corridor.

On the far side of the valley the mouth of Deadman Creek is bracketed by huge gravel terraces, enormously out of scale with the present-day stream. Turns out that the ancestor of Deadman Creek wasn't just a larger stream. It was a *river*, the size of the present-day Thompson or larger. On a topographic map or shaded terrain map you can see the long deep valley excavated all the way back up into the Cariboo Plateau. At one time the Deadman River may even have drained the mountains to the west, a huge piece of country. Imagine a Fraser River–sized torrent pouring out of that valley, carrying sand and gravel into the waters of Glacial Lake Deadman.

There's an intriguing body of research (by Timothy Johnsen, Robert Fulton, June Ryder, Jerome-Etienne Lesemann, Tracy Brennand and others) concerning late-glacial lakes in the valleys of southern interior British Columbia. These were huge lakes, sometimes surprisingly ephemeral, often following drainage patterns quite different from those of the present day.

Timothy Johnsen's master's thesis covers this very piece of ground, the Thompson River valley from north and east of Kamloops downstream to Skoonka Creek, seven or eight kilometres south of the little town of Spences Bridge.[12] His work identified two bodies of water that occupied the Thompson valley long enough to carve banks and beaches high on the surrounding slopes. The first and largest was Glacial Lake Thompson (High Stage), 140 metres deep, 220 kilometres long, extending from an ice dam in the deep valley south of Spences Bridge all the way to Kamloops, then far up the valley of the present-day North Thompson and also up the valley of the present-day South Thompson to somewhere around present-day Chase or Sorrento.

All that mass of gravel at the mouth of Deadman Creek, now stranded high above the Thompson River, would have been under water.

The present-day valley of Shuswap Lake as so choked with glacial ice that the waters of this Glacial Lake Thompson (High Stage), dammed at both ends by ice, spilled over the height of land into the network of back valleys between Chase and Tappen, near present-day Salmon Arm, and from thence into another enormous glacial lake, Glacial Lake Penticton in the Okanagan Valley, and from there into ice-free country to the south via the Columbia River system.

Eventually glaciers in the Shuswap downwasted sufficiently for lake waters to escape into the Okanagan via Cinnemousun Narrows or the Hunakwa Lake valley. Lake levels fell, exposing lake bottom sediments east of Kamloops.

The second of Johnsen's great glacial lakes, Glacial Lake Deadman (Lowest Stage), 50 metres deep and 160 kilometres long, ran from the ice dam at Skoonka Creek only as far as present-day Kamloops and up the valley of the North Thompson. But still it drained *eastward* up the present-day valley of the South Thompson River, carving the high clay bluffs east of Kamloops from those exposed lake bottom sediments.

Now here's the really dramatic bit. Sometime around nine thousand years ago the ice dam at Skoonka Creek failed catastrophically, emptying most of the contents of Glacial Lake Deadman, about twenty cubic kilometres of water, into the lower Thompson and Fraser valleys, carrying mud and debris downstream all the way to the Strait of Georgia and across to Saanich Inlet on Vancouver Island, and establishing the modern Shuswap and Thompson drainage pattern *westward* through the Fraser Canyon.

I'm in luck. There *is* good water in Jimmies Creek. Not as much as I might have hoped but enough to be going on with. And water at Jimmies Creek almost certainly means water at Brassy Creek.

Afternoon clouds are building now, it's quite dark to the east. There are even some scattered showers over that way, a blessing, keeping temperatures on the moderate side. Out west the sky is still clear blue, which makes sense. That's rain-shadow country over there.

The lower Thompson River valley and adjacent stretches of the Fraser River valley, tucked into the lee of the Coast Mountains, can claim British Columbia's hottest, driest climate. Even hotter and drier than the famously hot, dry south Okanagan. Ashcroft gets considerably less annual precipitation than the town of Oliver (near the south end of the Okanagan Valley) and summertime temperatures are higher here. On the other hand, winters are colder thanks to a river of frigid air flowing south off the high Cariboo and Chilcotin plateaus. Winters are also much longer here, with many fewer frost-free days annually. The future vineyards of Chateau Ashcroft will operate at a disadvantage.

By the time I drop down into the Brassy Creek valley it's evening. There's ample water, thank goodness, running out of a deep gully cut back into the hills to the south.

> *Here are your waters and your watering place.*
> *Drink and be whole again beyond confusion.*
> —Robert Frost, "Directive"

DAY FORTY
Monday, July 14: Brassy Creek to Ashcroft

> *As I went down to the river to pray*
> *Studying about that good old way*
> *And who shall wear the starry crown*
> *Good Lord, show me the way!*
>
> *Oh sinners let's go down,*
> *Let's go down, come on down,*
> *Oh sinners let's go down,*
> *Down to the river to pray.*
>
> — Traditional

Up in good time for the long day ahead.

Poking my head from the tent, breathing deeply of morning air scented with damp sage, I rejoice in the view: the sun just rising above the valley into an absolutely clear blue sky.

By the time I finish breakfast the day is already warm and the first few clouds have begun to materialize. I'm guessing that I can look forward to a repeat of yesterday's afternoon overcast or maybe something a little more dramatic.

The country west of Brassy Creek is rugged, with deep gullies and sheer faces falling away toward the floor of the valley. The little track

I'm following is forced down and down until eventually it just gives up, wanders feebly across the roadbed of the Canadian Pacific Railway and expires in a little meadow above the river.

Moment of truth!

I was hoping to find some sort of natural path or trail leading west along the base of the slope. But I can see now, looking west, downstream, that the only possible way forward is along the CPR right-of-way carved into the sheer rock. If I want to go on, I'll have to walk the tracks.

I don't like it but there doesn't seem to be any other way.

Let me tell you a story. When I first began to plan this section of the trip from Kamloops to Ashcroft, it occurred to me that I could avoid the long trek out of Kamloops on Highway 1 by following the Canadian National Railway's right-of-way along the north side of Kamloops Lake.

Wanting to do the right thing, I naively (and foolishly as it turned out) wrote a note to the CNR asking if I might have their permission to do the walk. In due course came the reply, loaded with unpleasant and pejorative terms like "trespass," and "forbidden," and "legal action."

I gathered I was not welcome.

As it happens, that was perhaps just as well. I've since realized that there are several long tunnels on that section of the main line, and I'm not at all sure it would have been safe or healthy to share one with a speeding CN freight train. Even so, couldn't they have simply explained that, in courteous terms, and asked me to refrain?

Anyway, I have *not* asked the CPR for permission to walk their tracks into Ashcroft. This troubles my law-abiding, rule-following, courtesy-loving soul. But I have no other choice.

So I go.

It's no problem, no problem at all. The engineers wave as they go by. I take pictures of them and their locomotives. Admire the trains.

God bless the CPR.

At one point I *do* feel obliged to step discreetly out of sight when I spot a track maintenance vehicle coming along the line, bearing down on me, with my now-paranoid soul whispering urgently that those cheerfully waving engineers might still have ratted me out—matter of ordinary procedure you understand, nothing personal, just doin' me job. But the truck rolls on past my place of concealment ("hiding place" seems so craven) without even slowing.

Incidentally, there is still something truly impressive, majestic, about a big train in full flight. One forgets. It's like an ocean-going vessel, that same immense scale.

I start counting the cars on one train, after the leading engine and perhaps the first twenty cars have already gone by. The last car, with no trailing engine for some reason, is number 117. The leading engine is long gone beyond the curve of the mountain, well out of sight and sound, so that the last car drifts peacefully away, massive and practically soundless, like a sailing ship under full press in light airs. (Of course on more demanding sections of track there would need to be a trailing engine to power and control such a huge structure.)

A long, hot, thirsty walk along the railbed above the river, much farther than I'd expected.

Not wanting to stop—I am still a little anxious about my welcome on CPR property, and there's no shelter anyway—I keep trudging along, kilometre after kilometre. Afternoon clouds gather, as expected, but they seem to have little effect on the heat. I wouldn't call it a beautiful country. Too harsh for that. But it *is* dramatic with that great river rolling along through the desiccated landscape, half concealed by swelling sagebrush hills and deep cutbanks of glacial till and river gravel.

It's a great relief, all in all, to finally step off the tracks onto the Queen's highway (actually just a dusty little lane, but a public thoroughfare even so) and totter down to the river for a break.

I manage to find some shelter from the heat and glare beneath an enormous old juniper (*Juniperus scopulorum*) right at the water's edge. The river, brown and laden with silt, races by with an audible hiss. The Thompson River, still bank full even this late in the season, is an impressive body of water, big water, by any standard.

I drink greedily (from my bottles, not the river), have a bite to eat and tune out for a couple of hours, dozing, watching the river roll, waiting for the slightly cooler air of evening before venturing along the last few kilometres into Ashcroft.

By the time I finally hit the road, afternoon clouds have gathered into ominous overcast. There's a curtain of precipitation across the summit ridge of the Cornwall Hills to the west, promising serious rain to come. I only just manage to reach the Ashcroft Legacy Campsite, downtown Ashcroft, before I feel the first drop or two. All very ironic considering what I wrote yesterday about this being rain-shadow country.

Anyway there is good water at the campsite and a patch of lush green lawn on which to pitch my tent. No cactus. No poison ivy. And a shower! What luxury! In this commercial, private-enterprise age of ours, I find something quite charming about the notion of a community that still offers a civic campsite down by the river for the comfort and convenience of us pilgrims.

And here's something more, laid on by the fates especially for my visit, no doubt. I've had a bit of a breather and am just preparing to set up my tent, hoping to beat the rain, when there comes a deep hoot from the rail yards above the campsite. I register vaguely that this is *not* the electric horn of a diesel locomotive but a *whistle*. I look up just in time to see—I swear this is true—a steam locomotive, huge black machine, puff-puff-puffing its way along the main line out of town, eastbound.

("*All aboard for Kamloops, Calgary, Regina, Winnipeg, Fort William . . .*")
That's got to be the ghost of historic Ashcroft rolling out of the mists
of time.

Before zipping myself into the tent (the urban backpacker once more,
politely discreet), I note a sliver of blue along the western horizon and a
hint of sunset, the bottom of the clouds tinted orange. That serious rain
never did materialize. Didn't I tell you? Rain-shadow country.

> *Deep river,*
> *My home is over Jordan.*
> *Deep river, Lord,*
> *I want to cross over into campground*
> *Oh, don't you want to go to the gospel feast,*
> *That promised land, where all is peace?*
> *Oh, deep river, Lord,*
> *I want to cross over into campground.*
>
> —Traditional

DAY FORTY-ONE
Tuesday, July 15: Ashcroft to Three Sisters Creek

Were it not for the Canadian Pacific Railway, Ashcroft wouldn't
exist. Hastily surveyed by Oliver Evans and his pregnant teen-
aged wife, Ellen, just before the tracks arrived in the autumn of 1884,
the town quickly became the region's chief place of business: the rail-
head and trading centre for a huge area of the countryside extending
far up into the Cariboo and Chilcotin.

Reading the histories, one comes away with the impression of
a town dominated by a fairly narrow commercial outlook. A never-
ending procession of wheeler-dealers, hoot and holler, out to make a
dollar. Buying and selling. Scheming and dreaming. And you've got to
hand it to them, they had drive. Entrepreneurship says it well. They'd

take on these projects: stores, hotels, offices, canneries, mines, market gardens, waterworks, lumber mills, power stations, irrigation schemes, ranches, any damned thing, and make them work.

Or go broke trying.

As it happens, in a modest way I'm part of that history. When I was an infant, my parents and I lived in this town for a couple of years. My father, a very young man in those days, worked for the Bank of Montreal, still doing business with people from all over the Cariboo and Chilcotin. So I have a stake in this little community. It's one of my hometowns. I take an interest.

And I have to say that the old place is looking a little forlorn. A town that lives by economics, dies by economics. Trains don't stop like they used to. The highway passes by. The Chilcotin and Cariboo take their business elsewhere. The mills and the cannery and the mines, many of the ranches, gone, all gone. Even the Bank of Montreal, one of the first branches in British Columbia, has packed it in. The town seems to be wilting, robbed of its *raisons d'être*.

And I think it's such a pity. Perhaps Ashcroft suffers by comparison with the Okanagan, hotter and drier in summer, colder in the winter, as I've been saying. But it has its own charm. An attractive ruggedness. All that sunshine. And the townsite is really quite lovely, down in the valley, a broad terrace enclosed by a bend of the rolling river.

You come down out of the hills some evening, just as the town is lighting up, and you think: *Wow, this could really be something special, like a Norman Rockwell print, with tree-lined avenues and stately homes and fine public buildings.* An oasis in a dry land. After all, this is one of the oldest towns in British Columbia. It should be splendid.

But it isn't.

That would be the legacy of those founding fathers, not to mention all the movers and shakers since, so obsessed with the idea of making fortunes that they had scant time or energy or thought to spare toward creating something of lasting beauty and worth in the little town they were building. A town as a work of art. A town that would be a joy and a pleasure and a privilege to live in, no matter what the state of the economy.

Another early start, another long day ahead. I'm suffering a mild case of the Ashcroft blues, but I know the cure. Hit the road, Jack. Eat some miles. Breakfast of champions.

I'm now entering the traditional territories of the Nlaka'pamux First Nation (also known as the Thompson Indians), the third of four Interior Salish traditional territories I'll pass through on this journey. From here, Nlaka'pamux traditional territory extends east to Nicola Lake, south to the little town of Lytton, then both upstream and downstream along the Fraser River from about the south end of the Fountain Valley, in the north, to Spuzzum and Yale on the Fraser in the south, and then yet farther south into the Cascade Mountains and across the international boundary into northern Washington State.

I eat lunch in the sweet-scented shade of a haystack, this year's crop of alfalfa just in off the fields.

Then it's a hot, never-ending climb into the western hills, with the road running mostly in the shady wooded valley of Oregon Jack Creek, thank goodness. (Oregon Jack, aka John Dowling, was a prospector and reputed hold-up man who lived and prospected here in the late 1800s.)

Oregon Jack Provincial Park turns out to be something of a jewel.

Three spectacular limestone cliffs, aka the Three Sisters, stand sentinel over a great hollow in the hills just inside the park's eastern boundary. Apart from the three beautiful if rather stern sisters, the elevation of the park and its northeastern exposure create a noticeably cooler microclimate, which is most welcome on this hot summer day. And I'm thrilled to see big old interior Douglas-firs scattered through the open forest.

No ghost forest here. For some reason the loggers have left this bit of countryside alone. This is the good stuff, some of the nicest bits of natural habitat I've seen on the entire journey.

And under a dry overhang on the northern flank of the nearest "sister," some anonymous walkers from an earlier age have left us a set of modest pictographs.

They're worth mentioning because not too far from here is the earliest known site of human habitation on British Columbia's southern interior plateau. I walked past it on my way up along Oregon Jack Creek. Catalogued by archeologists as EDRi 11, it is evidenced by a small collection of stone tools, tool-making debris, and butchered bones, mostly deer, dating from 8,450 years ago, plus or minus ninety years.

Archeologists divide the prehistory of the southern interior plateau into three broad phases: Early Period (11,000 years ago to 8,000 years ago), Middle Period (8,000 years ago to 4,000 years ago) and Late Period (4,000 years ago to around 300 years ago, at which point recorded history commences). The earliest levels of EDRi 11 were inhabited at the very end of the Early Period or the very beginning of the Middle Period.

These people may have been part of the Nesikep Tradition, belonging mostly to the Middle Period, small mobile bands focussed on the hunting of large ungulates, though doubtless efficient at exploiting the resources of each season in turn.

Let's call them "the deer hunters."

Of the three periods (Early, Middle and Late), the Middle Period seems to have been blessed with the most benign, biologically productive climate. It must have been ideal for small groups of highly mobile hunter-gatherers foraging their way across the landscape, taking advantage of whatever was available and plentiful in any given season, then moving on to the next thing: big game through the fall and winter; freshwater fish in the early spring; spring-beauty corms and avalanche lily bulbs in the late spring; roots and berries in the summer; salmon in the fall.

From our modern perspective it's a bit of a stretch to imagine human beings so fully integrated into the natural world and having so little impact on the ecosystems they inhabit.

And I get a kick out of thinking that here, this evening, across all that span of time, I'm sharing something of the experience of that little band of deer hunters camped in the Oregon Jack valley more than eight thousand years ago.

DAY FORTY-TWO
Wednesday, July 16:
Three Sisters Creek to Cornwall Hills

Some gorgeous views from the summit meadows of Cornwall Hills Provincial Park: west to the upper Hat Creek valley and the rounded alpine summits of the Clear Range; north to the abrupt boundary between the rolling uplands of southern interior British Columbia and the high forested plain of the Cariboo plateau; east to the harsh, hot, tawny landscape of the Thompson valley with the river winding past far, far below; and south to the high ridges between the Thompson and Fraser rivers.

From here I can see only the forested north-facing slopes of those ridges to the south, but I know that many of their drier south-facing slopes support broad open alpine meadows just like these on the Cornwall Hills.

In the warmer, drier conditions that prevailed when EDRi 11 was occupied, it's quite likely that even north-facing slopes in these highlands would have been open grassy meadowlands. A happy hunting ground for that little band of foragers.

Toward the end of the Middle Period, sometime around 2500 B.C., the regional climate began to cool. More snow fell. Deeper winter snowpacks persisted longer into the spring. Mountain glaciers advanced.

Forests spread. Life became more difficult. But nature takes with one hand and gives with the other: colder climates and closed forests may have meant fewer ungulates, but they also meant cooler, clearer rivers and an increase in salmon productivity.

It was about this time that a new ethnic group (quite distinct from the deer hunters of the Nesikep Tradition) appeared in the landscape, moving upstream along the major river valleys to exploit the larger salmon runs. These were Salishan speakers of coastal origin—the forebears of British Columbia's present-day Interior Salish peoples.

Call them "the salmon fishers."

Remarkably the two cultures, deer hunters and salmon fishers, seem to have coexisted, sharing this piece of countryside for something like a thousand years before finally merging.

As the climate continued to deteriorate, it must have become increasingly difficult, especially in the winter months, to sustain a foraging lifestyle, simply taking a living from whatever resources happened to be available at any particular season of the year. Winter starvation must have become a fact of life.

Perhaps in response to such dire necessity a new approach to subsistence developed at the beginning of the Late Period, around 2000 B.C. At times when food was plentiful the people of these southern interior valleys began to gather *more* than they could consume immediately, preserving and storing the surplus as a buffer against the meagreness of leaner seasons.

Archeologists call this new way of life the "Plateau Pithouse Tradition," characterized by significant storage of processed and preserved foods; a more sedentary lifestyle; an increased dependence on salmon; evidence of intensive exploitation and processing of diverse resources, not just salmon but ungulates, fruits and vegetables (particularly roots); and, most obviously, the construction of semi-subterranean, circular pit-houses, sometimes called *kekuli*, which provided wintertime shelter for families and a place to store food. The Plateau Pithouse Tradition proved a highly effective adaptation, surviving in various forms through the next four thousand years and on into the historical period.

Almost within living memory, hundreds of people from different bands and even from different tribes, primarily the Nlaka'pamux, but also Secwepemc and Lillooet, still gathered at Botanie Mountain and Botanie valley in the high country between the Thompson and Fraser rivers to collect spring-beauty corms and avalanche lily bulbs for processing and storage, a practice that continues in a more modest way even into our own times.

I manage to find a well-sheltered level spot for the tent just below the summit, tucked in among the willows. (I *love* the astringent smell of alpine willow!) It's just warm enough for me to sit outside watching the full moon rise before I go to bed. Another full moon on a mountaintop, perfect timing. It feels like a special blessing and grace to be here on this particular night.

DAY FORTY-THREE
Thursday, July 17: Cornwall Hills to Upper Hat Creek

The Hat Creek Road dwindles and dwindles until it's just two parallel tracks of gravel and dirt winding through the open forest, past a series of little ponds in a deeply carved valley above and beyond the Three Sisters. It's a canyon almost, with sheer limestone cliffs, cleaving the crest of the Cornwall Hills. And at the western end of that canyon an unexpected widening into light and space, the upper Hat Creek valley.

The grasslands of the upper Hat Creek valley are something of an anomaly, reminding me of the high-altitude grasslands I saw on the south-facing slopes of Crater Mountain last August. There are open bunchgrass meadows here at elevations of 1,500 metres or more on south-facing aspects. Again I think of them as relics of a much earlier time at the beginning of the Holocene, eight to ten thousand years ago, when conditions were warmer and drier than at present. The grasslands of southern British Columbia were not then confined to the deeper valleys but extended across a much larger area of upland.

I've an idea that the continued existence of these high-elevation meadows in the upper Hat Creek valley depends at least partly on the intensity of the rain shadow here, right in the lee of the Coast Mountains, mimicking that early Holocene climatic maximum.

Temperatures are cooler in these upper grasslands and there's more precipitation than at lower elevations. Indeed, there is almost (but not quite) enough moisture in the soil to allow the survival of seedling trees. (The conventional wisdom is that grasslands exist where forests cannot, where moisture in the soil is insufficient to allow seedling trees to survive.) So these are about the best growing conditions grasslands can have. Any more moisture and they'd be forest.

And it shows. The sparse, widely spaced bunchgrasses outside Ashcroft were already dry and bleached yellow by the heat. The grass here, in the upper Hat Creek valley, is still green and growing. And the growth is rich and thick, with very little bare ground between bunches. There's an obvious variety of species, too, a real biodiversity, not just of grass but of broad-leafed flowering forbs. It's a garden.

All of which must have seemed a real attraction to the people camping at EDRi 11, not to mention all the generations and cultures and traditions since.

When BC Hydro considered building a coal-fired electrical generating station in the upper Hat Creek valley during the 1970s (apparently the whole upper valley is underlain by a substantial bed of low-grade coal) one of the first things they did was to commission an archeological survey.

That survey and subsequent researches have unearthed (literally) widespread evidence of intense prehistoric harvesting and processing of root vegetables, most especially arrowleaf balsamroot. Balsamroot is plentiful on the slopes of the upper Hat Creek valley. And it is nutritious, a staple food once consumed in quantity by indigenous peoples all over southern British Columbia.

Archeology in southern interior British Columbia has tended to focus on winter pit-house village sites, usually situated at low elevations along major rivers, where migrating salmon could be collected and processed in quantity. But that bias has left us with a distorted view of life in those communities. As important as salmon undoubtedly were in sustaining the population (isotope studies of Plateau Pithouse Tradition human remains suggest that as much as two-thirds of dietary protein came from marine sources) there seems little question that those people would have efficiently exploited the whole range of resources available to them. And, in fact, some research now suggests that the bulk of their diet, especially in terms of calories, would have come from plants, fruits, roots and vegetables.

Balsamroot may be plentiful and nutritious, but there's a catch. The raw root is virtually inedible. It's very fibrous and much of the potential food value is locked up in an indigestible polysaccharide, inulin, that must be converted to digestible sugars, primarily fructose, by long, slow cooking.

What archeologists mostly find in the upper Hat Creek valley are the remains of circular, stone-lined "pit ovens" or "earth ovens" used to cook the roots into edibility. A pit would be dug and lined with a layer of stone. Then a fire would be laid and kindled on the stone, with more small rocks piled on top. By the time the fire had burned down, the rocks and the pit itself would be thoroughly heated. A thin layer of earth would then be sprinkled on the rocks, and a layer of fresh vegetation added. The peeled balsamroots could then be placed and covered by another layer of vegetation and a layer of matting and a final layer of earth laid over top. Sometimes water for extra steam was poured into the pit through a hole left for the purpose. Another fire would be kindled on top of the filled pit, and the balsamroot allowed to cook for between twelve and twenty-four hours.

This was a laborious and time-consuming effort, carried out mostly by women be it noted (at least we think so), but great quantities of root could be processed in each batch. Once cooked, the roots could be eaten immediately or dried for storage.

The evidence suggests that hundreds of pounds of dried roots might be procured this way over the course of a season. That kind of volume implies a very considerable amount of digging, and some researchers have gone so far as to suggest that this amounted to a form of cultivation, a shift from simple gathering to a kind of basic agriculture, the implication being (so I gather) a hitherto unappreciated level of sophistication to the whole operation.

I'm not sure I buy that. To me the genius of the thing was that, apart from a little incidental tillage, these people were *not* modifying the natural indigenous ecosystems to any great extent. They were *not* trying to replace natural ecosystems with some sort of artificial man-made scheme of productivity. On the contrary, they seemed content to collect a harvestable excess (and no more than a harvestable excess, evidently) produced by existing ecosystems. Surely that was the secret of their success, part of the essence of whatever it was that allowed their lifestyle to sustain itself over not just hundreds but thousands upon thousands of years.

DAY FORTY-FOUR
Friday, July 18: Upper Hat Creek Valley

Having fallen asleep under starry skies, I wake to heavy overcast threatening rain. The mountaintops are cloud shrouded. Break time. There's no point in fighting the weather, especially when I'm headed back into the high country. And I'm not unhappy with the prospect of lingering for a day or two in such a pretty and interesting piece of countryside.

At some point when I came hiking up out of Ashcroft the other day, I crossed from one fragment of the earth's crust, the Quesnel Terrane, onto another very different fragment, the Cache Creek Terrane.

Unlike the Quesnel Terrane, which began life as a volcanic island arc somewhere not too far off the west coast of North America, the Cache Creek Terrane seems mostly to comprise bits and pieces of ocean floor scraped from the Pacific Plate as it subducted beneath that island arc, about 200 million years ago. The high limestone faces of the Three Sisters, for example, probably represent the remains of coral atolls, millions of years' worth of coral growth piled high.

And material in the Cache Creek Terrane comes from much farther away than material in the Quesnel Terrane. Samples collected in the town of Cache Creek yield fossil remains of tiny fusulinids, single-celled organisms native only to Asian seas. Imagine that: the rocks in the hillside across from the Cache Creek Post Office ferried through millions of years of continental drift all the way across the basin of the Pacific Ocean on the back of a moving plate of the earth's crust, a vast geological conveyor belt, before being scraped off, at last, against whatever remained of the Quesnel Terrane's island arc.

Of course that's just one chapter in the story. Even as that material came into place and through all the millions and millions of years since, it was being shaped by all the irresistible forces of erosion: gravity, running water and glacial ice.

I can't think of another place in southern interior British Columbia where the relics of glaciation are so common and so obvious as they are in the upper Hat Creek valley. It's as if the ice has been gone just long enough for vegetation to cover the wreckage left behind.

There are "eskers" everywhere: serpentine ridges of gravel representing the beds of ice-age streams flowing across or through or under the glaciers. There are little cirques on the mountainsides where the ice lingered, gnawing at the rock. There are whole slopes of what glaciologists would call "hummocky moraine," where a static sheet of ice simply melted away like the Wicked Witch of the West, leaving its burden of eroded rock and silt piled and mounded willy-nilly (like the witch's clothing). There are parallel ridges representing gravel-filled crevasses where the ice sheet broke open across some sub-glacial barrier.

There are also parallel ridges of terminal moraine, apparently formed by repeated feeble advances of the dying ice sheet. You can picture the thing melting away, then taking heart and advancing for a bit, though never quite as far as the last time, then melting away some more, and so on, with each advance bulldozing a little of the muck left at the glacier's snout into a ridge, roughly paralleling the ridge from the previous advance.

Brighter by day's end.

DAY FORTY-FIVE
Saturday, July 19: Upper Hat Creek to Cairn Mountain

Sunny but cool this morning. Perfect weather for today's long climb into the Clear Range, the height of land between the upper Hat Creek valley and the Fountain Valley farther to the west.

The steep trail has me thinking again about those people harvesting roots in the upper Hat Creek valley. When the season was over they would have had to carry all their produce back to winter villages along the Thompson and Fraser rivers, where other members of their communities would be busy catching and drying salmon. I picture long lines of walkers, mostly women, all carrying heavy burden baskets.

Horses didn't show up in this part of the world until the early 1800s. The folks who tended those earth ovens in the upper Hat Creek valley were pedestrians, like me. Everywhere they went, they went on foot. Everything they needed had to be carried on human backs. And I've a feeling that those burden baskets would have made my monster pack look like sissy stuff.

What an investment of time and effort it must have been to hike all those many kilometres up out of the Thompson or Fraser valleys to harvest roots in the upper Hat Creek valley or on Botanie Mountain, and then to make the trip back home at the end of the season laden with cooked, dried roots. Obviously the size of the harvest would have been strictly limited by what the harvesters could physically carry away. Much of the countryside, apart from prime spots, would have been effectively beyond reach, a sort of natural reserve, just too far away, just too much trouble to bother with.

And what a blessing horses must have seemed. Where we walked, trudging, now we ride! Where we carried heavy burdens, horses now make light of the weight!

But horses were something new to the equation. An unknown and uncertain quantity thrown onto scales that had been in balance for a long, long time.

Horses eat grass, quite a lot of grass, sometimes right down to the roots, and they chew up the ground with their hooves. They're hard on these indigenous grasslands. And horses bring every little scrap of the countryside within relatively easy reach. Suddenly the upper Hat Creek valley is a morning's ride from the Thompson or Fraser rivers. And there's practically no limit to the amount of dried roots you could carry away.

In some measure, at least, it must have been the limitations imposed by a strictly pedestrian culture, strictly human-powered, that made that culture so sustainable. They simply didn't have the capacity to do much harm.

And it may well be that the arrival of horses and the increase in power and mobility that came with them marked the beginning of the end for that immensely long-lived lifestyle, the Plateau Pithouse Tradition. A destabilizing factor. First the arrival of horses, then white men bearing gifts.

I'm remembering the view I had from the Cornwall Hills, with the Coast Mountains far away on the horizon. Here, on the summit of Cairn Mountain, it's as if I've taken a couple of giant steps to the west. The Coast Mountains are right in front of me now, rising up sheer beyond the deep twin rifts of the Fountain and Fraser valleys.

A mountaintop view is like coming up for air and a look at the larger world. Somewhere far to the southeast is Crater Mountain, where I started this journey. And in the other direction, to the north-west, is Williams Lake, my ultimate goal. I've a sense of having reached the halfway point. Better than halfway actually. We're getting there.

DAY FORTY-SIX
Sunday, July 20: Cairn Mountain to Cinquefoil Creek

C louds of white butterflies and blue butterflies, backlit by the morning sun, hover and flutter above the last of the steep, open meadows. The lupines are still blooming. That lovely smell of alpine willow fills the air.

Goodbye and farewell to the mountains. Back to the valleys.

I was a mite anxious starting out, truth to tell. The ground is steeper on this side of the Clear Range and Cinquefoil Creek ravine is heavily forested. I've been taking it pretty much on faith, a sure recipe for disaster, that I'll be able to find *some* way down into the Fountain Valley.

I needn't have worried. There's a well-established trail and some-body's gone to the trouble of brushing it out and cutting away the deadfall. You could take loaded packhorses down this thing.

In two or three places the trail wanders out across steep slopes of talus, accumulations of broken stone below faces of exposed bedrock. On each of these sections a good deal of the loose stone has been shifted to create a relatively broad and secure trail on what might otherwise have been a very treacherous bit of footing. It's hard to imagine even the hardest-working horse packer going to such trouble.

I can think of several other possible explanations but can't help wondering if this isn't tangible evidence of what I was thinking about yesterday: the traditional traffic between the root-gathering and processing grounds of the upper Hat Creek valley and the winter village sites along the Fraser.

Perhaps it's just wishful thinking, but I relish the idea that this trail I'm walking might have such a long tradition attached to it. I like the thought of all those generations upon generations of walkers gradually shifting the stones beneath their feet into the semblance of a made trail.

The so-called Classical Era of the Plateau Pithouse Tradition, roughly corresponding to the Middle to Late sub-period of the region's prehistory, between about 850 B.C. and A.D. 750, was characterized by a set of unusually large village sites—Pavilion, Keatley Creek, Bell, Fountain, Bridge River, Lillooet and Seton—along the Fraser River near Lillooet. Not surprisingly the classical era also corresponds to the time when root crops in the upper Hat Creek valley were being most intensely harvested.

The Fountain village site, at the north end of the Fountain Valley, is not too far away. The Bell site is also quite close. Perhaps some of the traffic to and fro did come over this trail.

Most of the classical village sites have been destroyed, but Keatley Creek, Bell and Bridge River remain relatively intact. Of those three, Keatley, with 120 house pits, is the largest and best studied. Researchers estimate that there might have been perhaps fifty active households at any one time, a total population of perhaps five hundred to one thousand, which would have made Keatley Creek something like ten times the size of one of the era's more typical villages.

The house pits at Keatley Creek were also much larger than usual and were apparently inhabited by multiple nuclear families. And there seem to have been disparities between different family groups in the same dwelling: some families were evidently better off than others. Archeologists hypothesize the development of a social hierarchy, specialized occupations, a class of leaders and administrators. And conversely an underclass of poor relations, labourers and slaves. The discovery of infant burials richly endowed with grave goods tends to confirm the existence of some sort of hereditary aristocracy or, at least, wealthy pre-eminent families.

The really fascinating and strange part of the whole story is that this "classical" era, according to the evidence, came to an abrupt and mysterious end around A.D. 750, with the more-or-less simultaneous abandonment of all the larger village sites.

A short day. I camp near the bottom of the ravine.

DAY FORTY-SEVEN
Monday, July 21: Cinquefoil Creek to Rough Creek

Wild roses are fairest, and nature a better gardener than art.

—Louisa May Alcott, *A Long Fatal Love Chase*

A cluster of wild roses, still in bloom, sweetly perfumed, last of the season.

The trail becomes a track. Which turns into a lane. Which passes through the Chilhil 6 Reserve's little village and joins a road running along the bottom of the Fountain Valley. I've crossed into a fourth interior Salish traditional territory. These are Lillooet people here. Cinquefoil Creek turns sharply left around a spur of Blustry Mountain and heads south down the valley toward the Fraser River.

I follow.

Fountain Valley Road has a lovely countrified appeal, like something out of childhood, overhung by trees, winding past little lakes and farms. It *is* a tad dusty, with a deep floury dust that, again, I recall vividly from childhood. (I'd forgotten about that dust. Haven't thought about roads like that in years. We're so used now to gravelled, macadamized surfaces that we take them for granted.)

Fortunately for me there's very little traffic. I thank goodness for that because when the odd car or truck does roll past, it raises such a cloud of fine dust that I can hardly see or breathe until the morning breeze rolls it away, bringing back the clean air.

It's no great surprise when I come upon a highways maintenance crew with graders and tank trucks and whatnot laying down some sort of salt solution (magnesium chloride as it turns out) that is supposed to glue all this dust together into a hard surface.

I chat with the foreman while I wait for a break in the action. I tell him about my project, the pilgrimage, all this long distance I've walked, and how I'm hurrying in the hope of making it to Lillooet before the really hot weather arrives.

"Too late," he says. "Forty-one degrees in Lillooet when we left town at seven a.m."

This comes as a bit of a shock, especially considering how pleasant it's been up here in the Fountain Valley this morning. From what the foreman tells me, I can expect to start feeling the heat just down the road where the valley begins to dip more steeply toward the Fraser.

Growing on the bank above the road, a beautiful lavender blossom almost as big as the palm of my hand. Three slender sepals alternate with three broad petals. This is a sagebrush mariposa lily (*Calochortus macrocarpus*). *Calochortus* comes from the Greek *kalo* (beautiful) and *chortus* (grass); *mariposa* from the Spanish for "butterfly."

It's a lovely thing, seemingly out of place in this increasingly harsh environment. And it's a sure sign of the advancing year: sagebrush mariposa lilies bloom right at the end of the season—spring's last, generous, parting gift.

> *Deep in their roots, all flowers keep the light.*
> —Theodore Roethke, "The Stony Garden"

The air grows warmer with every step I take, like climbing down into an oven. And the terrain along the edge of the main valley is increasingly precipitous, with not a flat spot anywhere. Then a minor miracle. (One of those times when I think, *Somebody's looking after me.*)

I hear a faint gurgle from somewhere above the road and climb to find an open irrigation ditch running across the face of the hill. What's more, not too far along the ditch, at the base of a big ponderosa pine, there's a little patch of level grass just large enough to accommodate my tent. Perfect. Time to bivouac.

I've started thinking of this as the Nesikep camp, though Nesikep Creek is actually on the other side of the Fraser, and the Lytton First Nation's Nesikep Reserves are to the north and west. (We're back in Nlaka'pamux territory here.) But I get a kick out of making some little connection to the place where archeologists first identified features of the ancient Nesikep Tradition.

You'll remember that the Nesikep Tradition gave way to the Plateau Pithouse Tradition at the beginning of the Late Period, around 2000 B.C. And the Plateau Pithouse Tradition attained its most elaborate development in the classical era, the Middle to Late sub-period between 850 B.C. and A.D. 750, before terminating abruptly with the sudden abandonment of those outsized villages at Pavilion, Keatley Creek, Fountain and so on.

Reading the literature, one has the impression that archeologists are most thrilled by the level of cultural complexity in the classic period, that they lament its passing and tend to view all subsequent forms as a kind of decline.

Brian Hayden, who with colleagues was responsible for developing much of the archeology at the Keatley Creek site, has written that "there can be no doubt that compared to generalized hunter-gatherers, the Lillooet communities represented an apogee of cultural development for the interior. Subsequent reductions in the size of the villages, in apparent population density, in the maximum size of house pits, and in apparent settlement hierarchies are what we refer to as 'cultural collapse.'"[13]

Here again I'm not sure I buy that. As far as I'm concerned those are all changes in the right direction. Small populations living in little groups widely dispersed across the landscape. Their ecological footprint must have been very light indeed. Low impact. Indefinitely sustainable. (At least until a wave of aggressive immigrants arrived a thousand years later.)

And smaller village size seems also to have done away with the need and opportunity for a ruling elite. Aristocracies collapsed. The society that early observers described seems to have been egalitarian, democratic, neighbourly, altogether admirable.

David Wyatt, writing in *Handbook of North American Indians*, (Volume 12): *Plateau*, says of the Nlaka'pamux (Thompson):

Every individual was a member of a family, local community and either the Upper Thompson or Lower Thompson band, but ruled by none, for each man had a voice in the informal councils where hunting, war, and other matters were discussed. Leadership came from the wise and experienced, and there might be different leaders on different occasions. Women spoke and led in their own areas of expertise. [14]

Resources were held in common and sharing was obligatory.

Marianne Boelscher Ignace, writing in the same volume, says that although individual Secwepemc (Shuswap) bands had their own regular areas for hunting, fishing, gathering and trapping, all Shuswap shared proprietary rights over the resource-producing areas:

A strong ethic of egalitarianism and of sharing food resources prevailed. At the fishing grounds, the entire catch procured by participating fishermen was equally distributed, and further fish were distributed to elders and others unable to fish for themselves. Meat was likewise distributed to all participants of a hunting party and to others in need. "Stinginess" in this respect caused harm to the hunter or fisherman's reputation and invited bad luck for the future harvesting of game, fish, or plant species.[15]

There was a typical division of labour between the sexes. Men hunted, women gathered plants and attended to domestic chores. But this too was flexible. Some women had reputations as expert hunters of large game. And men assisted in berry picking, helped process fish and game, made their own clothing and cooked:

> Chiefs mainly functioned as mediators within the band, and as representatives of their people's interest to the outside, regulating food supply where necessary, "admonishing the lazy and quarrelsome," giving advice, and setting a good example for all others, without having any material or other privileges. The chiefs' role was to maintain consensus within the band and among families, rather than dictating the course of action.[16]

See what I mean? Admirable. Certainly I know that if I were of interior Salish descent I would take far more pride, enormous pride, in the egalitarian tradition of those last thousand years of prehistory than in the supposed aristocratic tradition of the "classical" era before it.

DAY FORTY-EIGHT
Tuesday, July 22: Rough Creek to Lillooet

When my alarm rings at five o'clock I find that the prickly heat of summer which so oppressed me last night has given way to much cooler air. There's a little breeze blowing. The skies are overcast and I can smell rain.

It's a sudden and unexpected change in the weather, a deterioration you might ordinarily say, but today most welcome. A blessing in fact. A steady downpour would be better than 41°C in the hot sun, north along Highway 12 to Lillooet.

This is a place rich with dramatic meetings. And a river runs through it, the mighty Fraser, hurrying downhill through its broad valley toward the lower mainland and the sea.

On the most basic landscape level, one teeters here on the edge of a tremendous gap, not merely between one terrane and another (as at Ashcroft), but between two completely different geological provinces. On this side of the river valley, the relatively gentle uplands of the Cache Creek Terrane of the Intermontane Belt. On that side, the Methow and Bridge River terranes of the mountainous Coast Belt.

It's very different country west of the river: high mountains, vast rock faces, sheer, deep, vertical-sided valleys. And a completely different timeline, too. The Intermontane Belt, on this side of the Fraser, was part of North America for a hundred million years before the Coast Belt, on that side of the river, came crashing ashore.

In human terms, too, it's a place of dramatic meetings between very different cultures. This was the ground where First Nations came most sharply into conflict with the immigrant gold-seekers of the 1850s and 1860s. But today I'm thinking of an earlier era, the very first contacts, meetings that occurred the better part of a lifetime before the goldrush years. Those first contacts differed in some essential ways from what followed, but subsequent events have tended to obscure and overshadow them.

We are traders, and apart from more exalted motives, all
traders are desirous of gain. Is it not self evident we will
manage our business with more economy by being on
good terms with the Indians than if at variance.
—John McLoughlin, 1843 (quoted by Robin Fisher in
Contact and Conflict: Indian–European Relations
in British Columbia, 1774–1890.)

192

The North West Company fur trader and explorer Simon Fraser would have passed this way with his companions on their dash to the sea in July of 1808, and again on their return trip up the river a few weeks later, the first white men to set foot in the traditional territories of the Lillooet and Nlaka'pamux First Nations.

In the wake of Alexander Mackenzie's historic journey in 1793 across North America to the Pacific Ocean, the North West Company had established a whole network of trading posts—McLeod Lake in 1805, Fort St. James and Fraser Lake in 1806, and Fort George in 1807—across a broad area of central British Columbia the company had dubbed "New Caledonia."

Farther to the south, David Stuart of the rival Pacific Fur Company spent the winter of 1811 to 1812 living and trading among the Secwepemc at the confluence of the North and South Thompson rivers. He returned that spring with colleague Alexander Ross to establish a permanent trading post. Not to be outdone, Joseph Laroque of the North West Company established a rival post, also in 1812. A year later the North West Company absorbed the Pacific Fur Company, only to be itself absorbed, in 1821, by the Hudson's Bay Company (HBC).

For the next thirty years the HBC was a presence in the valleys of southern interior British Columbia, trading not so much for furs as for provisions, particularly dried salmon, and in later years, more ominously, for gold. In fact, Fort Kamloops turned out to be a less-than-profitable trading post, maintained mostly as a way station for the Company's annual fur brigades, which carried goods out of New Caledonia and brought in fresh supplies, until the gold rushes of the 1850s and 1860s changed everything.

It's worth remembering that in the sixty-five years between Alexander Mackenzie's journey in 1793 and the abrupt arrival of gold seekers in 1858, the incomers were never more than a limited and scattered presence in southern interior British Columbia, resident only at the indulgence of the various First Nations.

Fur traders lived for the trade, bottom line. They were dependent on the goodwill of First Nations for the supply of furs and other trade items, for daily provisions and sometimes even for physical safety. It was not in a trader's interest to attempt any interference with First Nations communities or with the indigenous culture of those communities.

Which is not to say that First Nations communities were unaffected by the fur trade. The availability of a whole range of novel trade goods together with the introduction of horses at about the same time must have worked a profound change on the traditional way of life. Old respected skills, old ways of doing things, would have been suddenly passé. And the change from a culture based on subsistence to a culture based on commerce must have worked an even more profound and insidious change, not merely in the *way* things were done but in *why* they were done. The pursuit of wealth and status led to substantial changes in the relationships between different bands and communities, with some groups giving up subsistence activities to attend and defend their new and lucrative role as middlemen in the trade. It must have played havoc with the tradition of shared resources.

It seems to me that the arrival of the fur trade also triggered or foreshadowed a profound change in the relationship between human beings and the natural world in southern interior British Columbia. Of course indigenous peoples had been practised traders of natural resources for millennia before Alexander Mackenzie showed up. A given. But there's a fundamental difference between trading within a small community for subsistence items and trading with the HBC. In a small community there's a natural limit to the demand for subsistence items. But there's virtually no limit to trade with the HBC. They're supplying the world. Those first transactions, the awakening of that commercial imperative, represent the first steps down a long crooked road that leads eventually to that giant hole in the ground outside Kamloops or the vast clear-cuts of the upper Nicola watershed or the devastated rangelands on Mount Kobau. The no-holds-barred, down-to-the-last-tree exploitation of the natural world in pursuit of profit.

I come upon a domestic hen picking her way down the side of the road and I can't help thinking, *Now that is a free-range chicken.* Truant, I suppose, from the farmstead I've just passed, a little cottage with a bit of an orchard around the kitchen door and a picket fence. Nice.

My weather break evaporates as the afternoon wears on. Skies clear. The sun blazes down. The shimmering air over the blacktop gets warmer and warmer as I approach Lillooet. It all seems thoroughly appropriate for the official location of Canada's hottest recorded day: July 16, 1941, a toasty 44.4°C. I'm finishing this part of the walk none too soon and will hope for cooler weather when I come back in early September to do the next section north from Lillooet along the Fraser River.

Those who contemplate the beauty of the earth find
reserves of strength that will endure as long as life lasts.
　　　　　　　—Rachel Carson, "The Sense of Wonder"

But, look, the morn in russet mantle clad,
Walks o'er the dew of yon high eastward hill
　　　　　　　—William Shakespeare, *Hamlet*

I believe a leaf of grass is no less than the journey-work of
the stars.

　　　　　　　—Walt Whitman, "Leaves of Grass"

6

Straight Up and Straight Down— Early Autumn along the Fraser

Fraser River valley looking south toward Watson Bar

DAY FORTY-NINE
Friday, August 22: Lillooet to Six Mile Rapids

It's still only mid-morning when I cross the picturesquely named Bridge of the Twenty-Three Camels at Lillooet—commemorating an odd episode from the gold rush years of the 1860s—and hike up the hill through the little town on the far side of the Fraser River. Already the day is warmer than I would wish.

I'm back a little earlier than I'd planned. It's a long hike from Lillooet to Williams Lake, at least 150 kilometres as the crow flies and quite a bit farther on foot through the rugged country along the river. This is the wildest, most remote and most uncertain part of the whole journey. Once under way I'm more or less committed. I want to be sure of finishing before the first storms of autumn blow in. So I've decided to get a head start.

The little town of Lillooet has an extraordinarily rich history and prehistory. It sits at the very entrance to a dramatic gap in the Coast Mountains through the deep valleys of Seton Lake and Anderson Lake, a natural passageway. Through many thousands of years of prehistory (and even into the early historic period, until superseded by the Cariboo Wagon Road and Dewdney Trail in the 1860s) this was by far the most important trade route from coastal British Columbia to the southwest interior of the province.

The Lillooet First Nation comprises two main divisions: the lower Lillooet, living in the Lillooet River valley at the other end of that gap through the mountains, and the upper Lillooet, living on Anderson Lake and Seton Lake and along the Fraser River near the present-day town of Lillooet, at this end of the gap.

The lower Lillooet were said to have coastal affinities, culturally speaking, acquired from long dealings with neighbouring tribes, the Squamish, Sechelt and Klahoose. The upper Lillooet had more in common with other interior plateau cultures, the Nlaka'pamux and Secwepemc. But even the upper Lillooet showed greater coastal influence than other interior tribes: a more stratified society, privileged access to some resources and a semblance of the kinship groups or "clans" reminiscent of northwest coast culture.

The upper Lillooet, especially those living along the Fraser River, were twice blessed by a geography that gave them control over a major trade route *and* access to the best salmon-fishing location in the entire Fraser River watershed: the Six Mile Rapids, about fifteen kilometres long, from the mouth of Fountain Creek to the mouth of the Bridge River, three or four kilometres upstream of present-day Lillooet.

All through that section, where the generally north-to-south flowing Fraser River spills sideways through an east-to-west gap at the south end of the Camelsfoot Mountain Range, the channel narrows dramatically between rocky banks. There are riffles and eddies where the salmon can escape for a time from the fierce current. And, providentially, there are also good solid perches from which fishermen can dip-net or gill-net the resting fish. By the time migrating salmon reach this point they are at optimum fatness for preserving. And the hot dry climate makes it possible to wind-dry great quantities of fish without having to resort to smokehouses.

Archeologists believe that the prosperity of Keatley Creek, Bell, Fountain and all the other outsized villages of the classical era rested on fisheries such as this. And even in early historical times the Lillooet village of Fountain, at the head of Six Mile Rapids, was perhaps the most important trading centre on the interior plateau. Every year the Hudson's Bay Company sent horse brigades there to trade for dried salmon.

Not much happening on the rapids today, however, when I go hiking past, along Bridge River Road at first, then branching off to the right to follow the Fraser upstream along the West Pavilion Forest Service Road.

The racks and drying sheds are still in place on the rocky ground at the mouth of the Bridge River, but there are very few people about. And nobody is fishing. It *is* a little early in the season. The river is still low and the fish may be waiting for cooler weather and more water.

But there are other issues.

Apparently the autumn run of sockeye salmon this year is in deep trouble. According to posted messages the fishery is closed until further notice. Bad news by any measure, but especially when viewed from the perspective of a fishery going back thousands upon thousands of years. On this very spot. From these very rocks.

Something is altogether amiss with the world.

By the time I reach the top of the hill above the mouth of Six Mile Rapids it's late afternoon, a very hot day, the heat beating down on me from the rocky slopes overhead. I'm all in. And there's something wrong with my feet; I can feel an ominous prickling down there.

I find a bit of shade under a Douglas-fir and lie back in the grass, just breathing for a moment. I drop off, without really meaning to, and wake to find the sun a little lower in the sky, nightfall coming earlier, thank goodness, now that we're into late August. Time to quit.

The feet are worse than expected, both heels badly blistered. The left, particularly, is raw hamburger. I should have stopped at the first little tingle to protect them with athletic tape, but they didn't feel all that bad. Endorphins, I suppose. Or impatience. Or maybe just fatigue. I tape them now, cleaning up the damage as well as I can. A classic case of closing the barn door after the horse has gone.

DAY FIFTY
Saturday, August 23: Six Mile Rapids to McKay Creek

Hwah-hwah-hwah. It's a lovely morning with just a hint of autumn in the cool air. I can hear red-breasted nuthatches (*Sitta canadensis*) calling from the Douglas-firs when I wake.

I ease my boots on, gingerly tighten the laces and limp on down the road. At Blackhill Creek I stop to refill the water bottles and re-doctor my feet. I stop at Lee Creek too. Then again at Slok Creek. In fact, I stop at every little creek along the way; any excuse for a break. Happily, as it turns out, there are a fair number of creeks running down out of the Camelsfoot Range, even at this time of year, so there'll be no shortage of water on this section of the hike, a blessing in such hot weather. But it's slow progress. I feel like a cripple hobbling along. (Well, I *am* a cripple hobbling along.)

While I'm resting in the shade at Lee Creek, a car pulls up, stops. The driver steps out and climbs down to the creek to get a drink, filling *his* water bottles and cup from the clear water of the stream. After a moment's mutual surprise at encountering another person in this out-of-the-way place, he introduces himself and we chat for a bit. Then he tips back the cup a last time, wishes me a good day, stoops to rescue a woolly bear caterpillar from where it has marooned itself on a rock in midstream, and is gone. My kind of people.

The valley of the Fraser River is narrower here, a deep trench in the surrounding uplands, quite impressive, especially when seen from a perch on the West Pavilion Forest Service Road, high on the side of the mountain. Far below the ground falls away in a great sheer face to the water, which is a swirling, silty brown even at this time of year. There's a fine view of the ancient village site at Keatley Creek across the river. Through binoculars I can even make out the dimples left where the *kekuli* were dug into the ground.

It's possible, I think, to overstate these things. The archeological reports tend to make the place sound like a metropolis. In actual fact it's just a little meadow covered by several dozen craters where the pit-houses used to be. Not particularly impressive.

But when you consider that most interior plateau archeological sites from that era, the first millennium A.D, boast fewer than five *kekuli* pits, it's clear that something unusual was happening over there.

The present consensus among archeologists seems to be that Keatley Creek village grew and prospered beyond the ordinary measure by trading in dried salmon and by retrading all the other goods that would have come here on exchange, a fairly obvious conclusion.

But research has revealed a tantalizing enigma. The work of Arnoud Stryd, Brian Hayden and others suggests that all the house sites at Keatley Creek were abandoned more or less simultaneously around A.D. 750.

Abandoned after a thousand years of occupation but still over a thousand years before the arrival of European immigrants and European diseases. Abandoned quite calmly and deliberately: no evidence of massacre, no broken bodies, all food storage pits emptied and filled with earth. Abandoned and never reoccupied.

It was a mystery.

Now comes one of those lovely, elegant instances of consilience, where the findings of one science, all unplanned, illuminate another. *Eureka!*

Enter the geologists.

Just opposite Texas Creek, south of Lillooet, far above the river, Highway 12 narrows to one lane across a very steep slope of fractured rock. It's like something out of a past age, that one lane of highway supported by rickety cribbing of splintered timber above the crumbling precipice below. Bits of stone rain down from above. One has a feeling that the whole slope could break loose any moment. And, in fact, geologists June Ryder, Michael Church, Michael Bovis and others, working the ground across the river, have determined that at least two major slides big enough to dam and impound the whole Fraser River have come off that hillside already: the first (and largest) between two and five thousand years ago, the second about twelve hundred years ago.

And here's the thing. The abandonment of the Keatley Creek village and all those other unusually large, classical era Lillooet villages seems to have occurred at about the same time as that second Texas Creek slide. Archeologists speculate that the slide dammed the river, creating a cataract sufficient to seriously impair or destroy the salmon runs on which the prosperity of those villages depended. Six Mile Rapids might have been drowned below the surface of a lake. The villagers abandoning their homes were fleeing not just a geological but an economic catastrophe.

The grasslands of the Fraser valley, from Lillooet north to the confluence of the Fraser and Chilcotin rivers, are not dissimilar to those of the Okanagan-Similkameen or of the Nicola or of the Thompson. There's a family resemblance. Many of the same species dominate. And there's much the same general arrangement of lower and middle grasslands in the bunchgrass zone and upper grasslands in the ponderosa pine zone and Douglas-fir zone.

But there's enough of a difference to create a distinct flavour. The lower grasslands along the river, perhaps because of the extremely rugged terrain, have an aspect to them that is almost fierce, reminiscent of desert badlands, with a heavy growth of prickly pear cactus and (especially on ground recovering from overgrazing) whole meadows dominated by clumps of porcupine grass, aptly named for the barbed, sharp-pointed seeds equipped with enormously long awns that help drive the seeds into the ground (a plant really *worthy* of the sobriquet "spear-grass").

The climate, too, is similar to grasslands farther south. There's a general shortage of soil moisture, with most of the precipitation arriving in the later autumn, winter and spring. Winters are cold. Summers are hot and dry. But conditions here are more extreme than in the valleys farther south. This is the northern limit of Columbia Basin influence. That, together with an intense rain shadow in the lee of the Camelsfoot Range and South Chilcotin Mountains to the west, makes for very hot, very dry summers. And winters are subject to outbreaks of intensely cold polar continental air coming from the north.

It's not surprising, then, given the meeting and mixing of northern and southern climatic influences, that this stretch of valley should host a remarkable mixture of southern and northern species. Quite a number of Columbia Basin species are here at the northern limit of their range. And by the same token there are northern species, more at home on the Fraser and Nechako plateaus, that occur here at the southern limit of *their* ranges.

It's wilder country, too, not exactly pristine but a little less shopworn than the more populated landscapes to the south. In fact, it's an exciting piece of ground. Thrilling. These next few weeks are going to be interesting.

End of the day. Very hot. Very tired. At least my feet are no worse. I'm glad to get horizontal.

DAY FIFTY-ONE
Sunday, August 24: McKay Creek to Leon Creek

I've only just started walking when I decide to abandon the forest service road in favour of a faint sandy track, two ruts, leading off to the right, down toward the terraces above the river. Fiercer country, as I've said, with high steep slopes looming above and a limited view of sky. But it's not a bad day for walking. There's a bit of a breeze in my face, blowing from the north down the river valley. And it's not so hot as it's been. I follow the little ruts in and out, up and down. A set of relatively fresh tire tracks in the sand. Are they going in? Going out? We'll soon see.

The tracks lead me to Little Leon Creek and the remains of a village that might once have been pretty but is now more or less derelict. The log dwellings are going to pieces, but the tiny church, clad in sheet metal, endures. The place is utterly deserted. There's not a soul around of whom I might ask permission or a by-your-leave, so I go on, hoping for goodwill on the part of whoever speaks for this place.

There's nobody in the broken-windowed farmhouse above Leon Creek, either, nor down along the creek itself. I come to the end of the tire tracks, no vehicle. Must have been going out. I'm alone. Lots of old stuff scattered around with an air of sad abandonment.

But the mouth of the creek is an oasis, where clear water emerges from the deep ravine amid a leafy tangle of cottonwoods and alder, and splashes down across a steep gravel beach of rounded cobbles into the river. It's early yet, I could go on, but suddenly I'm in a holiday mood. I feel a little uncomfortable—above the high-water mark is somebody else's property, after all: the Leon Creek Indian Reserve, of the Ts'kw'aylaxw First Nation—but I can't resist the place. The pack comes off. The tent goes up. I bathe in the creek, rinse my clothes, even take the time to sew up a seam that's been unravelling. Most especially I dry and re-bandage my feet. And so, comfortably, to bed.

It is as lovely and dramatic a place as any I've seen on this journey, with the creek splashing down over the cobbles, the river hurtling by just feet away, and a great rocky slope looming up across the water. That slope is still radiating heat, not unwelcome at this time of day. Evening comes early at the end of August, and though the daytime thermometer may still read, emphatically, "summer," once the sun goes behind the mountain a sudden chill in the air says, quite clearly, "fall." I lie awake in the tent, listening to the talking of the nearby creek and river's deep hiss and rumble.

I like it here. I like it a lot. I envy the owners their pretty and agreeable property. I wish it were mine. And that covetous thought raises any number of unhappy echoes from the past in this place.

You have to remember that not very long ago, a little over 150 years, say, this whole valley was the traditional territory of various First Nations, the Nlaka'pamux farther south, the Lillooet here, and not too far to the north, the Secwepemc.

By the summer of 1857 the Hudson's Bay Company already knew there was gold, quite a lot of gold, in the gravel bars along the Fraser and Thompson rivers. The Secwepemc, Nlaka'pamux and Lillooet, all of them well aware by then of the metal's value to the HBC, were bringing quantities of the stuff in to trading posts. (In the spring of 1858, Chief Trader Donald McLean at Kamloops reportedly took in 130 ounces of gold dust over a period of just eighteen days.)

There was no way the company could keep a lid on that kind of information. The first four hundred gold seekers landed in Victoria during April of 1858, en route to the Fraser and Thompson. An estimated thirty thousand more followed through the rest of that spring and summer and autumn, forcing a profound change in the relationship between native peoples and incomers. And also in the relationship between native peoples and the land their ancestors had inhabited for many thousands of years.

Fur traders had been content to insinuate themselves into existing social structures, obtaining whatever goods they wanted by trade. In the fur-trade era, First Nations still possessed and gathered the resources of the country. Even after the discovery of gold, the Hudson's Bay Company encouraged First Nations to work the deposits for themselves. But with the arrival of gold seekers, the incomers and native peoples came into direct competition.

It's not something most British Columbians care to think deeply about. We prefer to picture a cartoon-character geezer with a twinkle in his eye and a cute donkey to carry the gear. But these gold seekers were in many ways the worst sort of people, brutalized by years of living rough in the gold camps of California, Oregon and Washington, ruthless, arrogant, racist, contemptuous of the law, obsessed with the finding of gold and with the dream of get-rich-quick that would catapult them into another, higher level of society. Many had direct experience in the "Indian Wars" south of the forty-ninth parallel.

They weren't interested in trading. They had come to take the wealth of the land for themselves and they were quite prepared to shoulder native peoples aside or sweep them away entirely.

Nlaka'pamux and Lillooet, living on the main points of access from the coast, naturally felt the first and sharpest effects. But the Secwepemc and Okanagan were not long spared, especially when a second wave of incomers—settlers and colonists—followed the gold seekers. Settlers and colonists took the invasion to another level. They were not merely seeking access to natural resources, as prospectors and miners were. Settlers aimed to possess and exploit the land itself. They sought an exclusive right to use and occupation. And in that era what settlers wanted, settlers got, even if First Nations were already in possession.

To his credit, the first governor of the newly created Crown Colony of British Columbia, James Douglas (an ex-HBC chief factor), made substantial efforts to defend First Nations' rights. He issued repeated instructions that the needs of First Nations be protected against the tide of incomers by the establishment of generous reserves (to be specified by the native peoples themselves). During Douglas's tenure native peoples had all the rights of any British citizen. But Douglas faced stiff resistance even within his own administration. And as soon as he left office in 1864, his successors, most notably Joseph Trutch, the colony's newly appointed Chief Commissioner for Lands and Works, and Peter O'Reilly, magistrate (who happened to be Trutch's brother-in-law), set about drastically reducing the size of earlier reserves ("redefining" was the term used) or eliminating them altogether in favour of settler demands. Monstrous injustices were committed.

And how did the land fare through all these dramatic changes? Under new management, so to speak? Not too well I would say. Certainly the comers-from-afar seemed to feel no particular respect for the land. Whole valleys were trashed in the search for gold, and great stretches of grassland destroyed by herds of ravenous cattle.

DAY FIFTY-TWO
Monday, August 25: Leon Creek to Watson Bar Creek

A friend of mine, a nurse, calls it the three-day rule. When a body is injured, whether by disease, by accident or by surgery, if that body is going to recover, it will start to rally on the third day. I'm still moving in low gear this morning but things are definitely looking up. I feel less tired, have fewer aches and pains. And you know what's really astonishing? My feet seem to be healing even as I hike. Isn't that remarkable? Isn't that amazing?

There's a nice view from the edge of the ravine, looking back upstream along Leon Creek: a river of cottonwoods and birches and Douglas maples winding down out of the mountains, brilliant green in a landscape of burnt browns and greys. A covey of Chukar partridge (*Alectoris chukar*) moves back under the cover of scattered big sage bushes above the river. I'm not sure if I've left the reserve yet. Perhaps it doesn't really matter. The whole landscape resonates to the issues and the history and the stories represented by that reserve. You can't be here and not think about such things.

It wasn't long before a cascade of further developments robbed First Nations of any power they might have had to intervene directly against the changes crowding upon them.

For one thing, the demographic advantage that native peoples enjoyed in the early colonial years soon evaporated. In 1880, native peoples still held a population majority in the province of British Columbia. A decade later the proportion of natives in the province's population had fallen to less than a third, with the number of non-natives in BC nearly doubling in those ten years between 1880 and 1890.

(Of course that profound shift from majority to minority status would have occurred even earlier in the more settled and populated districts: southern Vancouver Island, the Cariboo and the Fraser, Thompson and Okanagan valleys.)

Nor was it simply a question of invading numbers or the gold seekers' greed or the settlers' hunger for land. As that overwhelming tide of incomers flooded up through the valleys and across the plateaus of British Columbia, First Nations found themselves increasingly dependent on the colonial administration and, subsequently, the provincial government to intercede on their behalf against the never-ending demands and importunities of the immigrants.

But First Nations' reliance on the honesty and reliability and good-will of government proved seriously ill-founded. From earliest days, and most especially after the departure of James Douglas, all the efforts of First Nations to secure some sort of redress and protection against the changes being forced on them were resisted and deflected and sabotaged by governments that were, in fact, deeply prejudiced against native peoples.

Even after confederation with Canada in 1871, when the Crown Colony of British Columbia became the Province of British Columbia and native peoples might have expected a bit of relief, based on the (slightly) more enlightened policies of the Canadian federal government, provincial politicians and bureaucrats like Trutch and O'Reilly worked ceaselessly to foil any reform.

The Federal–Provincial Commission established in 1876 to address native grievances was systematically blocked, hampered, resisted and forestalled in every way until 1880, when Gilbert Malcolm Sproat was forced to resign as Chief Commissioner and the Province took control with the appointment of Peter O'Reilly as his replacement.

Almost as soon as Sproat was out of the picture, the few new reserves that the Commission had negotiated began to be "redefined."

As a community, British Columbians are still suffering the consequences of injustices perpetrated during those early decades. The ongoing land claims of the various First Nations will take years and years to sort out, and may never be satisfactorily resolved, the whole process costing the community endless effort and resources that might have been better spent.

Watson Bar Creek turns out to be quite a bit larger than Leon Creek, with a watershed that reaches far back into the Camelsfoot Range. I've been hoping all day for an oasis like the one I enjoyed yesterday evening. But I'm doomed to disappointment. Watson Bar Creek is evidently subject to periodic heavy flooding. The whole lower valley is "blown out," a waste of braided channels, piled gravel and scraps of tangled brush. I end up camping again on a bit of beach just above the river, near the mouth of the creek, but it's not quite the same experience.

DAY FIFTY-THREE
Tuesday, August 26:
Watson Bar Creek to Chisholm Canyon

The route ahead is unclear. I'd like to stay close to the river but the valley narrows dramatically to the north (that's Chisholm Canyon up there) and the ground is very steep. The map shows no hint of a track. Even through binoculars I can see no obvious way forward.

What I *can* see just ahead, spreading across the broad terraces on the other side of Watson Bar Creek, are the green hayfields of the Ward Creek Ranch and, down below, sheltered beneath steep banks in a bend of the river, the buildings and corrals of the home place.

As it happens, I have a name for the owner of that ranch, given me by mutual friends: Chris Albeitz.

I've made a point of avoiding the company of human beings on this journey. My business is with the countryside. But I badly need advice; it's time to make an exception.

As always, I'm astonished by the kindness of strangers. The man invites me in, gives me iced tea to drink and then finds a scrap of paper to sketch out a route that will take me north along the edge of the river and above the worst of the canyon to rejoin the West Pavilion Forest Service Road where it starts downhill toward the ferry at Big Bar.

By the time I reach the top of the ridge above the canyon it's evening and the light is fading fast. But my efforts are amply rewarded by a broad view northward, illuminated by the setting sun shining out across the very stretch of country I'm hoping to traverse in the next few days. That's the Churn Creek Protected Area coming into view for the first time, far up the valley. There may even be a distant glimpse of the Junction Sheep Range Provincial Park's grassy slopes (but the air is hazy and it's hard to be sure). It's a view of the promised land, really, the acme of all these dry valley landscapes, the ultimate destination of the days and weeks and months I've spent walking the trail. Getting close now.

There's a splendid view back south as well, across all the ground I've covered with such toil in the last two or three days (though Leon Creek itself is lost from sight in the twisting and turning of the river valley). It's one of those moments of truth, epiphany, the view from high ground, when past life and future hopes, where we've been and where we're going, merge together.

And surely that's one of the fundamental things landscapes can do for us, beyond exposing us to the transcendent beauty of the natural world. They remind us, as individuals or as a community, of where we've been and they cause us to think about where we're going. They are a mnemonic device, a repository or storehouse of memories, a reminder of the individuals and events, good or ill, with whom or with which they are associated. They furnish us with a sense beyond memory, perhaps, of our common purposes or aspirations or hopes.

Whether happy or sad, the stories that are associated with a particular landscape both inform and illuminate it.

And if my mind over the last few days seems to have been preoccupied by that whole era of contact and conflict between indigenous peoples and the comers-from-afar, I think it must have something to do with the nature of this landscape. History here seems so recent and immediate, all past events compressed, as if each of them might have occurred yesterday, the traces not yet erased, in contrast to the more settled and developed regions of the province where early events have been thoroughly overlain and effaced by other more recent developments.

I'm still thinking about that little church at Leon Creek.

Any impulse First Nations might have had to resist the changes being forced upon them in the second half of the nineteenth century were subject to a kind of "one-two-three" knockout punch. First came the tide of gold seekers and settlers, then conniving governments, then the Christian Church and its missionaries.

I do not subscribe to the view that missionaries were all monsters or fanatics or sadists. I think in most cases they were fundamentally decent individuals, products of their age, self-sacrificing, who devoted whole lifetimes to what they saw as a highly moral, eleventh-hour effort to save an otherwise doomed people.

Missionaries—notably the Reverend William Sebright Green; the Reverend George Hills, Bishop of Columbia; the Reverend J.B. Good at Lytton; and Father C.J. Grandidier, an Oblate missionary in the Cariboo—proved, not infrequently, to be the era's outstanding spokesmen and advocates for First Nations' interests, lone voices in the white community against government malfeasance or neglect.

But when all is said and done, the fundamental effect of their efforts was to further suppress any impulse of resistance and to reconcile First Nations to the changes in their way of life. Missionaries taught the dangerous habit of obedience to higher authority. They sought to bring First Nations into compliance with colonial and then provincial objectives.

On occasion, missionaries even acted as direct agents of government policy. The Federal-Provincial Commission recruited Father Grandidier, for example, to persuade the Adams Lake Indian Band not to join a meeting of other chiefs but to stay home and negotiate separately for a reserve.

I can't help thinking, though, that native peoples themselves had to acquiesce in all of that, willingly, even eagerly perhaps, when the old gods and the old ways seemed to have lost their power. The church and its missionaries had no influence over their congregations other than what the people themselves chose to give. Government had pomp and the law and soldiers and carrots to dangle. Missionaries had only talk and promises of a better life to come, which may have proven, I suppose, more potent and enduring than guns in the end. Witness the ironclad church in the little abandoned village above Leon Creek.

DAY FIFTY-FOUR
Wednesday, August 27:
Chisholm Canyon to French Bar Canyon

All around my tent this morning the rabbit-brush (*Chrysothamnus nauseosus*) is in full bloom The brilliant golden-yellow of the flowers (part of the essential flavour of British Columbia's southern interior in September and October) is in sharp contrast to the muted sun-bleached greys and browns of the landscape (including the rest of the rabbit-brush plant), giving something of the quality of a hand-tinted photograph to the scene.

The genus name *Chrysothamnus* means golden-crowned. The species name *nauseosus* refers, a little harshly I think, to the plant's cloying sweet smell, which I rather like. Reminds me of balsamroot, a hint of cinnamon, but more intense.

The West Pavilion Forest Service Road runs very steeply downhill for many kilometres, from the Reynolds Ranch at the crest of the hill to the Big Bar reaction ferry on the river. The sign warns motorists of a 17-percent grade ahead. I'm almost glad I'm walking.

I don't suppose the Big Bar ferry sees an awful lot of traffic. And whatever traffic there is must arrive at irregular intervals. Naturally, therefore, the ferry operates on demand rather than according to some fixed schedule. When I arrive it is docked, as usual, on the far side of the river, the east side. Some time passes before anybody notices me. (I'll bet they don't get many riders turning up on foot.) Eventually there's a stir, the clank of the ramp coming up, and the ferry moves away from the far bank and into the stream without any sound I can hear above the rustle and hiss of the river flowing by.

A reaction ferry is held in place by lines running from pulleys on a heavy cable strung across the river upstream of the ferry. The operator sets the vessel in motion by turning the rudders so that the hulls of the ferry are angled out, into and across the current. On arrival at the opposite bank, the ferryman adjusts the rudders again to direct the hulls straight back into the current and the ferry slows to a stop.

Once I'm safely aboard and the ramps come up again, I find myself waiting for the engine's rev and roar to signal impending departure and send us on our way. The usual thing. But no, there's a little extra rustle of turbulence around the hull as it turns back into the current and we're moving. It's almost startling, that quiet motion. Magic! And very economical, too, I should think. Except for a little outboard on the lifeboat, there is no engine. (It's not simply that the engine isn't running. There *is no* engine.)

The ferryman, David Garrett, proves extremely helpful. Business is slow this afternoon, so we repair to his office and living quarters. First things first. Reassurance for my watchers via radiotelephone: I've made it safely thus far. Then ice water to drink! Oh luxury! And a refill for my bottles as well. And a big slice of honeydew melon!

About the route north, my particular concern, he has less to offer. Apparently there is a clear track along the west side of the Fraser from Big Bar to French Bar Creek. But beyond that, route finding gets a little trickier. Apparently, years ago, Garrett rode with a local rancher, Ron Cable, all the way to Cable's place up the Lone Cabin Creek valley. That sounds promising, as far as it goes.

"Stay high," Garrett warns before taking me back across the river. "Stay well above the broken ground down by the water."

I end up settling for the night on a broad sandbar at the lower end of French Bar Canyon. It's tricky, camping in the lower grasslands of the Fraser Canyon. There's cactus everywhere. Not easy to find a clear spot to pitch the tent.

The dead pines on the slope above the river are (or were) ponderosa or yellow pine, very near the northern end of their range here. They were big beautiful trees, prime examples. I take their loss personally. That hillside, otherwise so dry and bleak, would have had an altogether different flavour to it when they were green and thriving. The world was a lovelier place with them alive. Death is the fate of all living things, I suppose, but it saddens me nevertheless.

And the grief doesn't stop there.

A friend of mine, Doug Banks, once took me flying in a small plane out across the pine forests of the Chilcotin Plateau, a little farther to the north. From the air, as far as the eye could see, from horizon to horizon, that forest was red. And farther north, along the Blackwater River, valley after valley, grey. It was monstrous.

I've been doing some reading.

For all the harm they've done, mountain pine beetles (*Dendroctonus ponderosae*) are tiny creatures, 3.7 to 7.5 millimetres long, with stout cylindrical bodies. Rice-grain sized. Little, black, fat rice grains. Except for a brief period when the young adults emerge from their natal trees and take to the air (seeking fresh victims), mountain pine beetles pass their entire existence within the sapwood of their host trees. They live life in four stages: egg, larva, pupa and adult. And the timing of their life cycle depends on ambient temperature. Under ordinary circumstances, in those areas of British Columbia subject to mountain pine beetle outbreaks, the beetles complete precisely one life cycle, one generation, every year.

Eggs are laid in late July to mid-August and hatch in approximately one week. The larvae feed through the autumn, overwinter in their galleries and resume feeding with warmer temperatures in the spring. They transform into pupae by June. New adults emerge from the pupae in late June to mid-July. After a week or two of maturation, they burrow out through the bark of their host trees and take to the air, seeking a new host. If all goes well for them, they will burrow into the sapwood of the target tree, mate and lay the next crop of eggs.

If the host tree is heavily infested, the larval galleries effectively girdle it, cutting off the flow of sap and killing the tree.

This strangling of the host is no incidental part of the business;

it's an essential part of *Dendroctonus ponderosae*'s strategy, effectively putting an end to the host tree's resistance.

And the beetle is assisted in the dirty deed by a couple of fellow travellers, two species of blue stain fungus (*Ophiostoma clavigerum* and *O. montium*). The dispersing adult beetles carry fungal spores from their natal trees to new hosts where the spores germinate quickly. Fungal filaments penetrate living cells in both phloem and xylem, further hampering the flow of sap.

And here's an interesting thing. Part of the maturation process of young adult beetles is a period of feeding on blue stain fungus, which seems essential for the development of flight muscles. At the same time, special pouches built into the beetles' mouthparts are charged with fungal spores for transport to the new host. It's a true symbiosis.

The timing of emergence is mostly governed by temperature. The beetles can fly between 19°C and 41°C, but the optimum is between 22°C and 32°C. Within that optimum range the tendency to fly increases with light intensity and relative humidity, decreases with windy conditions.

If there is wind, beetles will disperse downwind. Most will settle within a couple of days and within a relatively local area, but if there are suitable convective winds, a few may be carried many tens or even hundreds of kilometres.

DAY FIFTY-FIVE
Thursday, August 28:
French Bar Canyon to French Bar Creek

It's eight-thirty in the morning, exactly, when the sun finally touches the tent, lighting it up, making the world a brighter, friendlier place. Morning comes late at the bottom of the valley. I can hear the clatter of leaves on the little cottonwoods outside, moving in light air, shadow dancing on the wall of the tent.

The trail to French Bar Creek, across the high terrace that Dave Garrett called "Miller Flats," proves straightforward, just as promised, though it's washed out in a couple of places on the steep bank above the rapids at the mouth of French Bar Canyon. The Fraser at this point appears to be flowing across the top of a sunken ridge, creating a great wave that extends almost the entire width of the river. Looks impressive enough from high on the hill. Down at water level it must loom like a mountain.

There are decisions to be made. It's still only early afternoon when I reach French Bar Creek. Lone Cabin Creek can't be much more than twelve or fifteen kilometres farther up the valley, a distance I could easily cover before nightfall, all other things being equal. But the way ahead is uncertain and I'm uneasy.

I decide to declare a half-holiday. I want a whole day to tackle the trickier section of the route ahead. And, besides, I'll be glad to spend a sunny afternoon hanging out here.

French Bar Creek, like Watson Bar Creek, is evidently subject to major periodic flooding. The flats at the mouth of the creek are a broad expanse of mostly barren rock and gravel. But for now the water is clear and dazzling in the warm sunshine and it's a pleasure just to sit beside the stream, enjoying the happy sound and the play of light on the glistening many-coloured stones. I rinse my clothing and bathe, noting with satisfaction (and still some amazement) that both feet are now completely healed. I read my book and watch a little spotted sandpiper (*Actitis macularius*) foraging along the edge of the stream.

"Spotted" is both a name and a descriptor. Spotted sandpipers *are* spotted on breast and flanks, at least through the breeding season. This is the common little sandpiper that walks with an odd exaggerated bobbing motion, almost mechanical, like a tic. It forages for a bit, then takes flight for a short distance, a few quick wingbeats, then a glide, with wings held stiffly downward.

On the slopes above the mouth of French Bar Creek, more dead pines, dry and lifeless, needles faded red. Beetle-killed pines stay more or less green for almost a year after being attacked and killed. Then the needles turn red, fade over the course of two or three years, and fall. The end result is bare and grey, sad, a forest of standing dead trees. But the trees are already long gone when you first see red.

Under normal circumstances, *Dendroctonus ponderosae* is just one of many species of bark beetle that prey on the various native species of pine. Mature, healthy pines are well able to fend off the attack, mostly by walling off and smothering the attacking beetles with resin and dead tissue. Consequently, the various species of bark beetle, including mountain pine beetle, are restricted to trees that are at some disadvantage. Since resistance increases with age and size, younger, smaller trees are most commonly infested. Drought and injury also increase the risk of infection. Beetle populations are strictly limited by the number of suitable hosts and tend to persist at a low steady level.

But mountain pine beetles have evolved a strategy that allows them to break free of those limitations. If a sufficient number of beetles can be brought to simultaneously attack a single tree, the defences of that tree, even a full-sized, healthy, mature tree, can be overcome by killing it, stopping the flow of resin.

Mountain pine beetles can achieve that kind of coordination, partly through temperature-sensitive regulation of life-cycle development (so that all the young adults emerge for dispersal at more or less the same time) and partly through olfactory cues, kairomones and pheromones, that focus the attack on a few particular trees.

There are enormous advantages for the species in being able to exploit full-size trees. A four-fold increase in tree diameter, from ten to forty centimetres, yields a forty-fold increase in larval production.

Foresters recognize four phases in mountain pine beetle

populations: *Endemic*, where annual survival is just adequate to balance mortality; *Incipient-Epidemic*, where populations have achieved sufficient numbers to successfully attack full-sized mature trees, but can yet be suppressed, returned to endemic phase by adverse conditions; *Epidemic* (or *Outbreak*), in which the infestation, no longer localized, spreads rapidly across the landscape, out of control barring the occurrence of lethally cold temperatures, and continuing until most or all of the susceptible trees have been colonized and killed; *Post-Epidemic* (or *Declining*).

The different life phases of *Dendroctonus ponderosae* differ in their vulnerability to cold. Eggs are killed by sapwood temperatures of -18°C, for example, but pupae and adults can survive to -34°C. Larvae, depending on age and the degree of cold adaptation (the accumulation of glycerol in body fluids with the onset of winter), can survive to -40°C.

Temperature is important in other ways. If the climate is too cold or too hot, mountain pine beetles lose the perfect timing and precise coordination on which mass attack depends, and they never get out of hand, never break free of Endemic or perhaps Incipient-Epidemic levels.

Perhaps that explains why the big pine beside my Nesikep campsite south of Lillooet was still thriving. Too hot down there for the beetles to go crazy.

All this means that entomologists are able to use climate records to predict just which areas of the countryside are most vulnerable to mountain pine beetle epidemics. Too cold and the life cycle is stretched or the beetles are killed outright. Too warm and the life cycle is thrown off the other way. But where temperatures are just right, sooner or later the outbreak will take off like wildfire, sweeping across the countryside.

Thing is, conditions seem to be changing. Areas to the south, once prime candidates for mountain pine beetle epidemics, seem no longer vulnerable: the incidence of outbreaks has declined. Areas to the north, like the Chilcotin Plateau, epicentre of the present monster outbreak, the largest ever recorded, which were once too cold for mountain pine beetle epidemics, are now in the bull's eye.

And there is real concern, with changing climates, that vast areas of jack pine (*Pinus banksiana*) in boreal Canada (not to mention boreal pines throughout the northern hemisphere) could become vulnerable to *Dendroctonus ponderosae* epidemics, with the eventual, inevitable result: a plague of truly biblical proportions.

DAY FIFTY-SIX
Friday, August 29: French Bar Creek

Morning is autumn-chilly. The tent is dark. I go through all the usual preparations still bundled in my warm sleeping bag. Eating breakfast. Bringing the log up to date. Waiting for the sun to rise and light up my life.

Waiting.

Then, suddenly, I'm startled by a loud *thwock* coming from somewhere a few centimetres above my head. Something heavy bouncing off the tent-fly by the sound of it. Then, again, *thwock*. What could it be, way out here in the open? I unzip the tent and the fly and poke my head out for a look.

Rain, that's what.

I can hardly believe my eyes. The sky is completely overcast, the hills are shrouded with mist. Somebody has stolen the good weather while I slept. What a dirty trick!

Admittedly I've been taking the weather a bit too much for granted lately. That's a dangerous habit to get into. But when it's so lovely for so long, one becomes accustomed.

And there was absolutely no reason last night, a beautiful evening (apart from an odd rising wind after days of relative calm, now that I think about it), to expect anything other than another gorgeous blue-sky sunrise this morning.

By nine o'clock the rain is falling in earnest and I'm pretty sure that my trail, deep glacial silt, will already be too muddy and slippery for walking. There goes the ball game. Make a new plan, Stan.

Easier said than done.

Everything depends on how long this continues.

It's a thirsty country and we've had a bit of a drought. The ground could dry quickly if the rain stops soon enough; I might still get away today. On the other hand, I'm determined to bide my time until the trail is good and dry. Hate slipping and sliding. For now, anyway, there seems little I can do but hang out and see how things develop. I retreat back into the sleeping bag to read and doze.

I come awake again to find that the rain has stopped and the sky seems to be brightening. I pull on my boots for a bit of a walkabout. Everything is thoroughly wet, the sand soaked to a depth of maybe two centimetres. And, you know, if I weren't so concerned about covering more ground, moving on up the trail, I could enjoy this. In such dry country, the smell of wetness, wet soil, wet rocks, wet vegetation, is a beautiful thing, as I've said before, intoxicating, almost exhilarating. Cool, slightly acrid, moist. So different from the rest of my experience over this past week. Makes you want to breathe deep. And the place has an altogether different appearance veiled in mist: moody, almost mysterious, quite lovely (though the dead pines on the hill above the creek look all the more forlorn).

Still, the urge to go forward is almost irresistible. There's an edge of panic, a sense of being stuck here with time a-wasting. I can see a little patch of blue sky. Should I take a chance?

It's already noon. One swallow doesn't make a summer and one little patch of blue sky doesn't mean an end to the storm. Patience. Back to the tent.

Clouds roll in again. The blue sky disappears. About three o'clock in the afternoon, the heavens open. Very heavy rain with thunder and lightning. A front going through, perhaps. My decision to sit tight is confirmed and validated. Patience rewarded. Tomorrow's another day. Think about something else: those forlorn pines on the hill, perhaps. What's to be done? How do we deal with forests of dead pine?

Salvage logging is an attempt to mitigate the fire hazard posed by all those dead pines, and to retrieve something of their economic value.

It's hard to argue with that.

Even so, I'm not altogether convinced that it's always the best course. For one thing, there are significant ecological costs to salvage operations. Remember that even though the pines are dead, everything else in that bit of habitat remains intact until the feller-bunchers and bulldozers start romping around. From what I've seen, the equipment more or less trashes the whole ecosystem. And, of course, clear-cutting destroys surviving trees of whatever species and whatever age so that "reforestation" has to start from scratch. Even the loss of dead stems and roots is a cost: they would have helped stabilize the soil, providing shelter and organic material to nourish the next generation of trees.

Better to leave it alone, perhaps.

If we left these beetle-killed stands unlogged, the ground would be undisturbed, ready for planting, and the rest of the ecosystem would already be in place, intact and thriving, with the soil and drainage undamaged. The microclimate would still be relatively moderate, certainly compared to a clear-cut. And there would already be young pines, spruces and firs growing, with years of a head start on anything a tree planter could plug into the ground. It will be interesting in the next twenty, thirty, forty, fifty years to compare clear-cut beetle-salvage areas to non-clear-cut and see which are furthest ahead in terms of forest regeneration. My money is on the unlogged ground.

Even the economic value of beetle-salvage seems doubtful, at least for the owners of the resource (that's us). A salvage operation doesn't just take dead pines. It takes all the live ones, too. And it takes any other species that happen to be growing in the cutblock. And on all that timber, infected or healthy, live or dead, pine or not pine, operators pay the beetle-salvage rate of stumpage, virtually nothing. A sweet deal, but not for the people of British Columbia who own the resource.

I'm not even convinced that dead pines, especially once they've lost their needles, are more flammable in the full heat of summer than live pines bursting with resinous sap. Maybe that's just one of those handy assumptions that go round and round until they have the ring of common sense. I don't doubt that once the dead, dry stems are on fire, they burn intensely; certainly they make excellent firewood. But I wonder how dead stands compare with live stands in terms of how readily they catch fire and how rapidly the fire spreads.

Something else troubles me about beetle-salvage logging: I can't see that dragging infected stems all over the countryside is a very good idea. Infected logs often end up at mills or log yards hundreds of miles from where they were cut. I find myself wondering to what extent this monstrous outbreak has spread on the great rolling wheels of logging trucks as well as the busy little wings of the beetles themselves.

By evening, substantial clearing, a beautiful rain-washed sky, sunlight on the mountains. Sand now soaked to five centimetres. Trail slick with mud. No decisions until the morning.

DAY FIFTY-SEVEN
Saturday, August 30:
French Bar Creek to Bunchgrass Mountain

It's a go! The tent-fly is still soaking wet, of course, and some of the other gear, but I wake to mostly clear skies. After breakfast I sponge away the excess moisture and possess myself in patience, waiting for the pale sun to do the rest. Not such a bad thing, anyway, this bit of delay. The trail will be that much drier.

And here's another bit of luck. I've been anxious about finding my way on this part of the walk, but here, running up the trail in front of me, absolutely unexpected in this out-of-the-way place, freshly planted on the rain-pocked earth, are the tracks of a horse, shod, and a small canine. A mounted cowboy and his dog, I deduce. (*It's elementary, my*

dear Watson.) They must have gone past while I was hiding in the tent, eating breakfast and waiting for the gear to dry.

He (that may be an unwarranted assumption on my part, could be "she" I suppose) will know the trail. I will follow him/her. Problem solved.

As things turn out, it's fortunate I have some sort of guide because I'd never have found the way otherwise. Even with a guide it's a nerve-wracking climb out of French Bar Creek onto the relatively flat benchland above, with the trail threading its way along the sharp exposed crest of one hogback clay ridge after another. The ground is still quite soft from the rain and I know that if I once start to slide and tumble, I'll not be able to stop.

Things are more straightforward once I reach the terraces above. I begin to relax. A good trail up here and not a bad day for walking: broken cloud and much cooler, but enough sunshine to dry the vegetation and keep my spirits up.

The farther north I go, high along the side of the valley, the nicer the habitat: a parkland of widely spaced Douglas-firs, beautiful old trees, and a rich growth of bluebunch wheatgrass. "Bunchgrass Mountain," Dave Garrett, the ferryman back at Big Bar, had called it, describing his ride with Ron Cable, and for once there's nothing ironic about the name.

Time travel, that's what I'm experiencing here.

Not so very long ago the whole Fraser valley from Lillooet to Williams Lake would have looked like this. Ditto the Thompson. Ditto the Nicola. Ditto the Okanagan and Similkameen. It's a blessing that some of the good stuff survives into our own time. It's a privilege to see it and I'm grateful.

I meet my cowboy as he comes riding back down along the trail, herding a little bunch of heifers. Turns out to be the man himself, Ron Cable. We stop and chat for a bit.

Cable's reputation precedes him, as the expression goes. Said to be an *hombre muy duro*, bit of a wild man. But on this morning I find him courteous and affable. We talk a little about my long walk, getting on toward the finish now. He offers me the use of his place on Lone Cabin Creek if I can get that far this evening. ("Make yourself at home!") He does warn me that it's fairly steep going down into the ravine.

I say something about not having the best of traction with my light shoes and heavy pack. He allows that a man on horseback can go places where a man on foot would have difficulty. "But cows," he says, "cows, if they have a mind to, can go places that even a horse wouldn't go." Four legs. Two hooves per leg. Better than cleats. Those cloven hooves twist and turn and dig into the ground. All those edges.

As if to demonstrate, some of the heifers seize this moment to bolt. Straight down the hill they go. It's *steep*. Any steeper and the grass would have trouble hanging on. "Rugged country," says Cable, as a sort of disinterested, laconic observation, and takes off after them.

I reflect that the man must have considerable faith in his horse. And it must know its business. I notice he pretty much gives the beast its head. Some general direction, not a lot of close supervision. A superior management strategy. They're quickly out of sight and I turn to carry on.

That's the good part. The bad part is that the weather seems to be deteriorating again. It's pretty much overcast now, with the odd spit of moisture. Another turn of the screw. In fact, by the time I climb down off Bunchgrass Mountain and reach Lone Cabin Creek, it's raining lightly. Just a shower, soon past, but it leaves me feeling damp and chilly. Discouraged.

Thing is, I still haven't quite made it to Lone Cabin Creek.

I'm standing on the south edge of a deep canyon with Lone Cabin

Creek far below, hurrying down over the rocks toward the Fraser. Fortunately the trail is clear enough. It turns and heads upstream along the creek valley, across the steep slopes just above the canyon. Very steep slopes. The grass here *is* having trouble hanging on. Any steeper you'd need mountaineering gear. And I can see that part of the trail up ahead has sloughed away into the canyon. It's gone.

I know that Cable drives cattle through here. He told me so. And I believe him. But he isn't driving them along that trail. They must have come down across the steep grassy slope above the gap. This is what he was talking about. All those hooves working overtime, hanging on for dear life.

I want to go forward. I *need* to go forward. There's no other way. The rest of the countryside is straight up and down. What's left of my project, the climax of the whole trip, Churn Creek Protected Area, Gang Ranch country, Farwell Canyon, Junction Sheep Range Provincial Park, all of it, depends on me getting myself across that steep grassy slope. Everything I've worked toward, all that effort, all those days and weeks and kilometres on the trail.

But there's no way. Can't do it.

I couldn't climb out onto that grass if my soul depended on it.

Of course there are some perfectly sensible reasons why I shouldn't attempt this little passage right now. On this north-facing slope the ground is still soft from yesterday's rain and the trail is already greasy from the little shower just past. And that slope really is *very* steep. Even if the ground didn't actually give way and tumble into the canyon, the grass will be slippery with moisture. And my traction with light boots and heavy pack is not good.

Moreover, the consequences of a fall here hardly bear thinking about. If I survived the drop, I'd likely wish I hadn't. Nobody is going to miss me for a couple of weeks. And even once they start looking it would take them days to find me down there. (Fortunately, lying broken in the rain, I probably wouldn't last more than a few hours. And I'd welcome the oblivion when it came.)

But my reaction goes way beyond the prudent weighing of pros and cons, even beyond the normal anxiety of such a situation. I'm spooked. I've actually started shaking. Doubtless that's due in some measure to the damp and the cold. Also to fatigue and lack of food. But mostly it's fear, plain and simple, pure terror.

Never have I felt such a certain sense of my own death waiting for me on the trail, right there. Maybe it's premonition, second sight, an absolute certainty of what will happen if I start out across that slope. My feet will slip out from under me. I'll be left clinging to the wet grass, the heavy pack pulling at my shoulders. The grass will tear and I'll start to slide toward the brink. Say goodbye, Charlie.

So I turn and retreat. Flee, actually. Not quite running, thank goodness for that, preserving the last shreds of self-respect. (The monster pack wouldn't allow it anyway.) But certainly getting the hell out of there just as fast as I can. It's shameful. It's embarrassing. But I can't help it.

Once I'm clear of the steep bit and my heart rate slows a little, the sensible part of me clears its throat and speaks up: *Well, now, just wait a minute here. This will all look better in the morning. Let's have a little time out. Get your tent up, get some food, get warm, get some sleep.*

The part of me that's like a frightened horse can see the wisdom of all that, so I go looking for some place to pitch the tent and soon spot a nice level terrace perched high above the mouth of the creek, right at the edge of the canyon. Very picturesque, with nice views up and down the river valley. That'll do. But when I get there it turns out to be a flourishing field of prickly pear cactus from one edge to the other.

Okay, says the sensible part, *that's no good. What we need is something a little higher on the slope of the valley, a little more altitude. Perhaps somewhere back along the trail a bit . . .*

By the time I finally dump the pack I'm back at Bunchgrass Mountain, practically halfway to French Bar Creek, and it's getting dark. I set up the tent, mostly by braille, and crawl into the bag, way too tired to eat (though I know I'd be better for a bite). Mostly what I want is a drink of water. I've only one full bottle left from this morning and there's no creek here. Time to start rationing. Just a couple of mouthfuls to wet my whistle.

And tomorrow? Who knows? I'm not looking forward to hiking all the way back to Lone Cabin Creek for another look. Perhaps I'll feel differently in the morning, especially if I wake up to blue skies and sunshine. The alternative, hiking back to French Bar Creek with my tail between my legs, is even less attractive.

Either way, it's going to be thirsty work.

DAY FIFTY-EIGHT
Sunday, August 31: Bunchgrass Mountain

It's a restless night. Takes me forever to fall asleep. I'm terribly thirsty and fretting a good deal about my decision at Lone Cabin Creek. Was it rash, turning back so abruptly and with so little consideration? And what am I supposed to do now?

I needn't have troubled myself. I wake in the wee hours to the sound of raindrops on the tent-fly. By daybreak it's raining hard, raining steady, raining like it's never going to stop and that pretty much answers all my questions for me. If I was doubtful yesterday about tackling those slopes above Lone Cabin Creek canyon, today they're clearly out of the question.

And I can't afford to hang around waiting for conditions to improve. My supplies are already running low. I have no real alternative: at the first decent lull in the storm I'll be heading back to French Bar Creek, the Big Bar ferry and the possibility of a ride out.

It's not a comfortable wait. I think of the trail growing softer and softer in the rain. I think of hiking down those hogback ridges of greasy clay. (The locals call it "loon shit," though why loons should be singled out for this particular distinction I couldn't say.) This storm could go on for many days with conditions growing worse and worse. I'm half tempted to pull on the rain gear, collapse the tent and go.

But I understand myself well enough to know that's just the Windigo whispering in my ear. I remember the last time I let myself be hurried into daring the weather. I decide to stand pat, possess myself in patience, see what develops. I can always bite the bullet tomorrow morning if there's no improvement. At least there's water now.

It rains all day, a thorough rain. By the end of the afternoon there are signs of a break, even a moment of sunshine in the evening, lighting up the slopes on the other side of the valley. I poke my head out of the tent and take a deep breath. My camping spot is high enough above the Fraser that I'm actually looking *down* on the mist drifting along the river. Distant ridges fade, then reappear. A solitary tree stands in silhouette, like a Chinese print, only to be erased a moment later by shifting vapours. I catch a glimpse of the river far below. Drops of water jewel the grass stems around the tent, sparkling in the late sun. From somewhere not too far away a meadowlark starts singing, apparently just for the joy of it. A good sign.

DAY FIFTY-NINE
Monday, September 1: Bunchgrass Mountain to Big Bar

All this he saw, for one moment breathless and intense,
vivid on the morning sky; and still, as he looked, he lived;
and still, as he lived, he wondered.
    —Kenneth Grahame, "The Piper at the Gates of Dawn"
        in *The Wind in the Willows*

wake to a robin singing. Another good sign. It's a spectacular blue-sky morning, rain washed, with the sun just rising across the valley and scraps of mist still drifting along the ridgetops.

Now it's the meadowlark's turn again, chiming in from somewhere farther down the slope, joining the robin's chorus. It is months past breeding season. Maybe the two of them, robin and meadowlark, are just responding, like me, to the promise of the day.

Back in the tent I've just finished breakfast when I hear a faint, familiar gabbling, quite distinctive, coming down the wind from somewhere farther up the valley. I drop everything and get myself outside in time to see a flock of perhaps a hundred sandhill cranes

(*Grus canadensis*), big birds, impressive, coming into view, flying south along the ridge above and behind the tent.

The vocalizing of sandhill cranes is variously described as a trumpet or rattle. The Columbia Land Trust website says "their distinctive rolling *r-r-r-r* call sounds like something out of *Jurassic Park*." Wikipedia suggests the sound of a French-style "r," rolled loudly off the tip of the tongue. *R-r-r-r-r-r. R-r-r-r-r-r. R-r-r-r-r-r.* I rather like that. *Oooh la la.*

When the birds are almost overhead, they wheel and circle. And circle once more. Then they're off again, heading downriver.

As always, I'm struck by the dramatic flying silhouette, shaped like a cross, with the long outthrust neck, the equally long trailing legs, and the enormous wings, six to eight feet in span and very broad.

Seen up close, adult sandhill cranes are mostly a pale bluish-grey, with red forehead, white cheeks, black legs and feet. And a long, black, pointed beak, a stiletto of a beak, built for spearing and grasping prey. Considering that beak, I'd always imagined cranes to be committed predators, but it turns out they're omnivores, much like human beings. The bulk of their diet is plant material (roots, seeds, grains, berries), though animal matter is also important (snails, earthworms, insects, amphibians, snakes, nestling birds, eggs and mice).

Youngsters are reddish-brown above, grey below, and lack the red forehead.

What I've just seen is typical migratory behaviour: the flock finding a thermal to gain altitude, then flying or gliding on toward the next thermal.

It's possible these birds have come all the way from the Yukon or Alaska or even Siberia and are bound for the American southwest or Mexico. But it's much more likely that they spent their summer not too far north of here, on the Chilcotin Plateau or in the Cariboo Basin, where the bulk of British Columbia's resident sandhill cranes (estimated at somewhere between three and five thousand birds) rear their young.

And they may only be going as far as the Great Central Valley of California where most of British Columbia's sandhill cranes winter.

Sandhill cranes prefer shallow-water wetlands for breeding (I think of it as "moose pasture"): wet meadows, beaver ponds, estuaries, bogs, fens, marshes, swamps, often surrounded by coniferous forest for protective cover and privacy. They seem to like complicated, convoluted shorelines. To be useful, potential habitat must provide a secure nest site, roosting areas, feeding areas and at least the illusion of isolation from human beings. Sandhill cranes mate for life and return to the same general area every year to breed, though not necessarily the same specific site.

The actual nest is a mound of vegetation built on the shore or in shallow water. The female lays two eggs (very rarely one or three) and both adults share incubation duty over the next thirty to thirty-four days. Hatchling chicks are able to scramble away from the nest within twenty-four hours but it may be more than two months before they can take to the air. Again, both adults share the duty of feeding the chicks until they can forage for themselves.

On the macabre side, only one of the two hatchlings usually survives to fledging. There is intense competition between the chicks for food from the adults, and the more dominant chick usually starves its less forceful sibling to death. It's quite possible that every crane in that flock up there has committed fratricide.

Grus canadensis boasts a distinguished lineage. It's an ancient family with one of the longest fossil records of any living bird, going back at least two and a half million years, but possibly (according to disputed fossil remains from Nebraska) as much as ten million years.

It's interesting to think of sandhill cranes migrating across this landscape (just like these birds here today) through all that enormous span of time, as whole epochs of the world drifted by. I wonder how they coped with the cordilleran ice sheets? Maybe for that little time they had to modify their travel plans. Skipped the trip north. Stayed in California for the summer. Hung out at the beach.

My tent and gear take some drying, of course, but even so I'm away shortly after nine o'clock. The trail is still greasy, my boots pick up great heavy gobbets of clay. I'm anxious about the way ahead, but actually there's no problem. No problem at all. I move right along. The trail is still soft but it's already drying fast when I get to the hogbacks above French Bar Creek. I exercise due care and attention and reach the creek without mishap just after noon. The water is higher than it was but nothing I can't handle. I pause briefly for a little picnic, again relishing the warm sunshine and the play of light. Then I go on, climbing the steep trail to the edge of Miller Flats, past the view down into the rapids at the mouth of French Bar Canyon.

I'm still fretting about that business at Lone Cabin Creek. Second-guessing myself. Did I panic? Should I have gone on? Dealing with steep places, what mountain climbers call "exposure," has never been my strong suit. I fear falling the way some people fear snakes or dogs or spiders. You'll not catch me dangling from a rope and pitons, not this cowboy.

Such unreasoning fear can get in the way. Can even be disabling. But fear, after all, is fundamentally adaptive. A matter of survival. Better to be afraid of snakes or spiders or dogs—or falling from high places—than utterly lacking in caution. A bolder head than mine might well be hiking north now through the Churn Creek Protected Area, en route to the Gang Ranch and Farwell Canyon, that much closer to the goal. Or might be lying at the bottom of Lone Cabin Creek canyon with a broken neck.

Anyway, I yam what I yam. (And that's all what I yam.) These quirks and fears are just part of the hand we've been dealt, woven into the fabric of our lives. Can't wish them or will them away. And we're wise to play to our strengths rather than our weaknesses.

My strength is persistence. Perseverance. And my enthusiasm is reviving again with the sunshine and blue skies and easy walking. I've come too far to quit. I need to get myself out of here, put the gear back in order as quick as I can, re-provision, and get myself back to Big Bar in time to finish the trip this autumn. It's doable.

I suppose I could always take another run at that trail through the Lone Cabin Creek canyon. But I'm thinking there's got to be another way. Maybe I'll try the other side of the river, the east side. I can always recross the Fraser at the Gang Ranch bridge and continue north from there toward Farwell Canyon and Riske Creek as originally planned.

I'm back at the Big Bar ferry before three o'clock, like a horse going for the barn. Three days up, one short day back. Life is like that. So much depends on whether you're swimming with the tide or against it.

*No spring nor summer beauty hath such grace as I have
seen in one autumnal face.*

—John Donne, "The Autumnal"

For we walk by faith, not by sight.

—2 Corinthians 5:7

*And sleep as I in childhood, sweetly slept,
Untroubling and untroubled where I lie
The grass below—above, the vaulted sky.*

—John Clare "I Am!"

7

Journey's End—
Autumn in the Junction Country

Confluence of the Chilcotin and Fraser rivers

DAY SIXTY
Tuesday, September 9: Big Bar Mountain

The ground along the east side of the river valley north of the Big Bar ferry above French Bar Canyon, is extremely rugged, virtually impassable, with sheer cliffs and tumbled rock. But I reckon if I can get myself above and beyond all that, I should be able to make it north to Canoe Creek Road and the Gang Ranch without too much difficulty.

The first step is a long, brutal climb from the ferry landing to the ridge above. My map says there's a track up there and that's what I'll be making for. Happily for me the weather seems to have mended, for now anyway. It's a beautiful day, crystal clear with little puffy cumulus clouds and a bit of a breeze.

I locate the track, no problem, and the view south is spectacular, looking back down the Fraser to Chisholm Canyon, Watson Bar and beyond. All the ground I've covered. Then, as I hike onward, the view opens up to the northwest across the river: French Bar Creek, Lone Cabin Creek, Empire Valley and the Churn Creek Protected Area, all of it seeming very close now.

I've a suspicion that finding water is going to be a challenge on this section of the journey. This is definitely the drier side of the river, with no big mountain ranges to capture precipitation.

But I'm fine for this first night. Lawrence Joiner of the OK Ranch has given me permission to stay at his little cow camp south of Deadman Creek. I probably won't bother with the bunkhouse, just set my tent up as usual, but I'll be glad to have access to his well. Farther north I'll just have to hope for the best. Deadman Creek, Crows Bar Creek, China Bar Creek . . . with all the little seasonal creeks showing on the map, there's got to be water somewhere.

The OK Ranch is famous. It's one of the old-time spreads, subject of a book titled *Cariboo Cowboy*. The author, Harry Marriott, came to this country from England as a very young man, cowboyed for the Gang Ranch, enlisted in the First World War, survived and came back to establish a ranch of his own: the OK Ranch on Big Bar Mountain north of the community of Jesmond. Over these next few days I'll be hiking into the landscape of that book across the old Gang Ranch ranges from here to Canoe Creek.

DAY SIXTY-ONE
Wednesday, September 10:
Big Bar Mountain to Crows Bar Creek

The tent is wet with dew and the sun takes an awfully long time to clear the ridge, though the sky is pure cerulean. It's that time of year. Not exactly frosty at night, but chilly, especially under cloudless skies. And everything is soaking wet in the morning. Good thing I brought my sponge to help speed the drying of the tent-fly. Even so, it's well after ten before I finally get away.

Time and the running river have shaped the land between the cow camp and Crows Bar Creek into a series of broad terraces or benches, all of them well above the Fraser and separated from one another by deepish gullies draining down toward the river.

Out in the middle of one flat, a little band of four young bighorn rams, a nice surprise: the eldest with half-curl horns; two rams that are noticeably younger; and the youngest with horns just barely beginning their curl. None of the animals seem particularly alarmed when I come into view. They eye me carefully from a distance before finally deciding to head for higher ground. Handsome animals with grey-brown coats, white rumps, white muzzles.

These would be California bighorns. In North America there are actually only two different species of wild mountain sheep: bighorn sheep (*Ovis canadensis*), with their massive tightly curled horns; and thinhorn or Dall sheep (*Ovis dalli*), with more lightly built, less tightly curled, more widely spreading horns. But each species is divided into a number of fairly distinct races or subspecies. The pure white Dall sheep, found in Alaska and the Yukon, and the striking grey, black and white Stone's sheep of northern British Columbia are, in fact, the same species of animal. The massive Rocky Mountain bighorns of eastern British Columbia and the much smaller, more slightly built animals in front of me are apparently so similar genetically that some taxonomists question the subspecies designation, preferring to think of them simply as separate populations.

Whatever.

Mountain sheep, no matter what their designation, have a certain *je ne sais quoi* about them, an evocative aura that gives even a little glimpse like this a special thrill. I mean, they *are* beautiful animals, and scarce, not something you're going to see every day, but there's more to it than that. These are essentially prehistoric creatures, like the other species of ice-age mammals—grizzly bears, caribou, elk, moose and so on—that have somehow managed a fluky survival into our own times.

To come upon this group of four bighorn rams is a little like running into a woolly mammoth or a ground sloth or a herd of giant bison. It's time travel, a visit to the lost world. Just look at that exuberant head armour. (These are horns, just to be clear, permanently part of the animal, rather than antlers that are shed every year.) Doesn't it just shout "Pleistocene"? Like a sabre-tooth cat's fangs or the great curving tusks of a mastodon.

Bighorn sheep are grazers, they mostly eat grass, which makes them the most purely grassland-oriented of all the big native herbivores. It also puts them into direct competition with all forms of domestic livestock. And that competition is much more pressing than you might think. Only a small fraction of British Columbia's grasslands are accessible to mountain sheep. Bighorns depend on fleetness to escape their predators: cougars, wolves and coyotes. Fleetness, that is, *plus* a place of refuge. Biologists call it "escape terrain." Ground so rugged that pursuing predators cannot follow (or at least not very quickly). Mountain sheep themselves are well equipped with concave hooves and rough, flexible underpads for excellent traction and speedy flight on steep terrain.

Consequently, only those grasslands that are within sprinting distance of escape terrain are of any use to the sheep. That's what makes this valley so suitable for bighorns: rugged grassland with lots of escape terrain. Conversely, the absence of escape terrain renders much or most of British Columbia's grasslands virtually useless for mountain sheep. (The rolling open rangelands of the Nicola basin, for instance: wonderful grass, very little escape terrain.)

So when livestock are herded onto those limited areas of range that *are* suitable for bighorns, the bighorns, like as not, have nowhere else to go.

And domestic livestock, especially domestic goats and, most especially, domestic sheep, also carry diseases (notably Pasteurella pneumonia) that are deadly to wild sheep. Aside from competition for forage, the mere presence of domestic sheep on mountain sheep range means death to the bighorns.

So this little band of rams is more than just an interesting and evocative sight along the way. These four animals are a hopeful sign, good news, a positive indicator of this ecosystem's good health and, dare I say it, tangible evidence of somebody's good management. Call it God's stamp of approval. A lively canary singing in the mine.

That younger ram, incidentally, is not just hanging out with those older sheep. It's learning where the best grazing is, where best to spend the winter, where to go for salt, where to run when predators threaten. In fact, all the mountain sheep lore it needs to survive.

A second band of bighorns comes into view a little farther on. Ewes and lambs this time, about thirteen animals in all. Quite a bit more skittish than the rams. They've barely caught a glimpse of me and they're off in a cloud of dust, heading for the hills. This is apparently typical of ewe bands. They're more timid than the ram bands and tend to stick closer to their escape terrain, even to the point of denying themselves access to the richer but riskier grazing available to rams. The safety of the lambs is paramount.

Bighorns mate in November and December. Gestation lasts for six months, so lambs are born from late April to early June at a time when spring forage is at its best and the ewe's milk supply will be richest.

Lambs are weaned by October. Young males stay with the ewes until two or three years of age, then leave to join bachelor bands like the one I saw earlier. Most ewes breed for the first time when they are two years old. Males are capable of breeding at two years of age but usually must wait a further five or six years to acquire sufficient seniority to breed. Bighorns are surprisingly short-lived. In the wild, mature females survive only ten to fourteen years, males nine to twelve years. It's a hard, risky life, evidently.

Fortunately for me there *is* water at Crows Bar Creek: a little spring behind a tumbledown shack. This must be all that's left of the old Gang Ranch cow camp. Could this be the young Harry Marriott's cabin, the one he writes about in the book? I doubt it. That would be long gone. This might be its plywood and tarpaper successor.

DAY SIXTY-TWO
Thursday, September 11: Crows Bar Creek to China Gulch

When I finally get above the trees I discover that I'm perched directly across the river from my nemesis, that formidable canyon at the mouth of Lone Cabin Creek. Lots of escape terrain there if you're a mountain sheep. In fact, according to my map, the high ground on the north side of the canyon is actually called Sheep Point.

I can't help thinking that evolution is narrower, sillier and, well, unintelligent, than we like to think. And bighorn sheep are a case in point.

The massive horns and skull of a full-curl bighorn ram can weigh as much as all the other bones in the animal's body put together. The ram's skull has to be specially modified and strengthened to bear those huge horns and to protect the animal's not very large brain against concussion in its head-butting battles for dominance.

And the sole purpose of all that extraordinary growth is sexual display. Protection from predators? No. Safety on the cliffs? No. Getting food? No. The larger the horns, the more dominant the ram. The more dominant the ram, the more likely that ewes will find him an acceptable mate and that his genes will be passed forward to posterity.

It's a sort of capsule lesson in natural selection and Darwinian evolution: big horns enable a ram to breed more ewes and (all other things being equal) produce more offspring. And male offspring from that ram will likely inherit their dad's gift of large horns and his success in breeding ewes. Over time, then, the lines of smaller-horned rams will tend to dwindle and disappear, while the progeny of larger-horned rams will come to dominate the population. With that kind of selection going on, it's easy to see that, over time, horns will tend to get larger and larger, within the genetic limits of *Ovis canadensis*. (As long as the big horns don't actually interfere with survival or the physical ability to breed.)

Evolution in this case doesn't really have much to do with general fitness, with making a better or more advanced or superior animal. A super sheep. "Fitness" simply means horn size and, presumably, sufficient health and strength and vigour to carry those ridiculous appendages around. It has nothing to do with any other measure of fitness. Increased intelligence, say. Or adaptability. Or resistance to disease.

And that applies to social Darwinism as well, a concept that's out of fashion in polite circles nowadays but still very much implicit in the way most of us look at the world. An individual who has risen to the top of the social heap has certainly demonstrated his or her fitness. But fitness for what? And by what measure?

We human beings like to think of ourselves as the most highly evolved of all animals. But perhaps that should give us pause. What's our equivalent to ridiculous horns?

For mountain sheep, the measure of fitness is success in creating the next generation, a narrow measure. Ironically, the dominant rams, the most successful alpha males, tend also to be shortest lived. Evolution doesn't much care about individual well-being or longevity or happiness or accomplishment or personal excellence. Or making a better world. All those things we human beings might take to be measures of a life well lived. Evolution only cares about the next crop of babies.

I search uphill along the little dry creek bed. Nothing. I search downhill. Still nothing. I'm just thinking about hitting the trail again to try my luck elsewhere when I hear the blessed sound of trickling water from deep in the thicket ahead. Not much of a stream, as it turns out. It only runs a few feet before disappearing back beneath the stones (for good, as far as I can tell). But it will have to do. There's a change in the weather coming, clouds moving in from the north. Time to set up camp.

DAY SIXTY-THREE
Friday, September 12: China Gulch

I wake to a dark day, lowering skies, the smell of rain on the wind. Not a problem. I have shelter. Water close to hand. Ample supplies. Notes to write and a book to read. I can wait it out.

Sometimes I am even glad for a bit of a break like this. But not today. Today it's just tedious. Time is wasting. Autumn is coming. I want to get on with my walk. And there's something about the chilly inside of a tent on a rainy day, the slow passing of the minutes, that can bring out the worst in me. All those gloomy thoughts and misgivings. What am I *doing* here? To what end, all this effort?

The gloom deepens. By early afternoon it's raining heavily, drumming on the fly. Fortunately the tent is well placed and drainage is good. Inside I'm as dry and snug as I could be under the circumstances. The sleeping bag is warm. I doze. Later in the afternoon the rain eases off to showers and the showers ease off to nothing at all. The first bit of leafy sunlight on the tent catches me almost by surprise.

By evening the sky has cleared and there's a golden rain-washed early autumn light, with a bit of a breeze out of the northwest. I decide to take myself out for a look at the broad view down the gulch and across the river. And this, I suppose, is what the whole long journey is all about. This is what I'm here for. To bear witness to the beauty and grace of this whole huge empty sweep of country, this place and this time. This moment. To bear witness and then to testify. Hard duty and poorly paid, but somebody has to do it.

And the job is not without its rewards, in a special sort of coin: the splendid view out across the river on this fine evening. Or in the spring, saskatoon blossoms and balsamroot. Water in a dry land. Salmon in a clear stream. Orion rising over the ridge on a dark night in December. All quite impossible to price in dollars and cents, and therefore difficult to quantify. Perhaps beyond price. The stuff of a life well lived. Food for the soul.

DAY SIXTY-FOUR
Saturday, September 13: China Gulch to Churn Creek

The first person who fenced in a piece of land, ventured
to say: "This is mine" and found others simple enough to
believe him was the true founder of civil society.
—Jean-Jacques Rousseau, "Discours sur l'origine et les
fondements de l'inégalité parmi les hommes"

I t was bound to happen sooner or later. It's surprising, in fact, that I've managed to avoid it till now. Here we have an irate landowner, taking me to task for crossing his private property without permission. It's embarrassing. Regrettable. I have to say, in my own defence, that I have no clear idea when and where I came off Crown land onto this man's property. I saw no signs. The two or three gates I passed were wide open, almost welcoming. (You understand there are gates and fences to control the movement of livestock on public as well as private rangelands.)

But there's nothing to be gained by arguing. Least said, soonest mended. Happily, I'm already back on the public road when he accosts me. I make my most sincere apologies, wish him goodbye and leave as soon as I decently can.

I have every sympathy with the man. He's in a difficult position, as are all ranchers nowadays. Time was when a person could pretty much count on getting permission to cross somebody's private range (on foot, anyway). Just leave the gates as you find them, friend. And don't bother the stock. But times have changed. Apart from the whole question of liability (give somebody permission to come onto your land and the law will hold you responsible for their safety), any rancher who is too welcoming risks having every snowmobile–four-wheel-drive–dirt-bike–ATV yahoo from Prince George to Vancouver out there chewing up his range.

So the old-fashioned welcome is increasingly a thing of the past. Which is a great shame. It's regrettable that a landowner can't be civil and generous and welcoming without putting himself or his ranges at risk. It's even more regrettable, I think, that this hardening of attitudes among large landowners has created a growing barrier between ordinary people and the landscapes of home.

To my mind, this estrangement strikes at the very heart of what a nation is all about: that active sense of the beloved homeland, a sense of proprietorship that goes beyond legal ownership.

This particular rancher's private ranges happen to be part of one of the most spectacular landscapes in the country. And they lie smack across paths and routes along the Fraser River valley that human beings have been using for many thousands of years. (Since the last of the glacial waters drained away, I suppose.)

Does his title to the land, doubtless dating from the free-for-all days of the nineteenth century, give him exclusive right to and ownership of that landscape and those pathways? Or do other citizens, the nation, have some claim as well? Is this our country, our homeland, or just his?

These are charged questions. And I have no pat answers, though I'd like to think we all have some sort of stake or interest in the countryside, even if it's privately owned.

Evidently there are others who feel as I do. In some countries (the Nordic nations, for example, Norway, Sweden and Finland) the right of citizens to access the countryside through private land is enshrined in law as a specific freedom or right to roam. (In Finland it's called *Jokamiehenoikeus*, in Norway *Allemannsrett*, in Sweden *Allemansrätten*, literally "Everyman's Right.")

Those laws and regulations protect not only the right to access specifically defined ancient or traditional rights-of-way across private lands, but also, simply, the right of general access to the countryside across any uninhabited or uncultivated or undeveloped private lands.

With the right of access, naturally, comes a high level of responsibility based on respect for landowners and the countryside. There is a whole list of caveats and prohibitions specified by law and regulation. Those crossing private property are expected to do no harm. No littering. Generally no fires. No noise or disturbance.

The immediate vicinities of private homes and gardens are off-limits of course. So is any ground under active cultivation, though passage is sometimes permissible once the crops have been taken off, especially during the winter months. Livestock and wildlife are not to be harassed. Natural vegetation is not to be damaged. This is all simply common-sense courtesy, really, on the part of both visitors and landowners.

Access is strictly by foot or at least limited to non-motorized forms of transportation. Hallelujah! Commercial activities are prohibited without the owner's permission. Hunting and fishing without permission of the landowner are usually prohibited as well. Tent camping is allowed, but generally only temporarily, for a night or two in passage.

In Scandinavia the legal right to roam developed naturally from a long-standing cultural tradition of free access to the countryside. Perhaps because the Nordic nations were never feudalized, the exclusive rights of the landowning classes were never so fiercely asserted in law or in culture compared to many other areas of Europe.

In fact, the right of access to the countryside was taken so much for granted in those Nordic countries as being commonly understood, a basic and integral part of the culture, normal practice, that only recently, as the countryside has become more settled and developed, was it felt necessary to formalize those rights in legislation.

Which, I'd say, precisely echoes our experience in this country. Until very recently there was simply no need to legislate any right of access. The landowner's permission could be taken almost for granted as a matter of custom and courtesy.

But not anymore.

Perhaps the time has come for our own "freedom to roam" legislation.

Many large landowners aren't going to like that, though perhaps some would go along out of a sense of public spiritedness, noblesse oblige, simple patriotism, a desire to help build an improved sense of nationhood.

I doubt any of that would cut much mustard with this guy. He's pretty jealous of his property rights. But failing an appeal to his better nature, how about a little moderate *quid pro quo*. I'd bet that his operation absolutely depends on access to thousands of hectares of public grazing land. For six months or more out of each year, his cows and calves and bulls are fattening on public grass, *our* grass, which he gets at a very reasonable rate. Perhaps it should be a condition of his grazing leases or licences that he allow a bit of modest, well-controlled public access, a footpath, say, through his own ranges.

And while we're at it, let's have a little legislation to limit the liability of landowners for any injury or mishaps that casual visitors might suffer while roaming across private property. Something similar perhaps to the "Good Samaritan" laws that protect us when we stop to provide aid to the victims of an accident. Maybe that would help sweeten the bitter pill of "freedom to roam."

I cross the Gang Ranch Bridge at exactly five-thirty in the evening and end up camping for the night on a high sandbar near the mouth of Churn Creek, just south of the bridge, on the west side of the river. It's about the only place I can find that's free of cactus or poison ivy.

The sun goes down and then there's magic: a near-full moon rising from the rimrock on the east side of the valley to illuminate the soft, pale swell of the sandbar and reflect from the swirl of the main current and back eddy out in the river. It's a lovely evening, clear and calm, with just the hint of a breeze, almost warm, blowing south down the valley. The smell of cottonwoods in the air. I leave the tent flap open to the sound of crickets and the soft susurration of the river hurrying past my door.

DAY SIXTY-FIVE
Sunday, September 14:
Churn Creek to Sheep Point, Churn Creek Protected Area

It's another fine morning, with sunlight glinting on the brown river. The water doesn't so much flow as slide downhill, a great, sheer, liquid avalanche, moving fast, tumbling over itself in places, impatient for the sea.

I fill my water bottles (from the creek, not the river) and head out, full of anticipation and mixed feelings. I hope to spend the next two or three days on a little side trip south to Lone Cabin Creek and back again.

This is the Churn Creek Protected Area: all this west side of the river from north of Churn Creek to south of Lone Cabin Creek (a distance of perhaps thirty kilometres) and west up into the Churn Creek watershed (perhaps another twenty-five kilometres), almost thirty-seven thousand hectares of low-, middle- and high-elevation grasslands. This is another of those places that comes highly recommended by friends who know about such things, another must-see destination on any tour of southern interior British Columbia's grasslands.

And together with Junction Sheep Range Provincial Park a little farther north, this is my own personal promised land. This is the goal I've been hiking toward all these days and weeks and months. Here is the ultimate objective of my pilgrimage.

It had better be good.

The road—a little dirt road, mind, not something you'd want to drive in wet weather—climbs and climbs to the height of land and across into the watersheds of Koster and Grinder creeks, home to the famous and historic Empire Valley Ranch, now part of the protected area.

I've been looking forward to meeting John and Joyce Holmes, the young couple who operate the ranch under licence to the British Columbia Provincial Parks branch and who also seem to serve as general ambassadors, advocates and wardens for the protected area. They, too, come highly recommended, and I'll not likely get a better chance to make their acquaintance, though I've not been able to contact them directly and can only hope to catch them at home.

When I knock on the door I find they've both gone out haying for the day. That's disappointing though not altogether unexpected. Hay for winter forage is a crucial part of any livestock operation in this country and I'd guess that nearly every rancher in the valley is out on this beautiful autumn day, making hay while the sun shines.

The hay crop is doubly important here at Empire Valley. It's an essential part of the protected area's conservation strategy. An extra ton of hay for the Empire Valley herd means that much less pressure on native grasslands. And hay can't be imported into the protected area for fear of introducing invasive weeds.

Anyway, the rest of the Holmes family is here: Ellen, Hattie and Sam, along with Aunt Grace. The youngsters remind me of lighthouse kids. Still children, definitely, with all the usual enthusiasm and energy, but oddly old-fashioned and grown-up and competent. "Would you like to come in for tea?" asks the eldest. (*Why yes, ma'am, that would be very nice.*) Homemade bread with fresh plum jam. Can't ask for better. I get to fill my water bottles, too.

I needn't have worried. It *is* a spectacular piece of countryside, open grassland, aspen groves, Douglas-fir parkland. Every bit as good as I might have hoped. And it just gets better and better the farther south I go. Thank God it's got some sort of protected status, though, as it turns out the actual level of protection leaves quite a lot to be desired, being the product of a long and unseemly series of compromises. It's an interesting story, a sad and cautionary tale, a little complicated but somehow characteristic of our times. Bear with me.

The Churn Creek Protected Area probably owes its existence to a high-intentioned United Nations initiative, the World Commission on Environment and Development, chaired by Gro Harlem Brundtland.

The Commission's report, *Our Common Future*, released on April 27, 1987, made a substantial impression on the international community. In Canada, the Conservative government of Brian Mulroney responded in December of 1990 with the "Green Plan," which was supposed to be a national strategy and action plan for sustainable development.

Among other things, Brundtland's report suggested that the total area of land protected from development worldwide needed to be at least tripled to protect global ecosystems. The Green Plan committed the Government of Canada to establishing new national parks in the sixteen "natural areas" of the country not yet represented in our national parks system. And one of those unrepresented areas was the Interior Dry Plateau of southern British Columbia.

Parks Canada planners fanned out across the plateau, prospecting for areas with national park potential. Eventually they developed a list of five options: West Road River (an area of Nechako Plateau and Nazko Uplands between Quesnel and the Coast Mountains); Chilcotin Junction (at the confluence of the Chilcotin and Fraser rivers); Taseko–Fraser (an area north of the Bridge River comprising a good portion of the south Chilcotin Mountains); Bonaparte Lake (an area on the north Thompson uplands and Cariboo Plateau north of Kamloops); and Churn Creek.

Studies were done. Data were gathered. The candidates were duly assessed and compared for relative merit (scenery, biological diversity, naturalness, representativeness and cultural interest) and the best option turned out to be an area centred on the Churn Creek watershed in the southern Chilcotin.

Parks Canada originally envisioned a reserve of almost 450,000 hectares, many times the size of the present-day protected area. Although the land involved was still relatively undisturbed in those days, there were certainly other interests to be considered: mineral claims and mining, cattle ranches and grazing leases, guide outfitters and, of course, always the interests of the timber industry. To help make it happen and to accommodate the other "stakeholders" in that vast area, Parks Canada seemed willing to bend its own rules to an extraordinary degree. There would be continued access to existing mining operations at Black Dome Mountain and to existing placer claims on the Fraser River and Churn Creek (with the understanding that as those mineral claims were exhausted and abandoned they would take their place as part of the park).

Grazing leases and private lands were to be acquired only by negotiated settlement. Parks Canada's policy would be to purchase a rancher's entire operation, even though some of those lands would be surplus to requirements. The agency emphasized, and emphasized repeatedly, that there would be no forced sales. ("If a landowner does not wish to sell, Parks Canada does not buy.")

It was a bold, dramatic proposal, magnificent really, and would have been the equal of anything in Canada's system of national parks, right up there with Banff and Jasper and Wood Buffalo. Nobody expected the thing to be easy, of course. Just to assemble the land was going to take many years. But it seemed doable.

Early evening and I'm feeling a bit under the gun. I had hoped to camp tonight on the ridge above Sheep Point, just north of Lone Cabin Creek, and I wanted to get there in time to see the full moon rise. But it's getting late and I've still some distance to go.

No problem. I get there in plenty of time and make my little camp high on the ridge, where the views are broadest. I've just finished putting in the last of the tent pegs when the moon rises clear and full from the mountains across the river, beyond the headwaters of Crows Bar Creek.

I've been blessed with a whole series of remarkable full-moon evenings on this journey. Crater Mountain. The ridge above the Similkameen River. Kalamalka Lake Provincial Park. Chapperon Creek. Cornwall Hills. Moonrise has become a kind of theme, a leitmotif to announce some moment of extraordinary grace and beauty.

But this is the best.

A soft, surprisingly warm wind is blowing out of the west, sighing through the bunchgrass around the tent, smelling of the south Chilcotin Mountains and alpine fir. It's a gentle night. I tie the tent flaps back to let the breeze flow through. The last golden sunset light is now fading fast on the broad view along this sweep of river valley, from Canoe Creek in the north to somewhere beyond Big Bar in the south. The western horizon is a vivid blue-green promising more fair weather to come.

Stars are just starting to show in the sky above.

And in all this huge quiet landscape (for some reason reminding me very much just now of the Grand Canyon of the Colorado River) there is but one tiny pinprick of incandescent light far down the valley. Perhaps the ferry at Big Bar. In all this enormity, on this quiet evening, there's just me and the ferryman. It's a moment to remember.

> *The night walked down the sky—with the moon in her hand.*
>
> —Frederick L. Knowles, "A Memory"

DAY SIXTY-SIX
Monday, September 15: Sheep Point to Grinder Creek

A red-letter day!

Perhaps.

I've just started down the trail in the morning when I see movement ahead. An animal, approximately coyote sized, I'd say, though it's hard to be certain. Coyote-grey as well. Grizzled. But it doesn't look like a coyote. And it doesn't move like a coyote.

These are all the impressions of a moment, you understand, reviewed in the mind's eye afterward. I've no time to fish out the binoculars.

Whatever this thing is, it pauses for an instant, looks back, then vanishes into the grass beside the trail. I'm left wondering if I really saw a flash of vertical black and white striping on its face as it turned. Or was that just wishful thinking, a trick of the morning sunlight?

I'm not the most reliable observer. I've been hoping very much to see a badger (*Taxidea taxus*, subspecies *jeffersonii* here in British Columbia) on this trek and have been keeping my eyes peeled ever since Crater Mountain. But I've not had much luck apart from a couple of maybe-sightings like this one. And here we are, down to the last few days of my journey. It's now or never.

My lack of success in badger spotting is not all that surprising. For one thing, badgers are mostly nocturnal animals (though it's not particularly unusual for them to be up and about in daylight). More to the point, there just aren't that many of them. Badgers belong to the same sorry category as meadowlarks and mountain sheep and sharp-tailed grouse, and so on. They are the quintessential grassland animal and they should be as common as dirt in these southern interior valleys. They used to be as common as dirt, but they aren't anymore.

In fact, the entire badger population of southern interior British Columbia may now number under four hundred animals, further divided into two apparently distinct populations: Kootenay and Thompson–Okanagan.

There are a number of likely reasons for the species' decline.

In the past, badgers were heavily trapped. (The rather coarse fur was used for shaving brushes.) And badgers, or their burrows more precisely, have been traditionally regarded as a menace to livestock, cattle and horses, so that badgers were also widely persecuted as varmints, though in fact there isn't much real evidence that the burrows were ever much of a problem.

Of course many of the species that badgers prey on were also high on the varmint list (Columbian ground squirrels, for example, and yellow-bellied marmots, northern pocket gophers, meadow voles and various other species of rodent), and poisoning programs aimed at those rodents have probably affected badgers as well, perhaps through secondary poisoning or a diminished food supply.

Surprisingly, roadkill has also been a major source of mortality. Badgers are mostly nocturnal hunters and often use roadways as travel corridors. They are accidents waiting to happen.

And, of course, in common with all those other vanishing grassland species, *Taxidea taxus jeffersonii* also suffers from loss of habitat, mostly due to urban and suburban development. Ironically, badgers seem fairly tolerant of human beings. But they like lots of open ground and seem to have two major habitat requirements not usually found in urban or suburban environments: a plentiful supply of prey and good soil for digging.

A lot of digging.

If fish gotta swim and birds gotta fly, badgers, it seems, gotta dig, gotta burrow, gotta tunnel. And they're built for it, compact and muscular with powerful forelimbs, large front paws and outsized claws shaped for digging. Each individual badger will have many, many burrows within its home range. Burrows for cover and shelter, for food storage, for the birth and rearing of kits. Burrows up to ten metres long and three metres deep.

Incidentally, size-wise, badgers, which weigh in at six to thirteen kilograms (females smaller than males), are actually quite a bit smaller than coyotes (eight to twenty kilograms). And they're built differently. Coyotes are tall and thin, quite slender. Badgers are short and round, almost squat.

Badgers forage alone (except for family groups), mainly at night, and they're unique among our mammalian predators in typically digging for their prey, mostly other burrowing animals. Badgers will dig into the burrow of the animal they're pursuing at several different points, using their keen sense of smell to locate the prey. Sometimes they plug all but one of the entrances to the other animal's burrow, then excavate that entrance. Prey are usually killed and consumed underground.

Badgers mate in July and August. (Perhaps the animal I saw was still out looking for a sweetie.) Embryos don't implant for further development in the wall of the female's uterus until January or February. Young are born in March or April, which coincides, not incidentally I'm sure, with the emergence from hibernation of the British Columbian badger's two main prey species: Columbian ground squirrels and yellow-bellied marmots.

Badgers are not prolific breeders. Litters number up to four kits but average only two. One litter a year. Kits are weaned at about five or six weeks and have already started to disperse at ten to twelve weeks of age. Mortality, as you might expect, is very high among dispersing kits. Maximum life expectancy is about fourteen years.

Was that a badger down there on the trail? Who can say? The Churn Creek Protected Area is at the extreme northwestern edge of the species' provincial range. Badgers are extremely thin on the ground here, with extraordinarily large home ranges: up to 100 square kilometres for adult females (average 32 square kilometres) and up to 2,200 square kilometres for adult males (average 358 square kilometres).[17]

But it could have been a badger. Not out of the question. And wouldn't that be perfect, a badger in the Churn Creek Protected Area, with no persecution, no urban or suburban development, one little road, not much traffic. Just what the doctor ordered.

The little meadows on the ridge above the mouth of Lone Cabin Creek must surely be among the most pristine of British Columbia's native grasslands. There's no water here, of course, so high above the creek. That's probably what has saved these meadows from overgrazing. No water, no livestock.

I make a point of walking right to the brink of the canyon (considerably higher on this north side of the creek than on the south side). I'm looking out and down across a great span of air, perhaps a kilometre of space, to where I stood a couple of weeks ago. The trail on that side still looks dangerous, even from here. The first steep bit would have been just the beginning of my troubles. It's rough going all the way up the creek to Ron Cable's place. Would have been a nightmare in the rain.

My little detour along the other side of the river has cost me dearly in lost time and many extra kilometres of walking. On the other hand, I've seen some country that I'd otherwise have missed. Had some interesting experiences. Much of the good stuff in life happens on the detours.

I'm just turning to go when I hear the sound of falling stones on the far side of the canyon and see dust in the air. This time I do manage to get the binoculars out in time. More mountain sheep, another group of four rams. But these are the big boys. Three full-curl, near as I can make out from this distance, and one just short of full-curl. Majestic is an overused word, but there it is. Nonchalantly they make their way down the precipice into the canyon. Where angels fear to tread.

It's hard to leave paradise and I wish I could linger. But we're now well into September and I still have many miles to go while the weather holds fair. There's no time to lose. Also I'm down to my last few swallows of water. So it's back to Empire Valley and a campsite on Grinder Creek, well above the road for privacy. Tomorrow, north to Churn Creek again. With luck I might even get a quick swim in one of the deeper pools.

DAY SIXTY-SEVEN
Tuesday, September 16: Grinder Creek to Churn Creek

Hurrah for the northward trail! Emotionally and psychologically I've always rejoiced in warmth and light. I *should* prefer the southbound road, going to the sun. But my personal compass feels much happier today headed north, with the autumn sun at my back, a bit of breeze in my face and the clear deep blue of the northern horizon ahead.

For one thing, I'm going in the right direction again, back toward my ultimate objective. The goal is almost in sight. From the height of land beyond the Koster and Grinder Creek watersheds I can see all the way across the northern half of the Churn Creek Protected Area and the Gang Ranch ranges to the gap where the Chilcotin River spills down off the plateau to join the Fraser. Somewhere there, in the fork between those two rivers, are the open grassy meadows of Junction Sheep Range Provincial Park, the climax of this pilgrimage. And not too far beyond the distant horizon will be Riske Creek, Highway 20, Williams Lake, the end to all my journeying.

Also, I'm enjoying the walk. From the height of land the road runs downhill, more or less, all the way to Churn Creek. I'm in pretty good shape physically, everything seems to be working, no complaints today. And the monster pack is half empty. It's a stroll.

And of course the scenery can't be beat. The Fraser flows out of the north toward me, winding down its deep valley. The grassy slopes and terraces along the river, straw coloured at this time of year, give way to open forest at higher elevations. Most of the little Douglas maples (*Acer glabrum*) up and down the ravines have gone a brilliant orange-crimson, though the aspens down here are still more green than gold.

Words fail me, actually. How do you describe the reality of this kind of thing? The smell and colour and flavour of the wild country-side in autumn. I do love it.

In Canada, nearly all public lands outside the territories are controlled by the provincial governments. To have any chance of success, a national park proposal must have the blessing of one or more prov-inces willing to make the necessary land available to the federal government.

The 1980s and early 1990s were tetchy times, politically, in British Columbia, with ever-increasing levels of confrontation between envi-ronmentalists and the resource industries. The provincial government's answer to this escalating "War in the Woods" was the Commission on

Resources and Environment (CORE), established in 1992 with a mandate to develop a provincial land-use strategy and a series of specific regional land-use plans. Four "tables" were convened: Vancouver Island, Cariboo Chilcotin, East Kootenay and West Kootenay.

Parks Canada was asked to channel its Churn Creek proposal through the newly established provincial processes: the Cariboo Chilcotin CORE table and the Provincial Protected Areas Strategy.

And that was pretty much the end of Churn Creek National Park.

The CORE process was supposed to mediate between the need for environmental protection and continued industrial access to natural resources. The plan was to give all the various "stakeholders" a voice at the table. By 1993, twenty-four "sectors" were represented in the Cariboo Chilcotin CORE process. Decision making on land-use issues was supposed to proceed by consensus, with discussion among the various sectors leading to a compromise that all could live with. Sounds democratic, doesn't it? Admirable.

Unfortunately, it didn't work.

Industry, labour and business were adamantly opposed to the process, seeing it as a threat to the relatively unrestricted access to natural resources that timber and mining interests had previously enjoyed. The head of the Williams Lake local of the Industrial, Wood and Allied Workers of Canada would later boast how labour and industry had sabotaged CORE by manipulating procedural rules, by stacking the table with pro-industry sectors and by refusing to move from its original position during the fifteen months of negotiations.[18]

When Parks Canada finally got around to tabling a scaled-down version of its Churn Creek proposal in the winter of 1993–1994, it ran smack into this super-heated atmosphere, predictably got hammered by pro-industry interests and that was that.

(The Canadian Parks Service is not quite the force it was in the zealous era of J.B. Harkin, the first Commissioner of Canada's national parks. A bunch of shrinking violets nowadays, by comparison. Very shy of controversy. Willing to propose new parks, politely, but certainly not to publicly advocate or champion them. Pity.)

With the ultimate collapse of the Cariboo Chilcotin CORE process in 1994, Commissioner Stephen Owen presented his own series of land-use recommendations. And the Province of British Columbia went ahead on its own to develop the Cariboo Chilcotin Land Use Plan (CCLUP) in consultation with individual sectors. In 1995 the CCLUP created seventeen new parks and protected areas, one of them being a much-reduced version of the Churn Creek Reserve.

Well, better than nothing, wouldn't you say?

But here's the thing. The CCLUP's "90 Day Implementation Report" specifically directs that "all existing uses will continue in the Churn Creek Protected Area."

Swell.

So the grazing of domestic livestock continues (though happily at a reduced level and under the direction of the Holmes family). Pre-existing trapline operations continue. Pre-existing guide-outfitting operations continue. Fishing and hunting continue, including, I note, "the hunting of cougars, lynx and bobcat using a snowmobile," subject to the usual regulations. (In fairness, there aren't enough fish to attract any number of anglers. And with the general dearth of large predators, the hunting of ungulates may actually be required to keep wild herbivores at a population level consistent with healthy ecosystems.)

Snowmobiles are allowed but, happily, no ATVs. (Thank God for small mercies.)

Logging and mining aren't allowed, at least in theory. But existing Churn Creek placer gold–mining tenures, which were excluded from the protected area when it was created, still retain rights of access, use and development. And a "utility" corridor through the protected area will continue to provide access not just to existing industrial developments in the country to the west, but to all future developments, in perpetuity. Any future logging and mining development in the country to the west, any industrial development whatever, will have every right to walk all over the protected area, coming and going.

Still, I suppose the words themselves have some value and power. Simply by calling this piece of countryside a "protected area" we go some distance toward establishing it in the public mind as something of real distinction, something extraordinary, something *worth* protecting. And perhaps, with luck, it will eventually become unthinkable that anyone would do it deliberate harm.

We have to hope so, anyway.

DAY SIXTY-EIGHT
Wednesday, September 17: Churn Creek to Word Creek

Clay lies still, but blood's a rover;
Breath's a ware that will not keep.
Up, lad: when the journey's over
There'll be time enough to sleep.

—A.E. Housman, "Reveillé"

Does the road wind up-hill all the way?
Yes, to the very end.
Will the day's journey take the whole long day?
From morn to night, my friend.

—Christina Rossetti, "Up-Hill"

Considering that I'm almost at the end of my long journey, it seems odd that I should feel so weary and discouraged at the thought of going on this morning.

Perhaps that reluctance is part of the essence of pilgrimage. One desires very much to do the deed, to have the thing done. But the only way to get there is by physical effort, which is a good deal less attractive. The aching muscles and the sweat and the tedium of the long-haul walk are the inescapable price of accomplishment.

I'm not saying this very well.

In ordinary life we get so used to cheating. If we want to go from point A to point B, a long way down the road, we beg a lift or buy a ticket or fire up a vehicle to avoid the actual effort. We "save" ourselves the effort, but we also rob ourselves of the experience and the accomplishment of the journey. We don't really cover the ground at all. It's the machine that accomplishes the distance; we just go along for the ride like a sack of potatoes.

But on a pilgrimage we promise ourselves not to cheat. We're there for the experience, after all, and there is no shortcut to experience, no easy way. And that's okay because we discover, in the end, that we're up to it. That's the whole point.

The trick is to avoid thinking of all the distance yet to be covered. That's too discouraging. Just think of the next step. Maybe the one after that. Put one foot in front of the other. You can do that, no problem. Then do it again. And again. It's astonishing the distances you can cover that way. Of course you're tired. Maybe very tired. But can you take one more little step? Of course you can. Away you go.

In fact, it's best not to think of the walk as some sort of onerous project or chore, something to be got through. You know you've really got into the Zen of long-distance pilgrimage when walking becomes a way of being, an activity or a state you commence as a matter of course at the beginning of the day and leave off when the sun goes down. You're not there to cover a particular distance or achieve some sort of destination. Route and distance are immaterial. You're there just to be walking. Doing it. Moving your body. The man or woman in motion. Rhythmic movement is its own reward, like breathing. The world changes and flows around you. Places come and go. You walk on.

Does a fish think of swimming? Does a hawk think of soaring? All the effort they're putting in, how tired they are, how glad they'll be to quit? I doubt it. For them swimming or soaring is just part of being alive, like breathing. They stop only for death. They are swimming or flying machines.

And that's what I have become. A walking machine. A self-repairing, self-fuelling, self-directing walking machine. It's what I was designed for.

And in the end, when one has, in fact, done the deed, finished the route, it's curiously rewarding, even liberating, to know that one has the power, like any wild beast, to cover whole landscapes by the strength and endurance and power of one's own body, the work of the muscles and tendons and bones that one has been gifted with. One feels master of the landscape without the need of machinery, tools and devices.

Easy words.

Just a few steps from my riverside campsite the trail turns up the hill, and "up" pretty much describes the rest of the day. The trail comes to a road. And the road climbs a winding coulee to the pastures and hayfields and headquarter buildings of the Gang Ranch on the broad terraces above the Fraser. A little to my surprise (this is the main road to the Gang Ranch, after all; just imagine the thousands of head of cattle that must have passed this way) I find the slopes of the coulee covered in a rich growth of bunchgrass. A little falcon, a kestrel (*Falco sparverius*), hovers for a moment. I catch the flash of blue on its wings; it's a male. Then it whirls away in the breeze.

Killy-killy-killy.

The Gang Ranch, once the largest ranch in North America, was established in 1863 by two brothers, Thaddeus and Jerome Harper, from Harpers Ferry, Virginia, by way of California. As it happens, I have a nodding acquaintance with the ranch's present-day general manager, Larry Ramstad. We met at a Christmas party long ago and far away. And when I come hiking up the lane, there he is, talking to some other folks in front of the ranch's post office. Rather to my surprise he recognizes me. We chat for a bit. (It's not every day that somebody comes walking up the road from Osoyoos I suppose.) I'm just turning to go, we've said goodbye, when, as an afterthought, I ask if there's a tap nearby where I might top up my water bottles.

He tells me that the tap water can't be trusted. "Give me those bottles," he says. "I'll fill them for you." And off he goes, general manager of the Gang Ranch, to fill my water bottles. I'm mighty flattered, of course, that he would take the trouble. And I'm tickled, too, to find that the old-time tradition of hospitality for which the Gang Ranch was famous in the early days is still alive, even in these suspicious times.

The climb is unrelenting, from 330 metres at the river to 1,100 metres where the road finally, blessedly, mercifully, levels out before dropping into the Word Creek valley. I stagger along, feeling every ounce of the monster pack on my shoulders.

It's another spectacular bit of landscape. Essentially I'm climbing onto the surface of a thick accumulation of ancient lava flows, the foundation of both the Chilcotin and Cariboo plateaus. Near the top of my long climb the road emerges onto a broad meadow, flat as a tabletop, littered with round boulders, glacial erratics. Off to the right, a vast deep slot where the Fraser River has cut its way down through those beds of lava. Ice ages come. Ice ages go. The river continues to dig. It's almost surreal, that sense of visible time.

Sadly, the rangeland isn't nearly of the same quality as in the Churn Creek Protected Area to the south. The nicest grass I've seen all day was in that gully as I came up from the river.

In the era of the Harper brothers and for some time after, there was little of what you might call "range management" in the livestock industry. No sense of "carrying capacity." Cattlemen didn't boast about the condition of their ranges. They boasted about the size of their herds, the bigger the better. The more cows, the more calves. The more calves, the more money. And the range was supposed to provide, somehow, endless capacity, a bottomless reserve.

In addition to the Gang Ranch's own herds, all the cattle coming out of the Chilcotin to market in those early days would have been trailed from the top end of Hanceville Canyon, down along the southern rim of the Chilcotin River valley and across these very meadows, thousands and thousands of head over the years, grazing the grass down to the dirt as they went, damaging the range so badly that it hasn't yet recovered. And maybe never will.

It's autumn in the high country. The aspen leaves are turning gold along Word Creek, just a little stream winding down off the plateau, not yet started its plunge toward the Fraser. There's a real chill in the air as I set up the tent. Might even get a touch of frost tonight.

I hear a saw-whet owl (*Aegolius acadicus*) calling from somewhere on the dark mountain above, a passable imitation of a tiny file scrapping across a saw blade.

DAY SIXTY-NINE
Thursday, September 18: Word Creek to Mossy Creek

The Old Gang Ranch Road high above the river is very much the path less travelled, hardly more than an overgrown country lane, two dirt tracks separated by a strip of grass. I did most of my climbing yesterday; this morning's hike is a relatively easy stroll through little meadows, rolling parklands of Douglas-fir and lodgepole pine, copses of golden aspen with the first litter of fallen leaves still bright on the ground. It's a lovely autumn landscape on the edge of the Cariboo Chilcotin.

But hardly pristine. I'm still on the route of those old-time cattle drives. At least these meadows are not quite so barren as some I crossed yesterday. There is more moisture at this elevation, and an introduced species, Kentucky bluegrass, seems to have mostly replaced the long-vanished native bunchgrasses.

Range ecologists use terms like "plant succession," "potential natural communities" and "seral stages" to describe what's happening here.

When a natural ecosystem (a pristine bunchgrass meadow, say) is annihilated (completely burned, for instance, so that nothing living remains), its replacement, the ecosystem that colonizes and occupies the vacant space, will tend to morph over time, through distinct and recognizable phases, back toward something resembling the original community of species that made up the bunchgrass meadow.

That orderly and predictable progression of vegetation phases back toward the original community is what is meant by plant succession, and the phases are called seral stages.

First to colonize the vacant ground will be plants that are gifted with qualities that make them fast and effective invaders. Think of annual grasses like cheatgrass or forbs like fireweed: lots of seeds, fast germinating, quick growing, drought and heat resistant.

But as time goes by, those original invaders will be squeezed out, or shaded out or simply outwaited by longer-lived, deeply rooted secondary invaders: perennial grasses like Kentucky bluegrass, trees and shrubs like trembling aspen, snowbrush, redstem ceanothus.

In theory at least, Kentucky bluegrass and other secondary invaders will eventually give way to something like the original bluebunch wheatgrass community—perfectly adapted to the climate and conditions of a particular piece of ground—and that community will maintain itself indefinitely or at least until the next catastrophe. That stable, self-perpetuating community would be the potential natural community, sometimes called the "climax vegetation": the community of plants that would establish itself at a specific location if succession were allowed to run its course without further disturbance or interference.

Range ecologists talk about "early seral stages" (the cheatgrass) or "mid-seral stages" (the bluegrass) or "late seral stages" (something almost resembling the original bunchgrass meadow, but not quite).

Unfortunately, introduced species like cheatgrass and Kentucky bluegrass often take such a firm grip on a piece of ground—establishing a sort of "disclimax"—that recovery toward the potential natural community of native plants is stalled more or less indefinitely.

I have not given as much attention in these pages as perhaps I should have to the whole issue of invasive introduced plant species. In fact, introduced species may prove the ultimate threat to indigenous grassland ecosystems in southern interior British Columbia. Already great swaths of rangeland in the Okanagan and Thompson valleys, particularly, have been appropriated by introduced species: cheatgrass, Kentucky bluegrass, all the various species of knapweed (*Centaurea sp.*), houndstongue (*Cynoglossum officinale*), sulphur cinquefoil (*Potentilla recta*), crested wheatgrass *(Agropyron cristatum)* and so on. More countryside is lost to invasive plants every year and the pace seems to be accelerating. Some species, like sulphur cinquefoil and Dalmatian toadflax (*Linaria dalmatica*), are so robust and aggressive they seem able to insinuate themselves even into undisturbed stands of bunchgrass.

I know from the map that the Old Gang Ranch Road is supposed to drop steeply into the valley of McEwan Creek, to emerge, several hundred metres downslope, onto an open terrace above the confluence of the Chilcotin and Fraser rivers.

I've been looking forward to exploring that terrace. It's visible from Dog Creek Road on the east side of the Fraser and has always seemed intriguingly remote and hard to get to. A point of relative inaccessibility. And the views promise to be remarkable.

But I hardly notice the little overgrown track branching off to the right as I hurry past. The road I'm following continues to climb. It isn't until I round a corner and come upon McEwan Creek, just a trickle this high on the mountain, that I realize my error. I should have followed the path less travelled.

Already I've come too far to be happy about retracing my steps, so I decide to carry on. This is, after all, the road more travelled, and perhaps there's a reason why. It seems to be going in the right direction. And with a little luck the views will be even broader from this high on the mountain.

Unfortunately it doesn't work out that way. I can't see a thing through the trees. Every so often I get a tantalizing glimpse of wide expanses to the north, which I take to be the view across the canyon of the Chilcotin River. That will be the Junction Sheep Range over there. Somewhere beyond the horizon will be Becher's prairie and Riske Creek. But I can see hardly anything for the dense bush, nasty second-growth stuff, thick as hairs on a dog. The road passes a succession of logging landings and brush piles. I'm not sorry to leave it all behind.

A blue grouse (*Dendragapus obscurus*), large and dark, rockets from cover along the side of the road, crashes off into the bush. It's astonishing that it doesn't break its feathers or neck.

Eventually the old road comes angling back up the hill on the right to rejoin the one I've been following. A little farther along I come to a trickle of water between mossy banks, nameless on the map, wandering down from higher ground.

It's not much, but this looks like home for the night. The hour is late, I'm out of sorts. Time to make camp.

I could almost certainly reach the Farwell Canyon bridge by tomorrow evening. And doubtless that would be the prudent thing to do. Time is pressing. I'm starting to get a little low on supplies. And who knows how long this stretch of summery weather will last. Even so, I'm tempted to take a day and go exploring. I'd very much like to follow that old road back down onto the terrace, perhaps all the way down to the confluence of the two rivers, surely a sight to see: the milky-blue of the Chilcotin hurrying into the greenish-brown of the Fraser. I could backtrack as far as McEwan Creek, see what I've missed. For that, it might be worth pushing my luck a little.

It's another night for owls. As I lie waiting for sleep to come I hear a barred owl (*Strix varia*) calling from somewhere farther up the creek, not too far way: *Who cooks for you? Who cooks for you all?*

DAY SEVENTY
Friday, September 19: Mossy Creek

A lovely morning, calm and sunny. The summer weather looks to be good for at least another day or two. I decide to take a chance and indulge myself. It's a long downhill hike to start. And steep. At the bottom of the hill there's a fork in the road with a smaller track branching off to the left, and that takes me (this is a bit of luck) all the rest of the way down to the confluence of the two rivers. The way is far too narrow for ordinary vehicles, but there are quad tracks down and back.

A powerful place.

The Fraser, an opaque muddy-brown at this point and by far the larger of the two streams, rolls majestically southward out of a deep narrow valley to the north. The Chilcotin, relatively clear by comparison, is a milky-blue at this time of year. It spills out of Farwell Canyon (an even narrower slot cut into the high ground to the west), charges across the gravel flats around the confluence and dives into the larger river. For a time the blue Chilcotin water persists as a separate stream, swirling and billowing, like a swimmer trying to stay afloat, until at last it is swallowed and submerged by the brown.

It's a beautiful place, the flats at the mouth of the Chilcotin, but fierce, almost godforsaken, hot and dry, parched. Big sage and prickly pear cactus. The devil's garden.

Full of ghosts, too, I should think.

When Simon Fraser came by this place in the summer of 1808 it would have been Shuswap territory, the specific occupiers being the Chilcotin Mouth Band of the Canyon Division (*Sétlhemx*) of the Shuswap People. And I'm guessing the two parties would have understood each other pretty well. Like Fraser and his men the Canyon Shuswap were traders, a sort of interface between the Interior Salish groups to the east and south and the fierce Chilcotins to the west (relatively recent immigrants from the north who had occupied the southern and central part of what is now called the Chilcotin Plateau sometime during the previous four hundred years). The Shuswaps would trade salmon and salmon oil to the Chilcotins, receiving dentalium shells, woven goat's hair blankets, rabbit and marmot skins in return.

It was an odd, complicated, tense territorial relationship.

Sometimes Shuswaps and Chilcotins traded. Sometimes they killed each other, feuding over control of fishing or hunting territory. It's hard to get one's mind around that, an indigestible fact, a reminder that it's a mistake to assume that all cultures and peoples share the same basic mores of one's own time and place. A reminder, too, that life is complicated. Perhaps there were different people in each community, the traders and the warriors, always at odds with one another, trying to lead their people in different directions.

The smallpox epidemic of 1862 more or less wiped out the Canyon Shuswap. The few survivors moved across the river to join the Alkali Lake Band (now Esk'etemc First Nation), leaving the countryside west of the river to the Chilcotins.

The quad tracks end at the edge of the high-water channel. There's a pile of glittering Panasonic batteries, empty water bottles, empty cigarette packages, a dozen or more Budweiser beer cans in a neat stack. (Interesting fact: On my walk, discarded Budweiser cans have outnumbered other brands by a margin of approximately ten to one. Chance or a significant observation? Evidently it's the preferred beer of nitwits everywhere.)

Plus a nice little pile of human excrement decorated with toilet paper.

How could anybody, any civilized person, do this sort of thing to such a place? When I was still a very small child I was taught how to crap in the woods. At the very least, if I just couldn't hold it another minute, I could gouge a trench with my boot heel and cover it all up with dirt and rocks afterward. Leave the place decent for whoever might come along. Leave the place decent out of respect for the place. Even a dog knows enough to scratch dirt when he's finished doing his business.

And that, in a nutshell, is the problem with ATVs, quads, dirt bikes, whatever you want to call those things. They provide easy access, lazy man's access, to all the remote corners of the countryside for people who've got no business being there. People who don't know how to behave. People who have no manners. People who don't know how to crap in the woods. Quad-clods.

It's like taking a dog that isn't house-trained into someone's beautiful living room.

I know this is tarring the innocent and the guilty with the same brush. I'm sure there are conscientious riders. But honestly, it's getting so that when I see a couple of guys in a pickup truck with a quad up in the box I can't help feeling a certain prejudice toward them.

Probably Budweiser drinkers.

(There are people who make fortunes selling these machines. As far as I'm concerned they're also responsible for that pile of crap and litter beside the mouth of the Chilcotin.)

Back up the hill I turn south along the terrace. Grassy meadows roll on ahead with a dramatic drop to the river on the left and a steep, almost sheer, forested slope rising to the sky on the right. Somewhere up there, running across the brow of that hill, must be the road I walked yesterday.

These meadows are also far from pristine. There's no bunchgrass except on the steeper slopes. But they're well into the mid-seral stages: Sandberg's bluegrass (*Poa secunda*), needle and thread grass, stiff needlegrass, and Kentucky bluegrass where there's more moisture. Prickly pear cactus everywhere.

Eventually the track reaches McEwan Creek, fords the stream and disappears uphill into the bush on the other side. That's enough for me. No need to climb all the way up to yesterday's missed turn. The afternoon is getting on and it's a long hike back to camp.

The views across the Fraser are no disappointment. Not too far away up that valley on the other side of the river is the oldest ranch in British Columbia, in fact the oldest ranch in western Canada, the Alkali Lake Ranch, pre-emption registered in 1861 and still very much in business today.

Coyote.

No doubt about it this time. Trotting across the meadow in front of me like he owns the place. Which I suppose, in a sense, he does.

Canis latrans, "barking dog."

A medium-sized predator, just over thirteen kilograms on average (males larger than females) and 120 centimetres in length, about a quarter of it bushy tail. Colour: a buff-gray, grizzled, pale below, black-tipped tail. Yellow eyes.

Coyotes breed late January to late March, at which time they can be seen chasing each other madly around the countryside, yipping and ki-yiing and generally raising a ruckus as well as making whoopee. Gestation lasts from sixty to sixty-three days. Litters average six pups but can be much larger. Eyes open after nine days. Young begin to emerge from the den around three weeks of age and are weaned between five and eight weeks, graduating to food regurgitated by the parents. Male pups disperse at six to nine months. Female pups tend to remain with their parents, forming the basis of a loose social group. Coyotes attain full growth around twelve months, reach sexual maturity at about two years and can live up to eighteen years in captivity.

Mostly they prey on small mammals though coyotes will, seemingly, eat just about anything they can catch. Carrion is an important part of their diet. They eat fruits and vegetables in season. They are capable of taking much larger game: deer, antelope and, yes, domestic stock. They've even, apparently, been known to attack and kill adult elk.

I've always been pretty casual about coyotes, love to hear them singing up a storm on a winter's evening. I love, too, the idea of their being so totally at home in this harsh climate, not just surviving, not just getting by, but being fully equal to it, comfortable with it, in all seasons of the year. I feel friendly toward them.

Even so, I should perhaps be exercising a little more caution. Anything that can kill an elk could probably kill me. And human attacks have been recorded, though fortunately they're extremely rare. (And, indeed, most of the coyotes I meet are exceedingly shy, having learned from bitter experience that human beings are not to be trusted.)

In Secwepemc traditional cosmology, the Old One, *ck'ewelx*, brings order out of chaos, introduces many plant and animal species, and teaches the people some of the basic skills they need to survive. But this is a raw and dangerous world, the myth world, a work in progress, a beta version full of bugs and glitches.

So the Old One sends Coyote, *sk'elep*, to finish the job, make the place more people-friendly. Big mistake. Hard to get good help, you know. Coyote turns out to be a trickster, selfish, cunning and lazy. His vices, especially his eye for the pretty ladies, often lead him into foolishness. But almost in spite of himself, Coyote does good work. Most importantly, he's the one who brings salmon into the Thompson and Fraser rivers. So the Secwepemc hold Coyote in high regard. They're grateful to him.

And for once, at least, modern science backs up Secwepemc tradition. Unlike the grey wolf, which is a relative newcomer to this continent, having emigrated from Eurasia (along with *Homo sapiens*), the coyote is a homegrown North American product, evolving right here alongside the dire wolf, short-faced bear, American mammoth and such-like.

So it's true. Coyote was here, shaping creation, for a long time before human beings, the Secwepemc or anybody else for that matter, came over the hill and down to the river.

In modern times, unique among sizeable predators, the coyote has actually expanded and extended its range in North America as human populations have grown. Now the little barking dogs are found from Panama to northern Canada and Alaska. They've even embraced an urban and suburban lifestyle: a neighbourhood park or an abandoned automobile for a denning site; maybe a nice rat (or cat) for supper.

But old man Coyote is still out here in the back of beyond, patrolling the terraces above the Chilcotin and Fraser rivers, though the place is now inhabited only by ghosts. He's probably still running errands for the Old One. Look at him go there, trotting across the meadow, straight as an arrow, purposeful. Clearly a dog with a mission.

It's very nearly dark by the time I get back to the Mossy Creek camp. Nice to have a home to come home to.

DAY SEVENTY-ONE
Saturday, September 20: Mossy Creek to Farwell Creek

t's a strange morning. The skies are a beautiful blue, brilliant with sunshine when I wake. It's bright and cheerful inside the tent but windy outside, with a stiff breeze blowing from the south, gusting, stirring the trees. There's much creaking and sighing. Very odd.

I'm well into the usual morning preparations, notes, breakfast and so on, when suddenly, blink, the lights go out. That beautiful sunshine is gone so abruptly you'd think somebody had thrown a switch, leaving the tent dark and dreary. I look out to find the sky already half overcast and clouds flying northward on the wind. Soon the last scrap of blue is gone, swallowed up. And there's more than a hint of rain in the air.

Drat.

Double drat.

This is my comeuppance for slacking off yesterday.

What now? Should I stay? Should I go?

I know from bitter experience that walking in the rain is no fun. I also know that if I'm going to get weathered in it's best to stay close to a reliable source of water. I could probably pass a couple of wet days here in relative comfort.

But I'm desperately impatient to be gone. I'm so close to finishing this thing now. I just want to get it done.

I'm also a little anxious that a change in the weather could yet cheat me of my accomplishment The equinox, after all, is just three days away. I can feel the whole countryside teetering on the edge of that profound shift from summer to winter. Any day now the first storm of autumn will roll in. A week or ten days of foul weather at a stretch is not out of the question. My supplies are getting low. I can't afford to lose more than a day or two.

Still no rain. Is it brighter? Is it darker? Very much against my better judgment I finish packing, strike the tent and hit the trail.

At least the walking is easy enough, that's a blessing. But the weather continues to deteriorate. Out in the first meadow, where the view opens up, I can see curtains of rain all around the compass: across the higher ground north and south of the river and far to the east and west.

But my guardian angel hasn't altogether abandoned me. One way or another the tempest passes me by. I walk on and am spared, except for a little shower at noon. I take refuge under an old Douglas-fir, a real veteran, one of three or four along this edge of the meadow. I eat my lunch and wait for the squall to pass.

These meadows would likely have been much larger and more extensive back in the days of those old-time cattle drives from the top of the canyon. We have here a prime example of one of British Columbia's chief grassland management issues: the conversion of open range to forest. What a range ecologist would call "ingrowth" or "encroachment."

It's easy to see that not very long ago the wide spaces between the old Douglas-firs were open ground, covered in grass, part of the meadow. Now relatively dense stands of much younger trees occupy these spaces, with very little grass growing beneath them. This is called ingrowth: young trees filling the spaces between older trees.

Meanwhile, out along the edge of the meadow, a scattering of even younger trees is growing up. That would be referred to as encroachment: converting the meadow itself to forest.

Research suggests that the loss of grassland to invading forest in the last hundred years has varied between about 10 and 50 percent in different areas of the province with the rate of loss being highest where relatively cool, moist local climates favour the growth of tree seedlings.

It may even be that these meadows here are a sort of accident or artefact or artificial consequence of wildfire. They should be forest. Evidently the climate is sufficiently cool and moist for seedling trees to survive the hot, dry days of summer. But until relatively recently, perhaps, periodic wildfires destroyed the seedlings and young trees, limiting ingrowth and encroachment, maintaining the meadows as open grassland. In effect, the grasslands themselves are a mid-seral stage in a succession that will eventually yield a Douglas-fir forest. That's the theory anyway.

For a variety of reasons, including increasingly effective fire suppression and control, the last hundred years have seen fewer and less-extensive wildfires. These meadows are shrinking as trees take root, survive and grow, eventually shading out the grass.

There are those who advocate deliberate prescription burning as a sort of tonic to restore the open rangeland. The idea is that small, frequent fires would better mimic natural conditions, killing small trees and seedlings, maintaining the open ground, while leaving larger, older trees unharmed.

But playing with fire is a tricky business. Timing and intensity are everything. Low-intensity fires may favour grasslands. But hotter, high-intensity fires will kill bunchgrass as well as trees, favouring weedy invaders: cheatgrass, bluegrass, quackgrass, saskatoon, choke-cherry, snowbrush, willows, aspens, etc.

(And I can't help thinking that, really, there is no such thing as a "controlled burn," an oxymoron if ever I heard one.)

Besides which, fire is always something of a catastrophe to living ecosystems. Plants and animals are killed. Organic matter is destroyed. Soil nutrients are lost. Wind and water erosion is accelerated.

And the lack of wildfire may not be the only factor.

I observe that ingrowth and encroachment always seem most severe where ranges have been badly overgrazed or otherwise damaged. Perhaps that accelerates the process. Douglas-fir is a bit of a weed, thriving on disturbance. I've seen it growing in hedgerows along the line of old Caterpillar tractor tracks or on abandoned fencelines. Maybe healthy grasslands with a flourishing growth of bunchgrass and a solid biological soil crust are better able to resist the invasion of tree seedlings. Maybe overgrazing disrupts that resistance, giving ingrowth and encroachment a head start. If that's true, simply setting fire to a piece of countryside is not going to restore grasslands. There are more fundamental issues to resolve.

The Farwell Canyon Road turns out to be a broad gravel thoroughfare. I'm there by about half past two, and by four o'clock I'm at the bottom of the hill after a long winding descent into the Chilcotin River valley. The views are beautiful, with fantastic landforms and the river, a vivid glacial blue-green, winding past the earth-coloured hoodoos and cliffs of the canyon.

I camp well back under the cottonwoods on Farwell Creek, behind "Mike" Farwell's original homestead. I'm lucky to find a spot free of cactus and poison ivy. There's good water and a bit of shelter that I'll be grateful for if the weather should deteriorate further.

The next couple of days are going to be tricky. For one thing I've checked my supplies and find that I have barely three days' worth of food left in the bag. Maybe four if I'm careful.

And I still hope to make a side trip out along the north rim of the canyon into Junction Sheep Range Provincial Park. From the beginning I've looked forward to that side trip, the high point of the whole journey, the climax of my experience. It's the goal I've been working toward all this way. But it means a good deal of extra walking, one full day out into the park and one full day back.

Then there'll be another day of walking north to Highway 20 at Riske Creek.

That should pretty much use up my rations.

And I've got another problem. In all that country, except maybe somewhere up toward Riske Creek, there's not a single good water source I know of. It's going to be a thirsty trip.

But I do believe I can manage on what I carry away from here. I'll fill my belly with water before I start, of course, the human camel. And fill all the water bottles. As far as grub goes, I'll just have to be careful. It's a bit of a stretch, perhaps, but doable as long as nothing goes wrong.

DAY SEVENTY-TWO
Sunday, September 21:
Farwell Creek to Junction Sheep Range Provincial Park

Famous last words.

In the wee hours I'm roused by the dreary sound of rain on the tent-fly. And I wake in the morning to curtains of mist drifting across the distant ridges and a sky sombre with heavy cloud.

There goes the ball game.

Disappointed, I busy myself with breakfast, yesterday's notes, all the usual chores. There's no shortage of time to consider options. Certainly I'll not be going anywhere in this kind of weather. Out comes the paperback, carried all this way for just such an occasion, and I possess myself in patience. At least the precipitation seems to have eased off down here along the river.

By mid-morning the sky is much brighter. The rain has gone from the ridges and the sun is making a feeble attempt to break through. I begin to consider, just as an outside possibility, the chance that I might yet get away today. Time is passing and the days are short in late September. Designated decision time: eleven o'clock for a possible departure at noon.

Stay or go?

Go.

It's still mostly overcast but there are patches of blue sky. The ground is drying fast. I get the camp down in record time, pack loaded, water bottles full, and I'm back on the road shortly after twelve.

The Farwell Canyon bridge spans the Chilcotin River at a narrow point where the whole river pours and boils through a rocky gorge. Beyond the bridge the road climbs steeply, winding back and forth across the slope on the north side of the valley. I find it a strain (all that water I'm carrying doesn't help) but at least the day is relatively cool.

Halfway up the hill two young women in a little station wagon stop to offer me a lift. I regretfully decline. Gotta walk it. It would be a shame to weaken now that I've come so far and am very nearly there.

At the top there's a little track branching off to the right. I cache one of the water bottles and a few bits of extra gear under a handy bush. The less the weight the lighter the miles.

Now the going is relatively easy. The track leads through a landscape of gently rolling countryside, more or less level, mostly open grassland with scattered groves of trembling aspen, golden leafed. There are mixed woodlands down in the gullies and Douglas-fir forest back along the edge of the valley. As I walk, the day turns into something quite lovely weather-wise, with blue sky and bright autumn sunshine, though there's still plenty of scattered cloud, unstable air and distant squalls along the horizon.

Early in the afternoon I hear a familiar calling, that musical gabbling, rolled *r*'s, *r-r-r-r-r-r*, and look up to see a flock of sandhill cranes going over, perhaps a thousand feet up, heading southeast, evidently making for the Fraser. It's a big flock, larger than the one I saw at Bunchgrass Mountain, perhaps two hundred birds.

No, wait, make that two flocks. Here's a second one coming in from the north. Well, actually, wait again, because now I have three flocks in view. There's another one trailing along some distance behind. Must be five or six hundred of the big birds altogether.

It takes the whole procession quite some time to pass and I just stand there, rapt, watching, staring upward until they're almost out of sight. I wave my hat at the stragglers, wish them goodbye, safe journey, easy winter.

Enjoy California.

Don't stay away too long.

And I can't help wondering what it all portends.

Junction Sheep Range Provincial Park is an unusual park. There are no facilities. No effort is made to encourage human traffic. Certainly you wouldn't want to try driving the family sedan down that little track. And it's an awfully long walk from Farwell Canyon Road.

But worth every step as it turns out.

The place is all that I hoped it would be: beautiful bunchgrass, especially on the high meadows above the Fraser; lovely old interior Douglas-firs, gnarled and majestic; distant views up and down the river flowing through its deep valley, still very much a canyon here.

Evidently grace and beauty are still alive in my world and on an ample scale. No little backyard ecosystems here. This is a horizon-to-horizon scale, a suck-in-a-chest-full-of-air-and-rejoice scale. A fitting climax to my pilgrimage.

Hallelujah!

In 1973 the Lands Branch of the provincial government arranged a swap with Riske Creek Ranching (formerly the Cotton and Deer Park Ranches) to acquire land for a 4,573-hectare wildlife reserve at the junction of the Chilcotin and Fraser rivers. The reserve was intended to protect critical breeding, lambing and winter range for the largest population of non-migratory California bighorn sheep in North America, approximately five hundred animals, and, not incidentally, to protect essential habitat for many other hard-pressed grassland species as well.

In 1987 the reserve was renamed Junction Wildlife Management Area. Then in 1995, based on recommendations in the Cariboo–Chilcotin Land Use Plan, it was designated a provincial park.

Every pilgrimage needs a final shrine and a couple of saints. My track ends at a cairn perched on a hilltop high above the confluence of the Chilcotin and Fraser rivers. On the cairn is a brass plaque. And the brass plaque reads:

This plaque is dedicated to the memory of Harold Mitchell, Wildlife Biologist, and Wes Prediger, Wildlife Technician, killed in a helicopter crash March 2, 1981. These men worked tirelessly to have the "junction range" set aside as a permanent habitat for California bighorn sheep, historic residents of this natural grassland.

—Ministry of Environment, October, 1982

It is a much-needed reminder that committed, concerned people can make a better world, even in the face of inertia and determined opposition. Again I say, *Hallelujah*.

I reach the cairn just after six o'clock in the evening, do my seven circuits in the prescribed clockwise direction, thank all the powers that be for my deliverance and a safe conclusion to this long journey. Take some photos. Drink a little water. Meditate briefly on all the days and weeks and kilometres of walking that have brought me to this spot. Then it's time to think about finding a place to spend the night.

All day long the weather has cooperated, sending the squalls north and south and all around, giving me dry paths and sunny skies. But by the time I get the tent up, the sky to the west is one great mass of black.

This one is not going around. I've barely stowed the gear when the wind, which has been blowing fairly steadily all day from the south, swings abruptly to the west and rises in less time than you could believe to a shrieking gale, bringing the first few drops of the deluge. I can see it coming at me across the grass.

Moments later the heavens open. The tent shakes and flaps and quivers like a living thing but seems equal to the blow. For an hour or more the storm rages unabated before the wind finally eases a few notches. I read for a time by the light of my headlamp. It's still raining when I finally drift off, thanks to the earplugs I prudently included in the kit.

And what about tomorrow? God only knows. I don't want to get stuck here for any length of time. It's far too exposed and there's no water except what's left in the bottles (and what's coming out of the sky I suppose), a swallow for breakfast, not much more. The idea of slogging twenty kilometres back to the Farwell Canyon Road over a slippery, muddy track doesn't much appeal to me. But in a day or two I won't have much choice. I'll be out of food.

DAY SEVENTY-THREE
Monday, September 22:
Junction Sheep Range Provincial Park to Farwell Canyon

I wake in darkness to a tent still rackety with the wind. It's five o'clock in the morning by my watch. I can't tell, with all the tumult, if it's still raining. But I fear the worst, imagining the long wet day to come. Clouds low on the ridges. Tedious long hours stuck in the tent while the dirt track back to the Farwell Canyon Road, my escape route, grows less and less passable. All very discouraging.

So when the tent lights up shortly after seven o'clock, waking me from a shallow doze, and I look outside to discover the most beautiful blue-sky day imaginable, a few puffy cumulus clouds away to the west and south, I practically laugh aloud with relief and amazement. My guardian angel is still on the job evidently. Somebody's looking after me.

But it's chilly out there, with a cold wind blowing hard from the northwest. It's a very different sort of day from yesterday: a dramatic change in the weather and a change in season too, I guess, right on schedule. Perhaps that's what those cranes yesterday were trying to tell me: *Here it comes! Take cover! We're out of here! Goodbye!*

The tent-fly is already dry and the grass, too. Even the earth around the tent. No mud. All that moisture has been hoovered away by the wind ablowing all night long. Things are definitely looking up.

By the time I'm ready to start walking, the wind has eased off, thank goodness. I'll be heading straight into it today and the air is still quite brisk. For the first time in a long while I'm obliged to put on some extra clothing to ward off the morning chill.

One more visit to the cairn. A last look at the view. And an observation on the nature of pilgrimage:

You get to the object of your pilgrimage, the destination or goal you've been seeking all these long weeks and months. This holy, sacred place. You give thanks, rejoice a little, celebrate the accomplishment. Receive the blessing.

And then you move on.

You'd think that, having spent all the time and effort to get here, the pilgrim might want to hang about for a bit. Enjoy the fruits of their labours. But there's no point really. It's the getting here that's been important. It's the journey, the effort, and the experience of the journey that confers grace, not the being here.

(Though another time, in spring perhaps, when the grass is green and the flowers in bloom, I'd be glad for a chance to know this place better. It would be a different sort of experience, instructive in other ways.)

Maybe I've just become addicted to moving on.

It's a lovely walk and a lovely day for a walk. A rain-washed day, each distant feature sharp and clear. The monster pack (with the water bottles nearly empty and the food bag down to a bare two days' allowance) is a shadow of its former self, much reduced in weight, almost bearable. And the cooler, moister weather is actually a blessing considering that I don't have any water. I'll dehydrate much less quickly than I would on a hot day.

A couple of ravens fly by. *Whoosh, whoosh, whoosh.*

Five sharp-tailed grouse, perhaps a grown-up brood, flush from the side of the track some distance ahead. They're cautious birds evidently, a little nervous out here in the open, not at all like the spruce grouse and the blue grouse and the ruffed grouse back in the forest, waiting to take wing until they're almost underfoot. These birds are very different in appearance, too. They look pale, almost ghostly, as they sail away. And they seem much more at home in the air. They're strong flyers, not settling again until almost out of sight, several hundred metres downwind.

Today, September 22, 3:44 p.m., the equinox.

I reach the Farwell Canyon Road just after four o'clock, recover my gear and immediately empty a third of the spare water bottle's contents down my throat, tomorrow's water, never mind, pure pleasure. Then I spend a few moments considering my options. It seems a little early to be quitting. But darkness comes early these days and this will be my last opportunity to sleep in wild country. Tomorrow there'll be houses and fences and fields. No decision at all, really. I'll stay.

As it happens, the view from my campsite might almost have been chosen to carry me, in imagination, back along the line of my journey. First there's the Junction Sheep Range, south and east a little, still quite close in the middle distance. Then the Chilcotin River valley and the Fraser River valley winding away to the south. On the horizon the Marble Range mountains, high above Big Bar. There's fresh snow on some of those peaks from last night's storm.

Beyond that it becomes a work of memory. From Big Bar back south to Lillooet. From Lillooet back east across the Clear Ranges to Hat Creek, past the Cornwall Hills and into the Thompson River valley. East to Kamloops and the Lac du Bois grasslands. From Kamloops south to Nicola Lake and east across the Nicola basin to Bent Creek and Shorts Creek and the Okanagan Valley. South through the Okanagan to Osoyoos, up the Similkameen to the Ashnola and up the Ashnola to Crater Mountain. There, all done.

It's easy enough to recall individual places; the memories are clear and vivid. But it's harder to compass the whole continuous span and distance, step by step. The time and effort involved. I wonder how far beyond that horizon the Ashnola River valley and Crater Mountain really are? How long did it take to cover all of that ground? It's easy enough to say "seventy-three days," but that doesn't begin to capture any real sense of the minute-by-minute experience, hours and days, every single step of the way.

Below the tent a broad terrace, still high above the Chilcotin River. The range here isn't of the same quality as some of the pristine grassland I saw yesterday out in the park. That's to be expected this close to a major road. It's still very good though. Bluebunch wheatgrass, Sandberg's bluegrass, a bit of stiff needlegrass. All natives. A scattering of dark Douglas-fir. A grove of aspen off to one side, the foliage a little thinner than it was yesterday thanks to last night's gale, but still a brilliant fluttering orange-gold. And the scent of autumn in the air.

A sweet spot.

Except for one thing.

There's astonishingly heavy traffic on the Farwell Canyon Road. A steady procession of logging trucks, one after the other, like a convoy, like some sort of military exercise, each following hard on the last. The valley is full of noise, gearboxes and engines whining as the big vehicles, heavily laden, come crawling down into the canyon from the south and then back up again headed north. It was only a lucky chance that I happened onto the road during a weekend, Saturday and Sunday, when it was relatively deserted, thank goodness. It wouldn't have been much fun sharing those long hills with all that.

Most of those trucks will be carrying beetle-killed pine, salvaged. But I don't doubt there'll be some recently living logs too. Maybe even a few that come from the upper Churn Creek watershed, countryside that was once part of the national park proposal back in 1994. Countryside that was relatively untouched in those days. Well it's not pristine anymore.

Sometimes it seems to me that this kind of diminishment of the landscape must be almost inevitable given basic human nature, need and greed, all the powerful economic forces at work. But the lesson of that cairn out in the park is that it needn't necessarily be so. Determined people can make a difference, that's the point. We don't have to yield to devastation; it is not inevitable. Change may be coming, given the forces at work. But we can shape it to suit our purposes, our own needs and values. Surely this is the one thing that distinguishes our species: a capacity to defy the inevitable, to lift ourselves from the path of least resistance.

And there are other powerful forces at work in this world besides economics: human decency, love of beauty, a deep current of loyalty and affection for beloved home places. Harold Mitchell and Wes Prediger are not the only ones to have stood up in defence of the wild countryside. Everywhere, it seems, in every community, there are those, often working in isolation, certainly unheralded, who do their bit. Speak out. Write letters. Attend endless meetings. All purely for love of the land. My heroes.

DAY SEVENTY-FOUR
Tuesday, September 23: Farwell Canyon to McIntyre Lake

By the time the sun finally rises I'm in no great mood to appreciate it. The traffic through Farwell Canyon did ease off through the late afternoon and evening, and I managed to catch a few hours of sleep. But they were back at it again in the wee hours. It's a very early start for those guys. And consequently for me, too, more's the pity. I've a long day ahead.

Happily, the weather seems to be holding. It's another blue-sky morning but cold! The first real frost of the season glitters on the tent-fly, melting at a touch from the sun. Everything gets more difficult as the countryside moves toward winter. The days get shorter, one's hands grow clumsy with the cold. It's time to wrap this up, as those cranes were telling me yesterday.

My map indicates a forestry campsite at McIntyre Lake, around the spot where Highway 20, heading east toward Williams Lake, begins its long descent toward the Sheep Creek bridge across the Fraser River. That's quite a hike from here, thirty-five kilometres, give or take, to judge by the map. But it seems as likely a spot as any to spend the night.

As soon as I step onto the road, I know what kind of day I'm in for. The traffic is ferocious. Fortunately the surface has been treated with something and it's a good deal less dusty than it might be, but flying gravel is still a real hazard. The drivers are professionals. Without exception they do what they can to give me some room, slowing down, swinging wide. Much appreciated.

Nothing but little sticks up in the trucks' bunks today, all beetle-killed pine.

I've covered practically the whole distance to Highway 20 when I come across a tiny creek trickling down off the higher ground on the left side of the road. Who knows what's up that hill, but it hardly matters, I'm that desperate. I do the full treatment, filter and purification drops. The water tastes just fine and I'm very glad to have it. I fill all the bottles, just in case, and it's wonderful the sense of well-being I get, having all that water back in the pack. True wealth. (Heavy though.)

The Farwell Canyon Road runs along the western rim of a great open basin compassing Becher's prairie and the Toosey Indian Reserves 1 and 1A of the Tl'esqox First Nation. I've now passed into the traditional territory of the Tsilhqot'in or Chilcotin people, which includes most of the high country drained by the Chilcotin River and its tributaries between the Coast Mountains and the Fraser River, and also the headwaters of three rivers, the Homathko, the Klinaklini and the Dean, that flow westward through the Coast Range. The Tsilhqot'ins are Athapaskan speakers quite distinct from the Interior Salish.

I've long since left the wild country behind, as expected. It's all pasture here, domestic grasses, fences, houses, livestock. Just before the highway, on the rim of that basin, the road dips a little to cross Riske Creek.

It's already late afternoon, but I'm stubbornly determined to finish the day's walk at McIntyre Lake.

I turn right and set off briskly along the pavement, headed east. There's still heavy traffic, of course, but much less dust and no flying gravel, which is a relief. I force myself to stop once or twice for a rest, a drink of water and a meagre bite of food. (It's surprising how much even a brief stop can recharge the batteries.) I haven't gone far when I notice heavy overcast moving in rapidly from the west. By the time I reach McIntyre Lake, the blue sky and sunshine have gone. What's left of the day is grey, a bit bleak, fading fast. And there's a cold wind blowing out of the east or northeast. Doesn't bode well for tomorrow.

The McIntyre Lake forestry campsite is a disappointment. It's tidy enough, with no garbage or litter (which is a blessing; some of these little forestry campsites are a mess), but the place is infested with cattle. There are cows everywhere. Cows with digestive upset, evidently, because the place is covered in puddles of foul-smelling manure. The shoreline is churned to muck. Some joker's idea of "multiple use," I suppose. No tenting here.

So I retreat back into the bush, my natural habitat, alert for a bit of ground, open and level, where I can set up the tent. When that's done I gather dead brushwood to build a rough boma or kraal to keep the stock at bay through the night. By now, with that growing overcast, it's virtually dark. A black night. I'm thirsty, tired, very hungry and thoroughly out of sorts.

Then from somewhere in the gloom above I hear a great flock of geese coming in low (from the south, oddly), no doubt headed toward the pothole country I know lies just to the north. I can hear those birds talking to one another, the sound of beating wings, very close but invisible up there in the dark. Ghost geese.

Barely has the sound of their passage died away when I hear another flock, smaller this time, ducks I think, coming in very fast, right overhead, with the wind whistling across their set wings, tearing the air, the sound of tiny jet fighters in the night. Perhaps they're going to land on McIntyre Lake.

So there is magic and wonderment and grace in the world after all and the thought of that restores my equilibrium.

Tomorrow is very much up in the air, like the geese and the ducks. I'll have to see what this change in the weather brings. I've always imagined myself finishing my journey at Williams Lake, walking right to the depot, boarding the bus, rolling away. Finis. The end. Fade to black. Roll credits.

It would only be another thirty-five kilometres along the highway, the same distance I walked today, but I'm not enthusiastic. From here it's anticlimax all the way. And I'm very short of food, with just the scrapings of the bag left for breakfast tomorrow. Water will be a problem too. If the weather turns really awful overnight I may take it as a sign that I should call it quits right here. Hang out my thumb and see if I can catch a ride.

DAY SEVENTY-FIVE
Wednesday, September 24:
McIntyre Lake to Williams Lake

Hope is a moral obligation.

—Tony Kushner
(CBC interview with Eleanor Wachtel, September 25, 2011)

wake in the wee hours to the sound of raindrops on the tent-fly. A cozy sound if you happen to be someplace where you can wait it out in comfort. But the patter of raindrops quickly gives way to a steady downpour. No longer a cozy sound. And I know there isn't going to be any waiting it out. Not this time. The empty food bag and half-empty water bottles tell me so.

By first light the rain has pretty much eased off. That's a bit of luck, but my mind is made up. I eat a meagre breakfast, drink the last swallow of water, sponge most of the moisture off the tent-fly and start packing with hitchhiking in mind. I tidy up as well as I can. But I can't discard the filthy T-shirt and walking shorts just yet, seeing as I'm reserving my one change of clean dry clothing for the bus, in deference to the luckless fellow traveller who occupies the seat beside me.

Then I hit the road, which is to say: I walk back to the highway and down to the brake check at the top of the hill, dump my pack, stick out my thumb and wait.

There's a moderate amount of traffic, even on such a wet day, but it's a good hour before one kindly soul, Ron from Tsylos Park Lodge, finally pulls over to offer me a lift. (I can hardly blame the others who go whistling by. Doubtless I'm a sight to see after two weeks on the trail and a wet night.)

"So," he says, eyeing my travel-stained gear and worn-out boots, "where've you been?"

It takes a while to explain.

My good Samaritan drives me all the way to Williams Lake (thirty-five kilometres, a long day's hike, covered in what seems like the blink of an eye) and delivers me right to the bus depot. The southbound bus isn't due for a couple of hours, plenty of time to freshen up a little and get changed. Time for a cheeseburger and french fries at the café. Very tasty! The apple pie is tempting but I restrain myself, perversely, just to prove I can. All things in moderation.

And I guess that's it.

Done.

I have a simple and irrefutable answer to some of the questions I posed myself so long ago and so far away: Can I do this? Is it practical and feasible? Will I be able to get through?

It's done.

Answers to some of the other questions are more complicated. Questions like: Will it be worthwhile? Is there any pristine countryside left? Is there any hope for the future? I have some misgivings, but my answer is, essentially, yes. Most definitely.

It's raining again by departure time. The highway is slick and glistening, with heavy traffic splashing through the puddles. The bus turns left at the intersection of Highway 97 and Oliver Street, heading out of town past all the gas stations, burger joints and motor hotels.

Churn Creek and the Junction Sheep Range already seem worlds away, as remote and unreal as mirages and very nearly as ephemeral.

How long, I have to wonder, can the loveliness of such places survive in the face of all this? The pressure of humanity. The pressure of traffic. The fierce pressures for economic development, a steamroller, seemingly so overwhelming and inevitable.

I sense a terrible apathy here as well. Everybody is so busy, so focused on their own lives, their own pressing concerns and pleasures. How can they find time to worry about the wild and remote countryside? For most people *this* is what's real, this fierce urban life. The continued existence of a lovely, fragile bunchgrass meadow somewhere on a ridge high above the Fraser River, in the back of beyond, must seem as inconsequential as smoke to them. I mean, who cares?

Then there is outright hostility. This is the town, after all, where the Churn Creek National Park died, bleeding and broken, on the Cariboo Chilcotin CORE table.

And certainly all the processes that have so diminished the grassland valleys of southern interior British Columbia seem to continue relatively unabated: overgrazing, abuse by motorsports enthusiasts, careless urban and suburban development, invasive species. Protection for the few remaining relatively intact ecosystems seems half-hearted, a public-relations exercise rather than a sincere effort.

What hope is there for the long-term survival of indigenous ecosystems, the last bits of grace and beauty, in the face of all that?

Well...

The Churn Creek Protected Area and the Junction Sheep Range Provincial Park may seem several worlds away from the front seat of a Greyhound bus rolling south out of Williams Lake, but those wild and beautiful places *are* still out there. That's a fact.

And, too, there are all the other bits and pieces of more or less pristine countryside I've encountered during the last fourteen or fifteen months, some protected, some not: steep little meadows in the heavily populated Okanagan or Similkameen valleys; a corner of somebody's rangeland in the Nicola that somehow escaped heavy grazing; a fenced-off road allowance along the Thompson; a remote valley in the canyon of the Fraser River, bright with sunshine. And so on. It's true that the original pristine valley grasslands of southern interior British Columbia have been very much diminished in the last couple of hundred years by wear and tear, neglect and abuse. Undeniably so. But indigenous ecosystems do survive, here and there, in bits and pieces.

Including some quite large bits and pieces.

You just have to go looking.

And one of the really encouraging aspects of grassland

conservation is that you don't need a whole valley or mountain range to maintain a functioning ecosystem. You can have a very nice little bit of bunchgrass meadow or wetland or riparian woodland or ponderosa parkland in the back forty acres. Or in somebody's backyard, come right down to it.

Individual landowners, concerned ranchers, small community groups and forward-thinking municipalities can and do make a difference. This conservation effort doesn't require vast organizations, political consensus, massive funding. This could be an I-can-do-it-myself-without-needing-help-or-permission-from-anybody campaign, working on a small scale, adding up to something really quite significant.

The other encouraging thing is that even badly damaged grassland ecosystems may not be irreparable. If they're not too far gone, they can come back, though they might need a little help. And it doesn't take lifetimes. In all but the harshest environments you can see the results of conservation efforts in a few decades, sometimes just a few years. Very gratifying. There's hope for the future.

And there's further hope, I believe, in a growing public awareness of British Columbia's indigenous grasslands. At long last there's an increasing sense of the value of native grasslands and the urgent need to protect and shelter whatever fragments remain.

It has taken time for that awareness to develop. Grasslands are at a disadvantage in competing for a share of public attention with all those gorgeous images of soaring snow-capped peaks, crashing surf, forests of giant trees, the whole panoply of vivid environmental causes. The appeal here is softer, more muted, understated. A profound peace and quiet rather than tumult. A whisper of wind through the grass.

Even so, grasslands do touch us profoundly, they strike chords in heart and soul that no other environment can hope to reach. This is not so surprising, really. We are a grassland species after all, no matter where we have journeyed since. Grasslands are us. They appeal to the deepest levels of human consciousness. For me, for you, for all humankind, grasslands, including these arid valley grasslands of southern interior British Columbia, will always be a home of the heart.

The journey of a thousand miles begins with a single step.

—Lao Tzu "Tao Te Ching"

Epilogue

Two roads diverged in a yellow wood,
And sorry I could not travel both
And be one traveler, long I stood
And looked down one as far as I could
To where it bent in the undergrowth;

Then took the other, as just as fair,
And having perhaps the better claim,
Because it was grassy and wanted wear;
Though as for that the passing there
Had worn them really about the same,

And both that morning equally lay
In leaves no step had trodden black.
Oh, I kept the first for another day!
Yet knowing how way leads on to way,
I doubted if I should ever come back.

I shall be telling this with a sigh
Somewhere ages and ages hence:
Two roads diverged in a wood, and I—
I took the one less traveled by,
And that has made all the difference.

—Robert Frost, "The Road Not Taken"
(from *Mountain Interval*)

A thing of beauty is a joy forever:
Its loveliness increases; it will never
Pass into nothingness; but still will keep
A bower quiet for us, and a sleep
Full of sweet dreams, and health, and quiet breathing.

—John Keats, "Endymion: Book I"

Author's Note

It takes time to write a book and see it into print. A lot of water has passed under the bridge since I did the long walk on which this narrative is based and, inevitably, there have been changes in the countryside since I saw it, some positive, some not. McIntyre Dam has been modified to allow the passage of salmon (though they cannot yet pass the dam at Okanagan Falls). The long association between First Nations and the places we call Haynes Point Provincial Park and Okanagan Falls Provincial Park has been recognized, and that recognition has been marked by a change in names: Haynes Point Provincial Park is now sẃiẃs Provincial Park; Okanagan Falls Provincial Park is now sx̌ʷəx̌ʷnitkʷ Provincial Park. Shorts Creek Canyon, Fintry High Farm and the Fintry Protected Area suffered a major forest fire with extensive damage. The Kamloops Range Research Unit is now just an empty building, so I'm told—what a waste. The Frolek family has transferred much of the land it owned around Lac du Bois to the Nature Conservancy of Canada, a very welcome addition to the complex of protected areas in the Lac du Bois Grasslands. There's talk of logging in Oregon Jack Canyon. And so it goes.

It is almost certain in the course of such a long journey through the backcountry that I will have strayed inadvertently and without permission across parcels of private land. I will to take this opportunity to apologize to the owners of those properties for the discourtesy.

Acknowledgments

Special thanks to my agent, Carolyn Woodward, who stayed with me through thick and thin; to Allan MacDougall at Raincoast Books; to Rob Sanders at Greystone Books; to Scott Steedman and Michelle Benjamin who got me started. In a sense this is their book.

And I wish to acknowledge substantial financial support from the Canada Council for the Arts, the Writers' Trust of Canada, Shirley Langer, Kathleen and Gary Shaw, Valerie Langer and Nicole Rycroft, John Kerr, Vermilion Forks Field Naturalists (Princeton), Susan Bloom, Tena and Doug Pitt-Brooke.

I may have walked alone, but I had a good deal of help with logistics along the way. Many of those who helped are mentioned in this book but I also want to acknowledge Maria and Karl-Heinz Mascher, the Bishop family (Gail, Viny and Jude), Peter McAllister, Mike Kennedy, Terry Pitt-Brooke, Doug and Tena Pitt-Brooke, who became quite accustomed to dropping me off and picking me up in out-of-the-way places. Also my thanks to every driver who slowed down and swung wide.

I benefited enormously from the generosity and support of those who have provided me with a variety of places to live and work on this project over the years: Peter McAllister and Bernadette Mertens-McAllister; Brian Park and Andrea Mulder (the world's best neighbours); Ken Friesen and his associates; Mark and Anna Termuende; Sharon Lawrence; Doug and Tena Pitt-Brooke; the library and security staff—Jennifer Sigalet, Karen Friesen, Daniel DeGroot and Dave More—at the Kalamalka Campus of Okanagan College; Molly March; Heather Hilliard and Ken Farris; Mary Bewick; Pat McAllister; Josie Osborne and George Patterson; Georg and Rhonda Schurian; Daphne Wass and Greg Lang; Tony Wass and JoAnne Nelson; Jim and Jackie Finlayson; the Raikes family.

I also benefited greatly from those who donated equipment to the cause (computers, cameras, vehicles and camping gear) and helped with technical advice: the Mountain Equipment Co-op, John and Dale Kerr, Michael and Michele Gould, Jim Finlayson, Pat McAllister, Carole Ruth, Molly March, Samantha Flynn.

I want to mention my designated readers: Sharon Lawrence, Tish Woodley, Shelley Baumbrough, Molly March. Also John Lent and Mark Zuehlke, who wrote in support of a successful grant application. And Mark Hobson, Paulette Laurendeau, Josie Osborne, Margaret Eady and Sandi Rideout, who collected the mail.

And I need to express my appreciation, not least, to all those friends and family who have helped with much-needed moral support. It's been a long, crooked road. The list is very lengthy and I'm terribly afraid of missing somebody. You know who you are, all of you, and how profoundly grateful I am for the encouragement you've given me over the years.

A project like this builds on a store of knowledge and information hard-won by other people and I wish to acknowledge that debt. I talked with people like Dennis Lloyd, Rick Tucker, Bill Henwood, Don Gayton, Kristi Iverson and the people at the Grasslands Conservation Council of British Columbia (particularly mappers Ryan Holmes, Graham MacGregor, Bruce Rea and Ian Graeme). I read references too numerous to mention. And I benefited from a new tool, the internet search engine, which came to me partway through the project and changed the world. (Does anybody remember library card catalogues and *Books in Print*?)

And finally, my thanks to my editors and the staff at Harbour Publishing, particularly Nicola Goshulak, Cheryl Cohen, Daniela Hajdukovic, Sarah Corsie, Mary White and Audrey McClellan.

Notes

1.   Garrett Hardin, "The Tragedy of the Commons." *Science*, New Series, 162, No. 3859 (1968): 1243–1248.

2.   By Henry Miller from HENRY MILLER ON WRITING, copyright © 1944, 1957, 1964 by Henry Miller, Copyright © 1939, 1941, 1957 by New Directions Publishing Corp. Reprinted by permission of New Directions Publishing Corp.

3.   Ted Lea, "Historical (Pre-Settlement) Ecosystems of the Okanagan Valley and Lower Similkameen Valley of British Columbia, Pre-European Contact to the Present." *Davidsonia* 19, No 1 (2008): 3–36.

4.   BC Ministry of Forests and Range, "Fire Review Summary for Okanagan Mountain Fire (K50628)." 2003.

5.   Gary Filmon, "Firestorm 2003: Provincial Review: Final Report." BC Government, 2004.

6.   Annie Dillard, *Pilgrim at Tinker Creek*. New York: HarperCollins Publishers, 2013.

7.   Ibid.

8.   Excerpt from THE SOUND OF MOUNTAIN WATER by Wallace Stegner, copyright © 1969 by Wallace Stegner. Used by permission of Doubleday, an imprint of the Knopf Doubleday Publishing Group, a division of Penguin Random House LLC. All rights reserved." "CODA: Wilderness Letter" from THE SOUND OF MOUNTAIN WATER by Wallace Stegner. Copyright © 1960, 1988 by Wallace Stegner. Used by permission of Brandt & Hochman Literary Agents, Inc. Any electronic copying or distribution of this text is expressly forbidden.

9.   A.W.F. Banfield, *The Mammals of Canada*. Toronto: University of Toronto Press, 1974.

10.   Stephen Herrero, *Bear Attacks: Their Causes and Avoidance*. Toronto: McClelland & Stewart, 2003.

11.   Richard J. Cannings, "Status of the Long-Billed Curlew in British Columbia." *Wildlife Working Report* 96. Victoria: British Columbia Ministry of Environment, Lands and Parks, 1999.

12.   Timothy Frederick Johnsen, "Late Glacial Lakes of

the Thompson Basin, Southern Interior of British Columbia: Paleogeography and Paleoenvironment." Master's thesis, Simon Fraser University, 2004.

13. Brian Hayden and June M. Ryder, "Prehistoric Cultural Collapse in the Lillooet Area." *American Antiquity* 56, No. 1 (1991): 50–65.

14. William C. Sturtevant and Deward E. Walker, eds., *Handbook of North American Indians*, Volume 12: *Plateau*. Washington: Smithsonian Institution Scholarly Press, 1998.

15. Ibid.

16. Ibid.

17. Corinna Hoodicoff and Roger Packham, "Cariboo Region Badger Project: Year End Report 2006–07." Vernon: Summit Environmental Consultants, Ltd., and 100 Mile House: Ministry of Environment, 2007.

18. "Then Again, Some Don't: Arcand of the IWA Explains How to Break the Back of CORE." *Vancouver Sun*, April 8, 1994: A19. "How to Wreck the CORE Process, IWA Style." *Tribune* [Williams Lake], April 21, 1994: A4.

Reading List

BOOKS

Acorn, John, and Ian Sheldon. *Bugs of British Columbia*. Vancouver: Lone Pine, 2001.

Banfield, A.W.F. *The Mammals of Canada*. Toronto: University of Toronto Press, 1974.

Bell, Barbara L., Ken V. Ellison and Linda L. Wills. *Valley of Dreams: A Pictorial History of Vernon and District*. Vernon: Greater Vernon Museum and Archives, 1992.

Belton, Brian. *Bittersweet Oasis: A History of Ashcroft and District 1885–2002*. Ashcroft: The Corporation of the Village of Ashcroft, 2002.

Blacklaws Rick, and Diana French. *Ranchland: British Columbia's Cattle Country*. Madeira Park: Harbour Publishing, 2001.

Brown, Lauren. *Audubon Nature Guide: Grasslands*. New York: Knopf, 1985.

Campbell, Wayne, Neil K. Dawe, Ian McTaggart-Cowan, John M. Cooper, Gary W. Kaiser and Michael C.E. McNall. *Birds of British Columbia, Volume 4*. Vancouver: UBC Press, 2001.

Cannings, Richard, and Sydney Cannings. *British Columbia: A Natural History of Its Origins, Ecology, and Diversity with a New Look at Climate Change*. Vancouver: Greystone, 2015.

Cannings, Robert A., Richard J. Cannings and Sydney G. Cannings. *Birds of the Okanagan Valley*. Victoria: Royal British Columbia Museum, 1987.

Cannings, Sydney, Richard Cannings and Robert Cannings. *The World of Fresh Water*. Vancouver: Greystone Books, 1998.

Cannings, Sydney, JoAnne Nelson and Richard Cannings. *Geology of British Columbia: A Journey through Time*. Vancouver: Greystone Books, 2011.

Cox, Doug. *Ranching: Now, Then, and Way Back When . . .* Penticton: Skookum Publications, 2004.

Daubenmire, R.F. *Plants and Environment: A Textbook of Autecology*. New York: John Wiley and Sons, 1974.

Demarchi, Dennis A. *The British Columbia Ecoregion Classification.* Williams Lake: British Columbia Ministry of Environment, 2011.

Eder, Tamara, and Don Pattie. *Mammals of British Columbia.* Vancouver: Lone Pine, 2001.

Eyles, Nick, and Andrew Miall. *Canada Rocks.* Markham: Fitzhenry and Whiteside, 2016.

Fisher, Robin. *Contact and Conflict: Indian–European Relations in British Columbia, 1774–1890.* Vancouver: UBC Press, 1992.

Gayton, Don. *The Wheatgrass Mechanism: Science and Imagination in the Western Canadian Landscape.* Markham: Fitzhenry & Whiteside, 1999.

Harris, Chris, Ordell Steen, Kristi Iverson and Harold Rhenisch. *Spirit in the Grass: The Cariboo Chilcotin's Forgotten Landscape.* 108 Mile Ranch: Country Light Publishing Company, 2007.

Herrero, Dr. Stephen. *Bear Attacks: Their Causes and Avoidance.* Toronto: McClelland & Stewart, 2003.

Lynch, Wayne. *Married to the Wind: A Study of the Prairie Grasslands.* Vancouver: Whitecap Books, 1984.

Lynch, Wayne. *Windswept: A Passionate View of Prairie Grasslands.* Markham: Fifth House, 2004.

Marriott, Harry. *Cariboo Cowboy.* Vancouver: Heritage House, 2010.

Mather, Ken. *Buckaroos and Mud Pups: The Early Days of Ranching in British Columbia.* Vancouver: Heritage House, 2010.

Mathews, Bill, and Jim Monger. *The Roadside Geology of Southern British Columbia.* Vancouver: Heritage House, 2010.

Meidinger, Del, and Jim Pojar. *Ecosystems of British Columbia.* Squamish: British Columbia Ministry of Forests, 1991.

Parish, Roberta, Ray Coupé and Dennis Lloyd, eds. *Plants of Southern Interior British Columbia.* Vancouver: Lone Pine, 1996.

Safranyik, Les, and Bill Wilson, eds. *The Mountain Pine Beetle: A Synthesis of its Biology, Management and Impacts on Lodgepole Pine.* Victoria: Natural Resources Canada, Canadian Forest Service and Pacific Forestry Centre, 2006. Audio CD.

Sanford, Barrie. *McCulloch's Wonder: The Story of the Kettle Valley Railway.* Vancouver: Whitecap Books, 2011.

Savage, Candace. *Prairie: A Natural History*. Vancouver: Greystone, 2004.

Sibley, David Allan. *The Sibley Guide to Birds*. New York: Random House, 2000.

Stewart, Heather, and Richard J. Hebda. "Grasses of the Columbia Basin of British Columbia," *Working Paper* 45. Victoria: British Columbia Ministry of Forests Research Program and Royal British Columbia Museum Natural History Section, 2000.

Sturtevant, William C., and June Helm. *Handbook of North American Indians*, Volume 6: *Subarctic*. Washington: Smithsonian Institution Scholarly Press, 1981.

Sturtevant, William C., and Deward E. Walker, eds. *Handbook of North American Indians*, Volume 12: *Plateau*. Washington: Smithsonian Institution Scholarly Press, 1998.

Turner, Nancy J., Laurence C. Thompson and M. Terry Thompson. *Thompson Ethnobotany: Knowledge and Usage of Plants by the Thompson Indians of British Columbia*. Memoir No. 3. Victoria: Royal British Columbia Museum, 1990.

Webber, Jean, and Okanagan Historical Society. *A Rich and Fruitful Land*. Madeira Park: Harbour Publishing, 1999.

Wikeem, Brian, and Sandra Wikeem. *The Grasslands of British Columbia*. Kamloops: Grassland Conservation Council of British Columbia, 2004.

Wuest, Donna Yoshitake. *Coldstream: The Ranch Where It All Began*. Madeira Park: Harbour Publishing, 2005.

Yorath, Chris J. *Where Terranes Collide*. Victoria: Orca Books, 1990.

———. *Backroad Mapbook: Outdoor Recreation Guide—Cariboo Chilcotin Coast, Southwestern BC, Kamloops/Okanagan, Kootenay*. Coquitlam: Mussio Ventures, Ltd., 2015.

———. "BC Grasslands Mapping Project: A Conservation Risk Assessment (Final Report)." Kamloops: Grasslands Conservation Council of British Columbia, May 2004.

———. *BC Grasslands*: (The Journal of the Grassland Conservation Council of BC). (Past issues are available online.)

————. *Field Guide to Noxious Weeds and Other Selected Invasive Plants of British Columbia*. 8th ed. Williams Lake: Invasive Species Council of British Columbia, 2014.

WEBSITES

The Atlas of Canada—Toporama (http://atlas.gc.ca/toporama/en/)

BC Frogwatch Program. (http://www.env.gov.bc.ca/wld/frogwatch/whoswho/).

BC Parks (http://www.env.gov.bc.ca/bcparks) The source for information on BC parks and protected areas with maps, brochures and management plans available online.

British Columbia Ministry of Environment, Biodiversity/Environmental Information Resources e-Library (http://www.env.gov.bc.ca/eirs/bdp/) A prime source of information with many publications available online. Special emphasis on threatened species and ecosystems.

British Columbia Ministry of Forests Publications (https://www.for.gov.bc.ca/hfd/pubs /hfdcatalog/index.asp) Another prime source of information with many publications available online.

The Cornell Lab of Ornithology (http://www.birds.cornell.edu/).

E-Flora BC: Electronic Atlas of the Plants of British Columbia (http://ibis.geog.ubc.ca/biodiversity/eflora/). Maps and natural history information.

Grasslands Conservation Council of British Columbia (http://bcgrasslands.org/) A prime source of information on grasslands in British Columbia with publications and maps available online.

Hinterland Who's Who (http://www.hww.ca).

Invasive Species Council of British Columbia (http://bcinvasives.ca/) An excellent source for information on invasive species, particularly plants, including a downloadable version of their *Field Guide to Noxious Weeds and Other Selected Invasive Plants of British Columbia*.

Life Histories of Familiar North American Birds (http://www.birdsbybent.com/index.html).

Native Plant Society of British Columbia (http://www.npsbc.ca/).

Online Atlas of the Breeding Birds of British Columbia (www.birdatlas.
bc.ca/).

Royal British Columbia Museum and Archives (http://royalbcmuseum.
bc.ca/).

The Soil Landscapes of British Columbia (http://www.env.gov.bc.ca/
soils/landscape/).

Thompson Rivers University. The Reptiles of British Columbia. (http://
www.bcreptiles.ca).

Index